Hugh Martin
The Boy Next Door

by

HUGH MARTIN

TROLLEY PRESS
Encinitas, California

TROLLEY PRESS

Published by Trolley Press
P.O. Box 235268
Encinitas, CA 92023-5658

Publishing Consultant and Packager: BookStudio, LLC
www.bookstudiobooks.com

Cover and Interior Design: Charles McStravick, Artichoke Design
www.artichokepublishing.com

Editing: Lois Winsen
www.editorontap.com

Martin, Hugh, 1914-

    Hugh Martin : the boy next door / by Hugh Martin. -- Encinitas, Calif.
: Trolley Press, c2010.

       p. ; cm.
       ISBN: 978-0-615-36507-7
       Includes bibliographical references and index.

       1. Martin, Hugh, 1914- 2. Composers--United States--
Biography. 3. Musical theater--United States--History--20th
century. 4. Musical films--United States--History--20th century.
5. Musicals--United States--History--20th century. I. Title.

PRINTED IN THE UNITED STATES OF AMERICA

For Elaine, of course

Contents

Act One

Act Two

Act Three

Acknowledgments

$\mathcal{F}$OR THIS MEMOIR I have as many people to thank as a Hollywood actor on Oscars night.

When I first started naming the people who had helped my book along, I tried to personalize my gratitude toward each and every one. But as the list grew longer, it seemed more expedient just to call the roll: thank you, Reg Fulton, Bea Wain, Lester Fossick, Richard Lederer, Peter Dattilo, Duffy Brown, David Hummel, Ken Bloom, Miles Kreuger, Michael Feinstein, and Josh Ellis. Special thanks to Fred and Elaine Harrison, who not only gave me a perfect habitat for working, but also were sitting ducks when I yearned for a reaction. Since we live under the same roof, it's not easy to escape from me.

Special thanks to Robert Kimball, not only for his enthusiasm and encouragement; he also persuaded The Library of Congress to arrange a grant for me from The Leonore and Ira Gershwin Trust.

We have a faithful staff that greatly blesses our enclave. Thank you, Virgie Marlin, Ester Bonilla, Reyna and Edith Delgado, Socorro and Perla Diego, Yesenia Pulido and Juliana Chavez. My early efforts were processed by Sharon Peters and Nancy Grischkowsky.

When I first settled in Encinitas, one of the people without whom I would surely have crashed and gone up in flames was Beverly Betts Evans. Her stamina astounded us all. She accompanied me on several cross country trips, kept my head on straight, and got me to my engagements on time.

Likewise, the gifted Kitty Wolf of La Porte, Indiana, came to our rescue during the Broadway production of *Meet Me in St. Louis.* What a trouper!

A special word about Criscelle Santiago because she is a special person. I engaged her to be my secretary and during the ten years she has been with me, she gradually became a Girl Friday: whatever was needed, she did, a team player of the first order. Eventually she found her true value as a computer whiz. This book would not exist but for her untiring energy, skill, and willingness to be flexible.

I don't have to thank any ghostwriters because there aren't any. So if I have dealt a mortal blow to *Fowler's English Usage,* I did it single-handedly, with no accomplices.

All of you strengthened my fragile little ship immeasurably, and if we ever reach full sail, I shall sing your praises from the masthead.

— *Hugh Martin*
June, 2010

Foreword

by Michael Feinstein

IN A WORLD OF EXTRAORDINARY PEOPLE, I'm glad there is Hugh. He is truly a national treasure and, thank goodness, is much appreciated and cherished. In turn, Hugh has become an oracle for so many who regularly turn to him for information, guidance, history, encouragement, musicological advice, spiritual upliftment, humor, vocal instruction and just about anything else you can think of! The many facets of his personality radiate like a beacon of light through the fog of uncertain times and unmemorable art, assuring us that there is reason in the world, and life to celebrate.

Hugh Martin is first and foremost a prodigiously talented musician who writes both words and music with formidable skill, plays the piano poetically and with a sophisticated harmonic palette, sings like an angel and has contributed some of the most memorable vocal arrangements and musical routines of the last century. His behind the scenes influence on popular music began even before he started composing music, when he was aligned on Broadway with the most esteemed names of the musical theatre, such as Jerome Kern, Vernon Duke, Richard Rodgers and Irving Berlin. Hugh breathed fresh musical blood via his legendary vocal arrangements for a somewhat jaded Broadway musical stage, much to the delight of its composers. He fused a contemporary sensibility to thirties and forties musicals that brought a new energy and audience to the theatre. He found a way to be reverent and insouciant at the same time and evolved a new musical voice in the process. Once he started writing his own songs, it was as if someone had flipped a switch and they began pouring forth in his inimitable style: never cliché, always surprising, fresh, and stretching the limits of the 32 bar song form. He cannot stand the expected and always finds surprises in his music, not for the sake of being different but because he insists on finding another way of expressing that which is oft expressed. It is the inevitable and natural nature of the final result that has earned him so many fans, especially among his fellow songwriters. Stephen Sondheim has expressed special appreciation for his work and Tony Bennett named Hugh as his favorite songwriter.

As a person, Hugh, who is naturally kind and friendly, might at first might seem quiet, reticent and self effacing. Underneath is a person who is extremely strong willed and can be stubborn in support of what he believes is right. His sense of humor and whimsy is delicious and he has a way of looking at the human condition that can be ironic yet buoyantly helpful when we need to laugh at our failings. That sense of joy and aliveness also permeates his music. He is a discerning critic and being unthreatened, is the greatest fan and supporter of the work of others.

His years of self exploration and hunger for truth have led him to a place of peace and confidence in his spiritual path. By virtue of his unwavering faith and appreciation for life, he gives others a sense of security and comfort that is exuded in the way he lives and has thus become a magnet for those who desire to know his secret. Being a man of humility, Hugh is not someone to blow his own horn and certainly has his challenges to face, but they never get in the way of his sharing. I doubt that he can truly see how much he gives to all of his friends. It's so much, so often, and at an age that even with the diminishment of time does not dim the light.

Surely his songs are his legacy and they will be sung and heard for generations to come. There are so many more songs that will one day be heard and, if there is any justice, take their place amongst his best loved standards. Yet for those of us lucky enough to also know the man, we pity those who only know Hugh by his songs, great as they are. True, they reflect his essence and beauty and can regularly work magic on their listeners, but now you can also get to know the sweet soul behind the music and share a bit of a man who has truly made a profound difference in this world. Enjoy getting to know Hugh Martin!

— *Michael Feinstein*

April 1, 2010

ACT ONE

Off to a
Good Start

With Judy Garland, Palace Theater,
New York, 1951.

With Judy Garland, backstage at the Palace Theater,
New York, 1951.

Chapter 1

The Palace

*I*WASN'T BORN IN A TRUNK, but I did become a show biz junkie early in life, before ever glimpsing Broadway or Hollywood. In addition to a natural attraction to it, I had a theater-loving mother who regularly left home, hearth, husband, and Birmingham, Alabama, for New York City, starting when I was two years old.

Then there was *Variety*. Our public library didn't carry "the magazine of show business," but a local newsstand did. Lucky for me, the news dealer was a friendly soul who didn't object to a customer browsing for hours. I discovered *Variety* the year I entered junior high, and I was never the same after that. It introduced me to glamour, glitz, and glorious Technicolor, a welcome world to a dreamy youngster growing up in a city built around iron furnaces and steel mills.

According to *Variety,* the *sanctum sanctorum* of the entertainment world was the Palace Theater on the corner of 47ᵗʰ Street and Broadway. I lay in bed innumerable nights with visions of the Palace dancing in my head. These dreams never included my being on stage at the Palace, merely being a spectator. Yet, twenty-two years later, on the night of October 16, 1951, I found myself, to my astonishment, in a tuxedo, on the stage of the Palace at a nine-foot Steinway accompanying headliner Judy Garland as she sang these lyrics by Roger Edens:

> *I've played the State, the Capitol,*
> *But people said, "Don't stop.*
> *Until you've played the Palace,*
> *You haven't played the top.*
>
> *For years I had it preached to me*
> *And drummed into my head:*
> *"Unless you've played the Palace,*
> *You might as well be dead."*
>
> *A team of hoofers was the headline*
> *At the Majestic down in Dallas,*
> *But they canceled the day*
> *Their agent called to say,*
> *"You can open the bill at the Palace."*
>
> *So it became the Hall of Fame,*
> *The Mecca of the trade;*
> *When you had played the Palace,*
> *You knew that you were made.*
>
> *So I hope you'll understand*
> *my wondrous thrill,*
> *'Cause vaudeville's back at the Palace,*
> *And I'm on the bill!*

The improbable events that led to this fantasy-come-true started in the fall of 1951. I was living in New York and happened on an announcement in one of the papers that the Palace, after many inglorious years, was planning to re-open on a two-a-day basis with an old-time vaudeville show headed by Judy Garland. I have never been an opening night freak, but I adored Judy, had written the songs for one of her movies, *Meet Me in St. Louis*, and thought to myself, "This is one opening night I'd like to attend." Someone tipped me off that she was staying at the Waldorf, so I phoned her, hoping I wasn't being a nuisance. She was cordial as could be, so I screwed up my courage and asked if it would be possible to get a couple of house seats for the première.

"I have a better idea," she said without missing a beat. "Sitting in the audience is so ordinary. Why don't you sit on stage with me?"

Hugh: Judy, you shouldn't kid an old friend.

Judy: I'm not kidding.

I felt a little light-headed.

Hugh: Isn't Roger coming east to play for you?

Judy: He can't, he's in production with something for Arthur and they're right in the thick of it.

Roger was Roger Edens, her long-time and brilliant mentor; Arthur was Arthur Freed, MGM's top producer of musical films.

Hugh: Are you serious?

Judy: Never more so. I know you're terribly busy, but it's only for three weeks. I would so love it if you would.

Hugh: How much will I have to pay you?

She laughed that marvelous Judy Garland laugh.

Judy: I'll talk to Sid about it.

Sid Luft was her manager and soon-to-be third husband. I liked him immediately.

That was a watershed moment in Judy's career at a time when she felt threatened and rejected. Sid thought the time was ripe for her to get away from the cameras and back to her roots: vaudeville, the medium in which she had made her dèbut at age two singing "Jingle Bells." His first project for her was the London Palladium. He contacted the bookers, and he and Judy were gratified at the immediate interest. The British had always deeply loved her, and her four weeks there quickly sold out.

What next? Sid felt it had to be the New York Palace. Judy and Mickey Rooney, in their early juvenile "Let's put on a show!" movies, never stopped talking about playing the Palace, so what was more logical? The deal was set, and Roger Edens started writing an act for her. Old friends from MGM expressed a desire to help in any way possible; Chuck Walters agreed to stage the act, and Irene Sharaff to costume it. After I came on board, I was flown to Hollywood to observe the fruits of everyone's labors, and especially to be coached by Roger on how my piano accompaniments could bring out the best in Judy vocally.

Early in October we assembled at the Palace to start rehearsing. It was a larger then usual company for a vaudeville act because Judy had brought along seven male dancers from California. Most of them had worked with her in the "Get Happy" number in *Summer Stock*. There were other acts on the bill as well, so dressing rooms were at a premium. I ended up in a little cubicle so high up in the flies that it made me dizzy to look down.

When Judy learned that my dressing room was practically in another building, she was annoyed at the management. "That's crazy," she said, "and insulting to Hughie. Sid, go ask Sol Schwartz if he can fix it for Hugh's room to be next to mine." Sid told her that the dressing-room situation was tight and that there was no chance that mine could be moved. She was disappointed.

"I know," she said suddenly. "Hugh, look at this little annex in my room. I'll never use it. Is it big enough for you to dress in?"

"Well, sure," I said, "but what about your privacy? There's no door." She thought a minute. "What if we hung a sheet between us? Remember Clark and Claudette in *It Happened One Night*?"

I glanced at Sid. No frown. Good.

"Sounds fine to me," I said.

Sid told me later when we were alone that it helped solve one of his greatest problems—Judy's insecurity.

In my opinion and that of many others, Judy Garland was the greatest entertainer in the history of modern show business. But try to tell her that! In 1951 she felt like a failure, having just been fired by MGM, the only career home she had ever known. Perfectionist that she was, she often felt dissatisfied with her singing. Most devastating of all for a woman, when she looked into her mirror, she saw someone disturbingly older than her Esther in *Meet Me in St. Louis*.

More about the Palace later.

During my first piano lesson,
age 7.

Chapter 2

Memories of Birmingham

I WAS BORN IN BIRMINGHAM—Alabama, that is, not England—
in August, 1914, a month of world-shaping events quite aside
from my birth. Barbara Tuchman wrote a whole book about that
particular month entitled *The Guns of August*.

The trip I took back to "the Pittsburgh of the South" in
1985 had a dual purpose. It was a sentimental journey during
which I was to assist in a local production of one of my musicals.
With me was my traveling companion and best friend, Elaine
Harrison, whom I had talked into accompanying me from
California. It took a lot of talking because keeping me afloat on
these show biz hegiras is very hard work. I once overheard Elaine
say to one of her girl friends, "Traveling with Hugh Martin is
like moving an army."

Elaine was curious to know where I had spent my childhood,
so I took her first to 1900 South 14ᵗʰ Avenue, a large two-story
Victorian home that, at the time of my birth, had belonged to my
grandparents. I pointed out a large bay window. Behind it was the
room where I had been brought into the world one Tuesday in the
wee small hours of August 11, 1914.

Ellie Gordon Martin, my mother, the year before I was born.

When I was nine years old, my architect father built a little one story, wood-and-stucco cottage at 1919 South 15th Avenue, and we moved into it in 1923. Since it was just a block away from my grandparents' house, Elaine and I walked over and took a look at it.

Though it was twilight and a light rain had started to fall, I could almost see into what had been my mother's bedroom on the front side of the house. What memories I had of heart-to-heart talks in that bedroom. So many unanswered questions. So many plans, tears, and joys!

My mother and me.

Mother's fragile health required more central heating than Daddy could stand, so he built an open sleeping-porch in back. He and I slept there the year 'round, and I developed a lifelong hatred for the cold. I shiver just thinking about those long winter nights and the way the blood in my skinny body seemed to turn into ice on that wretched sleeping-porch.

I could see all of the front porch—a tiny affair of wood and red bricks, barely large enough to accommodate the two quarts of milk comfortingly deposited there by the milkman before we arose. When Dad flung open the front door each morning as he erupted from the house, he sometimes knocked over one or both glass bottles, providing a treat for whichever cat we owned at the time.

I gazed at the mailbox, still attached to the stucco wall at the back of the porch. It had brought me an occasional Valentine or love letter. But more excitingly, it had on three occasions held a check made out to me from *The New Yorker* magazine. The NEW YORKER! Daddy thought it frivolous nonsense, but Mother and I read it from cover to cover each week, starting with the very first issue showing Eustace Tilley scrutinizing a butterfly through a monocle. What a miracle for this high school bookworm to be accepted three times for snippets sent to "The Talk of the Town!" section.

But wait a minute. There was something unfamiliar on the wall opposite the mailbox. "Elaine, do you think the residents would mind if I went a little closer?" We climbed the twelve stone steps and peered at the thing on the wall. By then twilight had darkened into night, and my eyesight was not too sharp. "It looks like a plaque," I said in wonderment.

"It's a plaque!" Elaine replied. Nothing wrong with *her* vision.

"What does it say?"

"It says," she put her face closer, "Jefferson County, Historical Commission, Historic Structure, Hugh Martin Cottage, 1922."

I'm not prone to ego trips, but I was aware of a tiny one forming somewhere inside me. It was short-lived. "Ellie, don't get too proud of me," I said. "I just realized something. The 'Hugh Martin' on the plaque—it's not me, it's Dad. He was the town celeb. I was an afterthought."

"Aw," said Elaine.

"Even so," I rationalized, "it makes me feel kind of warm and fuzzy, growing up in a historic structure. It's like having your picture on a postage stamp."

Age 5.

Unlike Father, Unlike Son

I certainly didn't feel a part of history when I was in grammar school and junior high. I felt like a big round zero. Oh, my parents were splendid. To our intimates, mother was the heart and soul of the Martin family. But to the town of Birmingham—and it was a town then, not yet a city—my architect father was already an icon. When our pastor, Dr. Henry Edmonds, wrote his memoirs, he devoted a chapter to my dad. Here is a brief excerpt:

> *Hugh Martin's name must find a place in this list of friends. Yet to write about Hugh Martin poses difficulties. He was so unassuming, so unostentatious, so disregarding of himself, so gentle, that he is hard to lay hands on. He had fewer angles than any other man I have ever known. He was easy; easy with his family, easy with his friends, easy with his clients. There was no pose about him. He didn't need to pose. He was simply himself. He had very definite opinions but was never strident in stating them. He never seemed for a moment to intimate that you hadn't a perfect right to differ from him, indeed welcomed the opportunity for amiable discussion of those differences.*[1]

At the risk of sounding like a Father's Day greeting card, I have to say that my dad was a man for all seasons, a world-class saint who never knew it. There wasn't a selfish bone in his lean, strong body. He played a good game of tennis into his seventies. He had a great sense of humor. He loved everyone regardless of race, religion or station in life, and everyone adored him. If I could feel that Junior was remotely in the same league as Senior, I could exorcise all my demons in one afternoon. That never happened. I have always suf-

---

1 Edmonds, Dr. Henry M., *A Parson's Notebook*. Birmingham, AL: Elizabeth Agee's Bookshelf, 1961.

Hugh Martin, Sr.

fered from low self-esteem. The genesis of my problems was my physical weakness. Dad loved sports and, though he never reproached me, I knew—boy, did I know—that he would have been pleased to have had a terrific athlete for a son. Fortunately, he got his wish ten years later when my brother, Gordon, arrived on the scene.

I played a respectable game of tennis, but Gordon was a tennis whiz. All I could play was the piano, an accomplishment that impressed neither my father nor my schoolmates. It impressed my mom, though. She always insisted that she knew even when she was carrying me that I would be a musician. There's no magician like a woman's intuition.

I have never called my mother "Mother" or "Mom" or any of the other usual appellations. Her name was Ellie Gordon Robinson, one of those ubiquitous double names that Southerners are so fond of, and that's how I always addressed her: Ellie Gordon. She was an enchanting woman and the center of my life. It was my mother who educated and molded me; whatever she told me I accepted as gospel truth. It never occurred to me to doubt her. Fortunately, she was a virtuous and intelligent human being who never betrayed my trust.

But Dad was a hero to me, too, a sort of Prince Regent to the Queen. I'm only now beginning to realize how fortunate I was in having his care and mentoring. He and I didn't speak the same language in the way my mother and I did, but there were compensations. He was an avid reader and got me started on Kipling and Mark Twain when most kids my age were content with the funnies. And he took me with him to many wonderful places, traveling to woods and streams and, best of all, to the sites where he was building his beautiful houses and buildings. I loved the smell of wet cement and new wood, and I impressed Dad with my agility as I shinnied up and down the skeletons of his rising edifices.

Most of the local praise he garnered was for his houses, or for the University of Alabama in Tuscaloosa, but it was his exquisite Birmingham Public Library that thrilled me the most. It had a kind of simple glamour that instilled in me a lifelong love of public libraries. To complete the construction, Daddy had brought in a fine muralist named Ezra Winter, so in every room my juvenile fancies were stimulated by fairy tales and knights in shining armor and portraits of famous writers.

I Happen to Like New York

Shakespeare looked down on me, of course, and I soon learned that there was such a thing as "theater" and plays. I began to devour these works voraciously. However, around the time I entered my teens, it was not Shakespeare who got my attention, but a later compatriot of his named Noël Coward. I read everything of his that I could get my hands on, including a slim volume of nonsense verse called *Spangled Unicorn* that made me laugh out loud even in the quiet, dignified reading room. A few years later in New York, when I discovered to my sorrow that the book was out of print, my darling mother checked it out of the Birmingham Library and mailed it to me without a twinge of conscience. In her defense, she examined the rubber-stamped dates in the front of the book and found it hadn't left the shelf in a couple of years. I told Noël this story decades later, and I can still hear his hearty laughter.

The time frames of my parents, especially regarding the children they produced, were a little unusual. After my birth in 1914, they waited ten years to bring Gordon on the scene in 1924. Then they waited three more years to have Ellen in 1927. So when I left home to go to New York in 1933, Ellen was only six years old.

Music, and my facility for making it, although something I felt almost ashamed of at first, gradually turned out to be a windfall. When I entered high school, I was overwhelmed by the way my piano playing opened doors.

Ellie Gordon taught me the necessary etiquette for a young Southern male, but she was far more interested in my musical life than in my social life. She was not a stage mother by any stretch of the imagination. Indeed, she was without a trace of aggressiveness where my public image was concerned. At that time I was beginning to get a little publicity from the *Birmingham News* and the other two papers, the *Post* and the *Age-Herald*, and that gave Ellie Gordon the willies. She preferred me to keep a low profile even though her unswerving dream was for me to become a concert pianist.

My mother was, herself, a remarkable musician, proficient in piano and violin and the possessor of a beguiling soprano voice. Because of these gifts she had strong compulsions to flee Birmingham for New York, where the cultural action was. Her friends understood her drive, but others found her frequent flights from the Philistinism of Birmingham scandalous. Today Birmingham can hold its head up artistically, but in the 1920s it was all steel and smoke and slag. How you gonna keep her down on the farm, after she's seen New York?

If I have given the impression that she was too involved with her extra-Birmingham life to be a good wife and mother, let me say now it was not the case. She loved my father dearly and was an important part of his work. She loved architecture as much as he did and contributed significantly to his success. She kept copious notebooks filled with photographs and sketches of houses and buildings that impressed her. Whenever Dad needed an idea for a façade or cornice or dome or arch, he needed only to leaf through his wife's notebook and, "Eureka!," there was inspiration, everything from Palladio to Frank Lloyd Wright. Ellie Gordon did more. She began to design interiors for Dad's exteriors, and the beauty they created together was first-class.

After one of her eyebrow-raising trips in 1928, she returned with a strange new excitement in her voice and manner. She had been exposed for the first time to the music of George Gershwin, and had seen Gertrude Lawrence in *Treasure Girl* with a score by the Gershwin brothers. Out of her suitcase came the published piano solo version of *Rhapsody in Blue,* Gershwin's trailblazing work. I fell upon it and learned it in short order.

Within a few days the musical world, cherished by both my mother and myself, was forgotten along with the idea of my becoming a concert pianist. *Rhapsody in Blue* was the first of three phenomena that shaped my musical life. The second was *Show Boat* and the third was a film called *Love Me Tonight.* More about these later.

The timing was propitious. I was sixteen years old, and preparing for my high school graduation day. I was the class pianist, and when the program committee inquired what I would play, I opted for *Rhapsody in Blue.* The music supervisor of Phillips High School, Miss Kitt, thought otherwise. *Rhapsody in Blue* was *jazz,* a dirty word to Miss Kitt and, indeed, to practically all guardians of the bastions in 1931. There was definitely trouble in River City.

I'm a stubborn old man now, and I was no less stubborn when I was a teenager. I felt I couldn't play Beethoven or Chopin or Debussy; I was too on fire with this new sound that possessed me. I held my ground, and Miss Kitt finally surrendered to my exuberance. Graduation Day was a morning to remember. I've had my share of triumphal moments, but the cheers of my schoolmates that day still ring in my ears.

Looking back, there was one cancer in the idyllic loveliness of the South into which I was born: racial bigotry. I was aware of it but, to my deep discredit, I did nothing. How could I not be aware of it when there were nights when I could walk out my front door, look up and see, on the mountain overlooking my house, one of the Ku Klux Klan's satanic burning crosses? Thankfully, great progress has been made. But, as Edmund Burke wrote, "All that is necessary for evil to prevail is for good men to do nothing."

The classic soothing syrup for sluggish consciences is to go to the movies a lot, which was what I did. As a non-athlete I was happier in fantasyland than I was on the playing field. My natural habitat was the movie theater. It helped shape my life. When sound came in, I reacted in a big way to Al Jolson in *The Jazz Singer.*

But it was *Show Boat* that triggered my lifelong passion for musical theater. I never got to see the original Ziegfeld production. However, Universal Studios filmed a silent version in 1929. The studio, stimulated by the success of *The Jazz Singer,* put a soundtrack onto the otherwise silent film. Watching, listening, I became saturated with the glorious Jerome Kern melodies.

What excited me even more than the Kern songs was my first glimpse of Helen Morgan. The film company decided to tack on a prologue consisting of three of the numbers from the Broadway production with full sound, sung by Tess Gardella (whose stage name, believe it or not, was Aunt Jemima), Jules Bledsoe, and my beloved Helen Morgan. Miss Morgan was beautiful in a strange and vulnerable way, especially when she sat on a beat-up old upright piano and sang what is still one of my favorite songs, "Bill."[2]

I became obsessed with this mysterious lady whom Miles Kreuger, in his great book about *Show Boat*[3], described so perfectly as having "a persona like a wounded bird." Her phonograph records were few and treasured, and I played them interminably until my family begged for mercy. She occupied much of my waking time and not a little of my sleeping time.

I never expected to see Helen Morgan, much less meet this by-now mythical creature, but to the astonishment of my mother and me both occurred. Ellie Gordon had been commissioned by the University of Alabama to buy a carillon for its campus. In a moment of largesse, she had decided to allow me to accompany her to New York where she planned to shop for chimes.

My all-consuming thought was that I might, perhaps, get to see and hear Helen Morgan, but *Show Boat* had closed and *Sweet Adeline* had not yet opened, so the chances seemed slim. However my eagle eye detected a little notice in *The New York Times* that Miss Morgan would be honored for a single night at Leon and Eddie's, a dreary but popular night club in the West Fifties. I was there within minutes and booked a table for two for the Sunday Celebrity Night. The table they gave me turned out

2 Wodehouse, P.G., Oscar Hammerstein, and Jerome Kern. "Bill," from *Show Boat,* 1927.
3 Kreuger, Miles. *Show Boat*. New York: Da Capo Press, Inc., 1977.

1946.

to be a few feet from a swinging door out of which burst waiters with trays of drinks. But, *mirabile dictu,* from the same swinging door emerged my inamorata, the legendary Helen Morgan, toast of Broadway and queen of the super clubs.

The effect on 20-year-old me would not have been more startling if Helen of Troy had emerged instead of Helen Morgan. The first person she spotted was my little mother and in her slightly inebriated state, Miss Morgan took her for a childhood chum.

"Mabel!" she screamed happily as she hugged Ellie Gordon lovingly, "I haven't seen you in years—since we went to school together in Danville High School back in Illinois! What are you doing in New York?"

My mother rose to the occasion like a seasoned trouper.

"Why, we came hoping to see you, Helen. This is my son, Hugh. I told you about Hugh, didn't I?"

"Why no, Mabel. I didn't even know you were married."

More hugs, including one for me. Then Helen Morgan excused herself and walked to an upright piano on which she sat gracefully and sang "Bill." Truth is stranger than fiction.

Miles Krueger, incidentally, along with Michael Feinstein, is one of the great appreciators of past glories. Neither Miles nor Michael is old enough to have experienced the glories of the twenties and thirties when they first burst upon the scene, but they have enriched our lives by recapturing the memory of the great musicals and songs of that marvelous era.

Miles extends his nostalgia to include the great landmarks of New York, bringing back to life for us unforgettable buildings and theaters and restaurants. I share his ill will toward the moneygrubbers who have destroyed them, either with the wrecking ball or simply by forgetting them.

Show Boat was held over for three weeks in Birmingham, and each day, the moment our school bell rang at five minutes to three o'clock, I made a beeline for the Alabama Theater. It was one of those full-blown gaudy movie cathedrals complete with pipe organ, marble staircase, huge restrooms, and columns that would have been envied by the ancient Greeks. There, in that rarefied atmosphere, worries about my weak body and my awkwardness with the opposite sex and my less than brilliant grades in Latin and math faded away, and I became Gaylord Ravenal kissing the hand of the delicious Magnolia Hawks.

Later, the dark Miss Morgan almost lost me to a new blonde in town named Jeanette MacDonald. When Princess Jeanette walked onto a balcony in *Love Me Tonight* to sing "Isn't It Romantic?," it touched my foolish heart.

I used to go home after these exercises in hedonism and attempt to play the movie songs on my Mason and Hamlin baby grand. Usually my teenage fingers could somehow recall the harmonies and communicate them to my mother, but I came a-cropper with the song, "Lover." When I heard Jeanette sing it to a horse in *Love Me Tonight,* I was as captivated as Maurice Chevalier, who happened to be watching her; but I was totally thwarted when I tried to recreate it on my piano. Try as I might, I could not find the chords. Even today those Richard Rodgers harmonies seem offbeat and different, but then, to a neophyte musician, they were well-nigh impossible to reproduce.

I did, though. Even then I was single-minded. I plunked away at the piano for about a week; then, just as I was about to give up, my fingers fell onto the right keys. I'll never forget the exhilaration. It was like learning to swim.

The Blue Shadows, my first vocal group.
Olena Webb, Loulie Jean Norman, me,
and Edith Caldwell, 1932.

Chapter 3

Manhattan Fever

WHEN MY BUDDIES AND I WERE RUNNING from class to class at Phillips High School, we were unaware that, a few decades later, lockers in high schools might contain hard drugs, condoms, and hand guns. I'm not suggesting that a certain amount of hanky-panky didn't go on in our day, but we were blissfully unaware of it for the most part. And the same was true for the year and a half that I attended Birmingham-Southern College. We rarely locked our lockers; even petty thievery was practically non-existent.

However, there was a germ of addiction in our circumspect little house on 15th Avenue. I'm not referring to Daddy's cigars or Ellie Gordon's sleeping pills, innocent enough by today's standards. Rather, New York was the addiction. My mother had to have her trips as compulsively as today's druggies have to have theirs. It started almost as soon as I was born. She could not resist New York's pull on her. She would simply put baby Hugh in Grandma's arms and off she'd go, sometimes for several months at a time. She once received a holiday card from a neighbor wishing her a "Merry Christmas and a Happy New York." We were never sure whether it was a Freudian slip or a sly dig—probably the latter.

Can a child become addicted in the same way? You bet! A potent whiff of New York's culture clung to Mother when she returned to us provincials. I still recall the thrill of being allowed to watch her unpack her suitcases after a trip to the Big City. All kinds of goodies would spill out: programs from the operas, concerts, plays, and lectures as well as expensive and exquisite articles of clothing, including presents for all the family. These were limited in quantity as my mother was never extravagant, but her taste was impeccable, so the aesthetic level of her choices was, well, choice!

There were museum catalogues, too, from the Metropolitan Museum of Art and the Frick, as well as from some of the smaller galleries on Madison Avenue.

New York fever was catching. Both Ellie Gordon and I had an eye for beauty, so New York became synonymous in my mind with Ali Baba's treasure cave and the crown jewels in the Tower of London. New York seemed less a locality than a state of mind.

Hooray for Hollywood!

And Hollywood seemed even less a place than New York. We all loved going to the movies, but never thought of Hollywood as a city. We loved Douglas Fairbanks and Mary Pickford and Lillian Gish and Gloria Swanson, but were they people? More like figures in a dream. I know my mother's gorgeous younger sister, Aunt Olivia, who taught me how to dance the Charleston, dreamed frequently about Rudolph Valentino. And I'm pretty sure she thought of him as a fantasy figure, not a man.

Movies may have been a dream world to my family, but to me, everything that happened up there on that big screen was thrillingly real. My mother made the mistake of taking me to a local theater to see Pola Negri in *Passion,* a drama about the French

Revolution. I was about seven, and when Miss Negri, as Madame du Barry, was dragged to the guillotine, I unraveled. I still remember the subtitle that set me off; each word is burned into my memory. "Please don't kill me! Life is so sweet!" I began to scream at the top of my lungs, was hustled out of the theater, taken home, and put to bed. Dr. Snyder was summoned and he gave me a sleeping pill.

After that, mother was careful to expose me only to happier plots that featured the likes of Charlie Chaplin or Harold Lloyd. One day Gloria Swanson somehow got into the act and became my first heartthrob.

I Left My Heart in Pratt City

Ten years later I succumbed to a new infatuation. This time the object of my affection was Loulie Jean Norman, a local beauty. It was only a schoolboy crush and never went anywhere romantically, but it did bear fruit musically. Loulie organized a girls' trio that included herself, Olena Webb, and Edith Caldwell. The trio eventually became a quartet that included me. I was irrepressible when it came to singing. Though not blest with a large or impressive voice, I was long on musicality and style, so throughout my life I kept putting my two cents worth into any vocal proceedings I could. Peter Schickele, the creator of P.D.Q. Bach, remarked that singing with others is, for many, a sacred experience. It has always been so for me.

The three girls and I called ourselves The Blue Shadows and had no trouble finding opportunities to do our thing. Our first engagement came about when the original Warner Brothers film *42nd Street* opened at the ornate Alabama Theater in 1933. Our singing quartet was the live stage show they presented four times a day, along with the blockbuster movie. Movie musicals were still a

Loulie Jean Norman.

novelty. The film *Broadway Melody* had created a demand for theater music and theater ambiance. People were fascinated by films containing auditions, rehearsals, dressing rooms, chorus girls, "angels" who bankrolled shows, and understudies who went on at the last minute to become stars.

42nd Street was the prototype of all these stories and spawned scores of imitators. All four of us were affected by it, each in a different way. Pretty Olena thought it was a huge joke and continued to dream of husband and children. Perky, audience-pleasing Edith was startled to find herself making money from something she had always done for fun. Beautiful, multi-talented Loulie Jean was the only one who was not afraid to dream big. She knew, somewhere deep inside herself, that she had been given something rare and marvelous, though she had no idea where it would lead her.

As for me, I sat in my tiny dressing room and tried to figure out why I was having such wild, visceral feelings. Gershwin had touched a nerve; now I was exposed to this sensual, overwhelming theater music (it *was* theater music even though it was reaching us by way of film), and I became giddy listening to it.

A Busby Berkeley extravaganza kicked off the movie's title song sequence. His in-your-face choreography included masses of lightly dressed chorus girls forming giant squares on the stage. (In my opinion, Busby Berkeley was a giant square himself.) There were also hundreds of extras: Ruby Keeler tapping like someone "Arthur Murray taught dancing in a hurry," along with tarts, pimps, midgets, Dick Powell in fine vocal fettle, a young girl taking a flying leap out of a third story window and subsequently being murdered, all to the accompaniment of the entire Warner Bros. orchestra. There was no way I could escape the blasting, as I sat in my tiny dressing room on the other side of a thin wall from a huge loudspeaker.

But it wasn't this Hollywood extravaganza that gave me a new direction one fateful day. It was a simple line of dialogue, casually spoken, that put a crazy idea into my adolescent mind, blotting out my previous plans and schemes, and totally changing my life.

Bebe Daniels played Dorothy Brock, the star of *Pretty Lady,* the musical within a musical. The scene was an on-stage rehearsal, and Miss Daniels was about to run one of her songs, "You're

Getting to Be a Habit with Me." She stood next to the upright piano and after singing a few bars in E-flat she said to her accompanist, "Jerry, take it up a half tone, will ya?"

Without waiting for the pianist to modulate, she launched into the refrain in E-natural. The song is a beauty, one of Harry Warren and Al Dubin's best. The lovely chords of the first two bars intoxicated me as she sang them. Her voice took on a richer patina in the new key, and the Harry Warren chords sounded warmer and more seductive than before. I stood up and announced in a loud voice to my empty dressing room: "*I'm* going to be in show business!"

The Blue Shadows sang almost every evening on WAPI, our local NBC affiliate, for practically no money, but radio was in its infancy and just to be on the air was thrilling. The heaven to which we all aspired was WEAF, the Blue Network, and WJZ, the Red Network in New York. Only a tiny notch lower in our hearts was CBS at 485 Madison Avenue. Both NBC and CBS presented national programs of high quality; *The Rudy Vallee Show* for Fleischman's Yeast was *The Ed Sullivan Show* of those days. There was also *The Paul Whiteman Show with Mildred Bailey*, and The *Show Boat* program, and *Amos 'n' Andy,* and *Kate Smith,* and *Ruth Etting.* There was *The Voice of RKO,* and *Crumit and Sanderson,* and *Jessica Dragonette.* My personal favorite was *Willard Robison and His Deep River Orchestra.* Willard was a singer of infinite sweetness and tenderness, and he wrote songs with the same qualities. He sang with an orchestra of some thirty musicians, considered huge as the program had no sponsor. His announcer was the mellifluous Basil Ruysdael, who read short poems and fragments of literary works. The program emanated from the WOR studios on Broadway at 40th Street.

WAPI-Birmingham decided to run a talent contest; the grand prize was a two-week visit to New York, all expenses paid. Contest fever raged among those of us who could carry a tune or play an instrument. Groups were barred from entering as the budget allowed for only one winner. Since The Blue Shadows couldn't compete as a group, we all entered individually. I sang and played *Mad Dogs and Englishmen* and rehearsed and coached the three girls. I swiped Ethel Waters' arrangement of *Stormy Weather,* taught it to Edith, and she won! We were all happy for her because she was a good singer, a modest and dear person, and dirt poor. She hopped onto the Birmingham Special (train) as soon as she completed a hasty shopping trip to Pizitz Department Store and its competitor, Loveman, Joseph, & Loeb. To the delight of The Blue Shadows, WAPI, and the entire city of Birmingham, she connected instantly in New York. A then-popular band leader, Ted Black, engaged her to be his girl singer, and when Black retired, Orville Knapp took her on. Suddenly our little Cinderella was wearing haute couture gowns and singing her heart out in the Starlight Roof of the Waldorf!

Loulie and Olena and I decided to spend our own money to go to New York to see Edith at the Waldorf. Once there, we cased the situation, especially those majestic network studios, but we were content to be tourists basking in the glow of Edith's success. Secretly, Loulie Jean and I knew we would some day have to return.

Back in Birmingham, The Blue Shadows, now a trio again, continued to entertain whenever we could get a job. Radio was big in the 1930s, and soon we were getting offers to sing at banquets, church groups, Chambers of Commerce, Elks, Moose, Shriners, Masons, and Rotary Clubs. A few of these paid us a modest stipend.

Our first gig for money was in a hall attached to the First Baptist Church of Pratt City, Alabama. We were very excited that people were actually willing to put down their money to hear us sing harmony. It was not much money, mind you, but it made us feel like real professionals. Perhaps this was going to be our gateway to the wonderful world of entertainment. We might even bust out of Birmingham and break into New York show biz. Today the summit for young performers might be television or Broadway, but Loulie and I had our sights set on radio. NBC! CBS! Rockefeller Center had not been built yet, but "the Networks" was a phrase fraught with glamour. We tingled with excitement.

At the church in Pratt City we launched into "I Can't Give You Anything But Love," and our soft, blended voices quickly captured the audience. Olena sang "Them There Eyes." I played a bit of *Rhapsody in Blue*. We put Loulie Jean in the next to closing spot because she had always been our big gun, our showstopper. Sadly, I was too young and inexperienced to choose a suitable solo for her. I had selected an Ethel Merman song from *Girl Crazy* called "Sam and Delilah."[1] Loulie Jean walked to center stage front and I started to play the introduction. Since I knew a bit about the Merman delivery, I had coached her to belt out the song as much like Ethel's style as possible.

"Delilah," trumpeted Loulie Jean, "was a floozy. She never gave a damn."

I changed key, up a whole tone. Loulie's voice rose fortissimo and hackles began to rise with it. Half of the audience got up silently and started a mass exodus for the door.

Loulie looked startled but went bravely on. "Delilah got in action, Delilah did her kooch. She gave him satisfaction, and he fell 'neath her spell with the aid of love and hooch."

The exodus was almost complete now. A few curious souls stuck it out, presumably to see how far these Birmingham hoodlums would carry this outrage.

We looked at each other in disbelief. We didn't realize the lyrics were risqué. We thought it was a nice bluesy little song with lovely Gershwin harmonies and toe-tapping syncopations. Jazz was still very new and unexpected in 1931. As for the lyrics, we had never really thought much about them. Teenagers in the early

---

1 Gershwin, George, and Ira Gershwin. "Sam and Delilah," from *Girl Crazy,* 1930.

1930s were rather naïve compared to what goes on nowadays. "She gave him satisfaction" to us suggested Delilah had cooked her cowboy a nice steak dinner with perhaps a shot of whiskey on the side.

The last stragglers departed. Our long-awaited debut had been a bust. We wiped away tears and wondered how such a pleasant, jazzy little Gershwin song could have emptied the auditorium. After all, Ethel Merman was stopping the show with it eight times a week at the Alvin Theater on Broadway. I had fully expected it to stop our little show in Pratt City.

We stopped it all right. Cold!

Jean Sablon and Carmen Miranda,
in The Streets of Paris, *1939.*

Chapter 4

South America, Take It Away!

ABOUT THIS TIME, Harrison Cooper, a popular musician in Birmingham, offered me a job as vocalist with his orchestra. They were gearing up to embark for Argentina for an engagement at the *Club Charleston*, a posh nightclub in Buenos Aires. The thought of being away from New York for a season almost caused me to decline, as I had done with Mae West. Why did I say "Yes"? I'm afraid I have to admit I'm a frustrated singer. No one had ever offered me a job singing solo, and I was a boy who "cain't say no." Off we all went in the dead of winter in the USA and emerged in an exotic South American summer.

I wish I could say we knocked 'em dead at the elegant *Club Charleston*. Alas, we were a resounding flop. The *avant-garde* Argentineans thought they had booked a dance orchestra specializing in Le Jazz Hot. We were a mild affair, playing sweet, sentimental pop tunes in the Guy Lombardo style. Off with our heads! We were sacked with brisk, no nonsense efficiency. But we stayed for a couple of months because it took the club that long to find an authentic jazz band.

Our contracts called for return passage first class, but our employers double-crossed us. We found ourselves in the hold of a

Japanese freighter called *Rio de Janeiro Maru*. From my first look I began to wish I had gone on tour with Mae West. The food was sushi if we opted for Japanese fare. If we were determined to be "Amurrican," there were powdered eggs and powdered milk. Either way, it was definitely not Cordon Bleu. Our quarters looked like the galley ship in *Ben Hur*—tier upon tier of primitive bunks one above the other, and the place teemed with cockroaches. For months after we were liberated, my subconscious recalled the sensation of huge roaches dropping from the boards above us onto our faces. The nightmares that resulted lasted long after we docked in New Orleans one sunny June morning in 1932 after three weeks of filth.

There was one memorable experience, however, from the South American trip, so memorable it made up for the cockroaches and the cuisine. The orchestra did a daily broadcast over Radio Station LR3. After we did our thing in the largest studio, I wandered down the hall one day to see who followed us on the air. There was a sign in Spanish on the door of the small studio: "*No Pasar.*" My curiosity was piqued and I looked around until I found a little glass viewing window. Everything was soundproofed, but the sight that met my eyes was so intriguing that hearing the music seemed almost unnecessary. I saw a beautiful young woman singing to a microphone as if it were her lover. She smiled, she caressed, she danced, she almost kissed the unfeeling metal object. She wore a simple black dress with no accessories. I didn't realize it at the time, but I was peering at a phenomenon who would soon conquer Broadway and then move on to Hollywood to become the Brazilian Bombshell. And, stranger than fiction, I would be in the Broadway musical with her.

I sought an English-speaking technician. "Who is that dame?" I asked.

He almost laughed at my wide eyes and breathless voice. "That's Carmen Miranda," he said.

With Ralph Blane, 1941.

"Why does she give a total performance just for a little radio program?" I wanted to know.

"That's the way she is," he told me. "I asked her the same question one day. She said moving that way puts the excitement in her voice. She says if she just stands there and sings, her voice is flat, lifeless."

I was so thrilled by her visual performance that I made a point to watch her program every day through the peephole, even though I was never able to hear a note of what she was singing. I took myself to a music store before we sailed home and asked if they carried any Carmen Miranda records.

"Yes, we have her solo and also with her sister, Aurora."

I bought a stack of them and prayed I wouldn't break them on the journey back to America.

When the *Rio de Janeiro Maru* finally docked in New Orleans after three weeks of cockroaches, filth, stagnant air, and horrible food, my darling mother was on the quay. After the tedium of filling out masses of forms in customs, I was released from my prison and into Ellie Gordon's waiting arms. I think most of us vividly remember the scene in *Our Town* where Emily, in her grave, is told she can return from the dead and re-live one day of her life. She chooses her twelfth birthday, and what follows may be the most emotionally devastating scene in American playwrighting. If I should be given a similar opportunity, I think—no, I know—I would choose the evening Ellie Gordon and I spent together in New Orleans after I got off that horrid Japanese freighter. A taxi bore us to the Roosevelt Hotel, and we were given what seemed to me an utterly palatial room. I took a hot bath, my first in three weeks, followed by a Ramos gin fizz, a specialty of the Roosevelt. We then descended to the dining room where we had oysters, I remember, and an artichoke, the first one I'd ever seen.

"Son," my mother said, "while you were gone, I saw a sensational movie—*Roberta*. The music is by your favorite, Jerome Kern, and there are two youngsters named Fred Astaire and Ginger Rogers who are out-of-this-world dancers. Would you like to see it tonight?"

Would I? I would. I fell asleep that night almost the moment my head touched my clean, white pillow with no cockroaches on it. My dreams were a montage of mother's face at the dockside, Ramos gin fizzes, oysters, and artichokes, and Fred and Ginger happily tapping away on my ceiling.

Chapter 5

Decisions, Decisions

*I*N 1934, I FINALLY GOT UP THE NERVE to hop on the Birmingham Special to give New York my first big try. I hit the networks first, of course, but got absolutely nowhere, so I offered my services to anyone and everyone in the music business. Still no takers.

In the midst of all this rejection, I received a startling phone call. It was from someone who said she was Mae West. I thought it must be a friend with a propensity for practical jokes and a gift for impersonation. I responded with facetious small talk that made the caller quite angry because, as it turned out, it *was* Mae West. I was flabbergasted and embarrassed, but she merely said, "Never mind. Skip the apologies. I have a hard time sometimes convincing people that I am who I am. Let's not waste any more time."

Hugh: Yes, Ma'am.

Mae: I've written a nightclub act for myself and four men. We need some singing arrangements. I think we should get together and talk about it. Are you interested?

Hugh: Well . . . why yes, of course I'm interested.

Mae: We have to get going right away. We're opening in

Minneapolis in two weeks. That's our break-in spot. After that we'll play all the big cities.

Hugh: Including New York?

Mae: No. This is strictly a road tour. I'm opening in a new play in New York next year and I don't want to take the edge off.

Hugh: Can I do the arrangements here in New York before you leave?

Mae: Impossible. You'd have to travel with the act because I'm always changing and rewriting.

Hugh: How long would I be gone?

Mae: Six months.

Hugh: Oh, golly.

Mae: Whaddaya mean, "Oh golly?"

Hugh: I can't leave New York for six months.

Mae (angrily): Are you crazy? Who do you think you are, turning down Mae West? What have *you* ever done?

Hugh: Well, I, I haven't done anything—

Mae: This is a great opportunity for you, Hugh.

Hugh: I know it is, Miss West. I'm really dying to do it. It's just that I can't leave New York.

Mae: Why can't you leave New York?

Hugh: I don't exactly know why. I guess I've got to make something of myself and it has to be here—in New York.

Mae: Hugh, how old are you?

Hugh: Twenty.

Mae: And how old will you be in six months?

Hugh (sheepishly): Twenty

Mae: So what's your hurry?

Hugh: I can't leave New York, Miss West. And I can't even explain why.

Mae: You're insane!

She hung up before I had a chance to tell her that I agreed with her.

The experience shook me. Maybe I *was* insane. My compulsion to break the New York jinx bordered on insanity. But I was single-minded and even Mae West couldn't sway me.

I went from radio station to radio station, theater to theater, bôite to bôite, saloon to saloon, rejection to rejection. Rejection can get *toô* you after a while. So can homesickness. Winter in New York can be austere.

I had a ready-made excuse for failing (The Great Depression), but my self-esteem was already so low that I never even thought of it.

I was cold, lonely, and blue. I had no friends. And it was almost Christmas. I couldn't keep pounding the pavement. I had to have a break. I packed my suitcase and headed for Pennsylvania Station and the Birmingham Special.

For the next two weeks, I set aside the hopes and dreams I had been so relentlessly pursuing. I reveled in the beauty of Ellie Gordon's Christmas tree and Dad's buildings under construction. I walked in snowy woods just a mile or two from our home, and enjoyed worship services at various churches, including one for blacks where the music was a unique, upbeat feast for the ears. I rekindled old friendships, danced with some girls I thought had forgotten me, and replenished my beaten-down spirit.

Kay Thompson with her Rhythm Singers, CBS, New York, 1936.
Ken Lane, me, Al Rinker, and John Smedburgh.

Chapter 6

Watershed at 522 Madison Ave.

I REALIZED THAT THE MOMENT HAD COME to leave Birmingham once more and try my wings in New York City. But I was faint at heart; my home in Birmingham seemed a palace to me because of all the love that filled its tiny walls, and I knew I was prone to homesickness. So when I got an offer from a local orchestra, conducted by Bill Rollins, to be their pianist and vocalist, I took the easy way out and said "Yes."

The Rollins gang was a jazz band, and though I loved jazz, I had no flair for it. Bill had a habit of suddenly crying out, in the middle of a piece, "Take it, Mike!" or "Take it, Charlie!," the cue for a virtuoso improvisation by our trumpeter, clarinetist, or whomever. He yelled, "Take it, Hugh!" a few times, but soon learned better, because that exhortation caused me to freeze in my tracks. There would ensue a deadly stage wait while I floundered around on the keyboard for a thirty-two bar chorus that seemed to go on for thirty-two years. It was depressing, for Bill, for my colleagues, for the dancers, and most of all for me. After a few weeks of "Take it, Hugh!" I took it—the train that is—and returned to New York.

I was now back with Loulie Jean. We were constantly toot-
ing each other's horn, forever on the lookout for a break of some
kind for either or both of us. Providentially, she auditioned for
a new girl in town, a Miss Kay Thompson, just arrived from St.
Louis on a tide of advance excitement declaring her the hottest
new voice in the world of jazz. Miss Thompson quickly landed
an important showcase, a thirteen-week series sponsored by
Chesterfield cigarettes that would debut on CBS in 1936 with a
backup jazz choir of thirteen girls and three boys.

Loulie Jean was chosen to be one of the lucky thirteen and,
true to form, promptly made a pitch for me. What she did was
a little sneaky, but greatly appreciated. She suggested to Kay
that she might enjoy having a rehearsal pianist so that she could
occasionally get away from the piano. Kay must have been in a
good mood that day because she latched on to the idea immediately and agreed to engage me.

When Loulie broke the news to me, we were both intoxicated by the possibilities. Loulie was all joy, but I was scared.
At 8 A.M. the next morning I went to Miss Thompson's residence at 522 Madison Avenue, to give her a chance to turn me
down if I wasn't what she was looking for. I was too green to
know that 8 a.m. is the middle of the night for show people. Of
course I woke her up and tried to slink away, but she grabbed
my arm in a vicelike grip.

Kay: Oh, come on in. I'm awake now. You might as well have
coffee with me.

Hugh: I don't want to put you to any trouble. I just thought I
should play for you before rehearsals start—in case I'm hopeless.

Kay: How can you be hopeless? Jean says you're wonderful. Are
you wonderful?

Hugh: Um. Yes, I am.

Kay: Then that's settled. I'll see you Monday.

I turned to go.

Kay Thompson and Quartet. 1936

Kay: Wait a minute!

That *voice!* It was like the trumpet of Caesar's legions.

Kay: Are you free at noon today?

Hugh: Yes, I am.

Kay: There's a young man coming here to audition for me at noon. Could you play for him?

Hugh: Of course.

When I came back at noon, I found that the young man Kay had referred to was already there. Ralph Blane was five feet eleven as was I. He was shy, soft-spoken, and his face had a warm, sweet geniality that made us eager to know him better.

Kay: Did you bring any music, Ralph?

Ralph: Yes, I did. I hate to ask you to play this thing, sir.

Hugh: Call me Hugh.

Ralph: It's a real tapeworm, I'm afraid.

He reached for a scroll and began to unroll it. It seemed to go

Kay Thompson and her Rhythm Singers
in the movie Manhattan Merry-Go-Round, *1938.*

on for miles. He placed it on the music rack of Miss Thompson's black spinet where it flopped over on both sides. Miss Thompson was amused but persistent.

Kay: Didn't you bring a pop song? "Blue Skies?" "Dinah?" "Ain't Misbehavin'"?

Ralph: I'm sorry, Miss Thompson. I just arrived from Oklahoma, and my voice teacher wouldn't let me sing pop songs.

Kay: Where in Oklahoma?

Ralph: Broken Arrow.

She was afraid to laugh out loud; he looked so earnest, but I could see a quizzical little smile playing upon her lips.

Kay: What's the name of your song?

Ralph: "The Organ, the Monkey, and Me."

That did it! We all allowed ourselves a good laugh, and it broke the ice. Ralph launched into his big number, a shoddy little art song.

But hold everything! The voice coming out of that cherubic face sounded as if it had been devised by divine command. We were enthralled. His tone was rich, golden, opulent, a voice that could hold its own on any operatic stage. When he finished singing, Miss Thompson was almost speechless.

Kay: That's quite a voice, Ralph. Can you read music?

Ralph: Not very well.

Hugh: He's got a great ear, Miss Thompson. Perfect intonation, right on the nose. I could teach him anything you give him to sing.

Ralph shot me a thank-you look. Miss Thompson cogitated.

Kay: See here, do you know what a riff is?

Ralph looked blank.

Kay: A jazz riff?

A faint glimmer lit his round face.

Kay: All right. Now here's what we're going to do. I'm going to sing to you a riff, a jazz lick. And you will try to sing it back to me. Just imitate me the best you can.

Miss Thompson sat at her piano and sang:

Ta tiria dot dah ,
Dot dot ta tiria dot.
Ta tiria dot dah,
Dot dot ta tiria dot.
Ta tiria dot dah,
Dot dot ta tiria dot. WHOA!

This is not an easy lick. I got it instantly because of the group singing I had done in Birmingham, but Ralph struggled. He struggled so determinedly that his cheeks became quite red, and tears welled in his blue eyes. Miss Thompson was in a dilemma. She had hit a roadblock and was deciding whether to back up or roll over it.

"Miss Thompson," I interposed. "Miss Thompson, could you go have a cup of coffee or something? Give me five minutes with Ralph—no, ten—and let me see what I can do."

She did. And I did. Most important, Ralph did. He came through like the champ he always was, and it was the beginning of three things: the songwriting team of Martin and Blane, day one with the guru that Kay Thompson was to become to me, and the watershed I had been seeking for years. I'm sorry I woke you up that fateful morning, dear Kay, but it was the beginning of the rest of my life. God bless you!

I find it ironic and a bit sad that Kay should be remembered more for writing the *Eloise* books than for her magnificent singing and dancing. There is almost no one I'd rather watch than Kay Thompson doing her thing, either alone, or with the Williams Brothers, or in *Funny Face* with Fred Astaire and Audrey Hepburn. Inevitably my eyes go to Kay, no matter whom she's with.

Willard Robison and His Deep River Orchestra

Another lucky break came indirectly through my old high-school-days hero, Willard Robison, whose radio program on Friday nights, *Willard Robison and his Deep River Orchestra,* had been such an inspiration to me. I wrote to radio station WOR and they mailed me a ticket to one of Willard's programs. My excitement was almost more than I could bear when I was admitted to a large studio where I saw Mr. Robison himself sitting at a piano in a corner. Grouped around him was a thirty-piece studio orchestra and a tangle of microphones. No wonder, I thought, that the orchestra sounded so rich. Someone at WOR must have admired Willard the way I did because this was a sustaining program, unsponsored, with the studio itself paying the bills.

After the program I timidly approached the piano and introduced myself to him, to tell him how profoundly his music had impacted me during my high school years. He must have been touched by my intensity because he introduced me to his brilliant orchestrator, William Grant Still. Still was far more than an arranger; he has been called "The Dean of Afro-American Composers," and some of the music he has written is among the most glorious to be heard in the concert hall.

It's ironic that of all my adolescent heroes, the first I would meet would be Willard Robison. I had been warned by family, friends, and Warner Bros. that New Yorkers were cold-blooded, hard-hearted, gun-toting rascals. And here, first crack out of the barrel, was Willard, as warm and gentle a human being as ever came out of America. You won't find sweeter music than Willard's untrained voice turned into gold by the gorgeous sonorities of William Grant Still.

Willard asked me about my interest in music. I told him I sang, played piano, and did vocal arrangements. I told him about The Blue Shadows and described a few of the harmonic vocal gimmicks I had used.

I visited the program several times, and one night Willard invited me to his private studio, where he asked me to play the piano for him. I think he felt, as I did, that we were kindred souls. About this time he finally landed a commercial, five-times-a-week fifteen- minute program on NBC during prime time. With him and his orchestra would be Mildred Bailey, whom I had adored as much as I adored Willard, and a girls trio. To my astonishment, he invited me to join the program as vocal arranger for the trio. I thought I must be dreaming, but it happened just as Willard said it would, and I was paid the grand salary of fifteen dollars a week! Regrettably, I seldom saw the fifteen dollars because Willard borrowed it almost every week and never paid it back. I soon learned that Willard had a little problem with alcohol, and I suspect that my fifteen dollars a week went into the coffers of the Crown Bar on 50th Street and Broadway. But I would have given him the shirt off my back, so I wasn't about to worry about fifteen dollars.

Willard had the mistaken notion that because I had a feeling for blues and black music in general, I was a jazz pianist. Lee Wiley, who was a great jazz singer, called Willard to say that she was desperate for a pianist. I was Lee's rehearsal pianist for two uncomfortable weeks. Then she fired me. Willard said that she had called him and said, "I wasn't *that* desperate."

Georgia on My Mind

About this time an invitation to visit Franklin and Eleanor Roosevelt at their retreat in Warm Springs, Georgia, took me back south. A local boys' choir with a national reputation had been asked to do a command performance for the President and his wife. Their accompanist had suddenly taken ill, and their leader phoned me to ask if I'd be interested in subbing for him. Would I! I loved FDR, and I loved Eleanor even more.

After the performance, we filed past President Roosevelt, and he shook everyone's hand. "Great bunch of kids, aren't they?" he said to me. Then I managed to screw up enough courage to wander over to Eleanor, who was standing quietly in a dark corner observing the scene. I had my opening remark all ready.

"I'm a good friend of your orchestra leader, Mrs. Roosevelt. Willard Robison gave me my first job in the big city."

It was a perfect entrée. Everyone loved Willard, and Mrs. Roosevelt was no exception. She beamed and chatted with me warmly about her commercial daily NBC series, "My Day." It is a moment I still cherish.

Chapter 7

Those Dirty Chesterfield Singers

Much of what I am able to tell you about this group is courtesy of Bea Wain, who was a member of the original Kay Thompson Rhythm Singers. Bea lives about a hundred miles from me, so we are able to see each other occasionally, and when we can't, we phone. She filled a few gaps in my memory about those glorious days in the sixteenth floor rehearsal room at 485 Madison Avenue, where Kay put together the arrangements for her Chesterfield Series for CBS.

Bea, in addition to a lovely, lyrical, wide-ranged mezzo-soprano voice, has a stack of hit recordings and darn near total recall. She remembers things I would never remember—the paychecks, for instance, which came to $31.50 per week for each singer. It wasn't much, but frankly, I was so bedazzled by the company in which I suddenly found myself, I would gladly have paid the Chesterfield people more than $31.50 for the privilege of being there.

In those days, singers had no union, so we could be worked to death unless we wanted to drop out, which, of course, none of us did. We rehearsed six days a week, morning until night, without even a lunch break. That's how we became "those dirty Chesterfield singers." We brought in whatever it took to survive—coffee, Cokes, popcorn, an occasional sandwich—and we were too tired to clean up when we left at the end of the day. Consequently, when the CBS bigwigs glanced in, the sixteenth floor rehearsal room looked like a disaster area.

But to us it was Buckingham Palace, and Kay was the Queen because the marvelous sounds that came out of our throats were royal. Kay invented the arrangements on the spot. We were her instruments, the keys on which she played, the horns through which she blew. The vocal ensemble consisted of three young men and thirteen young women. Kay plucked us from many sources, some a little vulgar by CBS standards. Coming on the heels of the typical personnel of the day, we must have seemed a motley crew. There was Loulie Jean, of course; Bea Wain, the Mullen Sisters and the Vass Family, young, fresh-faced girls from the South; three good female singers from a popular CBS foursome, The Blue Flames; and Elizabeth Newburgher, who fell in love with and married one of Kay's male singers, Al Rinker. Al was the younger brother of Mildred Bailey. Al's singing partners were Ken Lane and John Smedburgh, and eventually, much to the displeasure of the original trio, me.

I doubt whether there were any happier people in the world at that time than Kay's group of thirteen girls and four boys. We might have been considered "dirty," but we were having fun and full of giggles. We loved Kay, we loved jazz—especially Kay's unique take on it. We were young, healthy, and good-looking. And we were working, drawing salaries in the middle of the Great Depression. Oh, they were meager salaries, to be sure, but enough to cover food and rent because we lived simply. We figured we had the last laugh, and we laughed often.

Kay tended to over-rehearse us; she could drive us pretty hard, and she did. Fortunately, we were all in love with her— *and* the music—so none of us ever watched the clock. We almost forgot to get hungry. Kay was aware of our submissiveness, but she had conscience enough not to want to push us too far. When she kept asking us to keep singing a new arrangement for the umpteenth time, she tried to cover up the endless repetitions by making us laugh. "Once more!" she would bellow. "Once more don't hurt nobody!"

Kay wore us out each day, yet she never seemed to tire. Rehearsal would begin with Kay seated at the piano. After an hour or two, when the routine was beginning to take shape, she would leap to her feet and say to me, "All right, Hugh. The piano is yours now." At first, hearing this clarion call to action brought traumatic memories of the old days when I was pianist in Bill Rollins' Orchestra and Bill would suddenly yell, "Take it, Hugh!"

But though that had been a mere two years ago, I was a little tougher now, a mite less easy to intimidate, and I startled Kay, the group, and myself by sitting down and reproducing more or less exactly what I had heard Kay play. This was my college, my university of higher learning. I began to experience some of Kay's genius. Every day I got a clearer view of the wheels clicking in that strong, dynamic Thompson mind.

It was a heady experience. After getting the hang of copying what she did, I went a step further and tried to analyze why she did it. The next step was trying to anticipate what she *might* do. This was probably the most exciting sensation, musically, that ever happened to me. When I tell interviewers that 99 percent of what I know about vocal arranging I learned from Kay, I am not whistling Dixie.

Chesterfield had to pay me a bit more than my singer friends because, as an instrumentalist, I was a member of Local 802, the Musicians' Union. Kay went a step further and asked André Kostelanetz to let me be the pianist in his orchestra on the series. To my joy, he agreed. This meant my salary would double, perhaps even triple. But my joy was about to be short-lived.

The big day arrived. I seated myself at a Steinway to join with Mr. Kostelanetz and the cream of New York's musicians in playing the opening orchestral number, "April in Paris." Along about the second chorus, the arrangement called for the strings to play F, F, F, D#, E, followed by a simple "plink" on my piano (G). The strings did their thing followed by silence. No "plink" issued from my nervous fingers. I had never played under someone with a baton in his hand, only in rinky-dink affairs where the leader man would yell, "Take it, Hugh!" That was intimidating enough, but to my frightened eyes, the great André Kostelanetz looked ten feet tall and that little thing in his hand was almost invisible. He indicated a downbeat and I almost "plinked," but at the last moment I froze. An officious little man, it might have been the contractor, was at my side in nothing flat. "Your services will no longer be needed, Mr. Martin. Thank you," he said.

With that, Mr. Kostelanetz took his place in a long string of eminent people who fired me. It was devastating the first time, but after a number of firings it became "So what's new?" Joshua Logan told me I should wear each firing as a badge of honor, a sign I knew what I stood for and was not ready to sell out for the sake of expediency.

This was obviously not the case with Mr. Kostelanetz. I had flunked my first test with Kay and thought she'd be ashamed of me. On the contrary, she was sorry it meant a financial loss to me. It was clear that in addition to a mentor who was changing my life, I now had a loyal friend, as well.

I think I was good for her, too. She could leave me on stage with the group and know I would protect her from any indignities, musical or otherwise. She trusted me, and I treasured her trust. She began to turn the sessions with the orchestrators over to me: "Hugh knows what I want, Leo. He'll break the whole number down for you. Forgive me, I've got to run."

Opening night, our debut broadcast finally arrived and met everyone's expectations, even ours. Kosty was in white tie, his musicians wore black tie, as did the male trio. The thirteen girls were outfitted in unobtrusive evening clothes, but the gown Kay wore was stunning. She looked as well as she sang—which is to say, "Terrific!"

Our first number was "I'm Shooting High" from *King of Burlesque*. It was what Kay called "rat race" tempo, and it must have brought fireworks into a million homes that night. The response nationwide was all that Kay and Kostelanetz and we, their support team, might have hoped for, not to mention the Chesterfield people.

We continued to do slave labor on the sixteenth floor, and I was happy to be a little cog in this musical juggernaut. But in show biz no one ever stays content very long. We are always looking for greener fields. I loved living and learning in Kay's shadow, but I longed to share the joy I saw in the faces of those sixteen singers. Singing has always been an obsession with me, bordering on religious fervor. One afternoon during rehearsal, I could stand it no longer. Kay had just said to me, "You're frowning. Don't you like the arrangement?"

Hugh: I love it.

Kay: Then?

(Pause)

Hugh: Those chords the boys sing back of you in the bridge—

Kay: Yes?

Hugh: It would sound fabulous in four-part harmony.

Kay: But I only have three boys. And each one has only one head.

Hugh (gulp): Kay?

Kay: Yes.

Hugh: Kay, I don't suppose by any stretch of the imagination you would let me sing with the group?

Kay: Do you sing?

Hugh: I sing.

Kay: Do you sing well?

Hugh: Not bad—on pitch—good rhythm—I'm not Bing Crosby.

Kay: They wouldn't pay you. They're a bunch of skinflints.

Hugh: Kay, I don't want to be *paid,* for goodness sake! I just thought, "Boy, what she could do with that fourth part!"

She looked thoughtful, then led me to the piano and sang me a very complicated fourth part that only dogs could hear. Dogs and Hugh Martin. I sang it back perfectly.

"You're in!" she cried. "Boys and girls," she announced, "meet your new member—Hugh's going to sing with us!"

The girls cheered. The boys did not. In fact they looked daggers at me and at Kay. I sang every week with the Rhythm Singers from then on and never failed to feel the hostility of the three men. They glowered at me, rehearsed with me only grudgingly, and tried to position me as far away from the microphone as they could get away with. It didn't faze me; I was having too much fun.

Kay did a movie about this time and brought me along to sing with the group. A featured player in the film was Joe DiMaggio, who had been persuaded to sing a song. He wanted Kay to accompany him, but she considered it beneath her dignity to do that, so she asked me if I would be his accompanist. I was delighted to oblige because I thought it might impress my baseball-playing brother, Gordon.

Chapter 8

Shangri-La on the Hudson

NEW YORK IN THE THIRTIES was indeed a "Wonderful Town." It's still wonderful and my heart leaps up each time I fly into JFK and look at that beautiful but hostile skyline. ("I'll lick you yet, you city with no heart!") But it's not the Utopia that I fell in love with in the thirties. Winters there were a little grim, but I was twenty plus and could take the cold and snow. I couldn't now, but back then everything was new and challenging and fun. The air was cleaner, the people friendlier. No, it's not my imagination, and it has nothing to do with generation gaps. Take consumers, for instance: when we went into a store, be it ever so humble or posh, we were treated with courtesy, usually even with warmth. Real people with real voices asked us how they could help us and seemed to want to know. We were never left hanging on the telephone while canned music assaulted our ears.

The theater was flourishing; scores of playhouses were open and playing to good business. Plays and musicals made sense, with a beginning, a middle and an end—an end that more often than not left the theatergoer satisfied, fulfilled, and edified. The musicals flowed with melody even when the libretto didn't make much sense. And the weightier plays profoundly comforted the afflicted and afflicted the comfortable. It was a healthy, vital era of theater and one for which I find myself wistfully longing. It's obvious that I am a grumpy old man, but I suspect I have plenty of company.

Someone who shared my point of view was my friend, the great choreographer, Agnes de Mille. She was a wizard with words, so let me quote from an extemporaneous interview she gave to the BBC in the 1980s:

> *I think that dancers can make their living (and they can make a pretty good one) so they have decent homes, and they have decent clothes, they're educated, they eat regularly, and all those agreeable things—but something's missing that we had before, and I don't think it's just because I'm an old woman sitting in a rocking chair remembering how things were in the lovely days. There was an excitement, there was an adventure, there was a marvelous sense of things happening, of being in the middle of dynamic, creative change. It exploded! The audiences really rushed out to talk about things. They rushed to come back. Now I think they're rather jaded in a way, and I don't think the dancers themselves—the youngsters—I don't think they have the devouring excitement to do little things. When you think of Martha Graham's girls who worked day and night—they all had to wait tables. They all had to earn their living—but then they would all come and give her five hours every single afternoon and night including weekends for the whole year 'round for nothing. No money. They got ten dollars a year, just for the privilege of stepping on the stage with her and being in a masterpiece, and they knew it was going to be a masterpiece. Now that, I think, that's almost religious—and that is gone as far as I know. And in a way it had to go, because you couldn't have the awful injustice. But on the other hand, this excitement is inspirational, and you're going to have to have that if you're going to have any more great new dancers.*

Central Park was healthy and vital, too. The trees were a green such as one sees in New England or Northern California;

they had not yet become smog dingy. And, as I mentioned before, it was relatively safe. My friends and I, especially when slightly stressed, often walked around the park after sunset and never felt threatened. It wasn't the Vienna Woods or the Bois de Boulogne, but it sufficed.

There was a certain decorum then, also. One was not allowed to dress too revealingly. I once lay on a rock in Central Park minus my T-shirt to get a bit of ultraviolet, and a nice Irish policeman suggested that I kindly put it on again. He said it so nicely, in fact, that I was only too happy to oblige.

The stores were positively Ali Baba-ish. Macy's was my first love. When I was a child, Ellie Gordon, always the indulgent mother, allowed me to drive everyone nuts as I barreled up all the down escalators. I loved Macy's so much I never got across the street to Gimbel's. But I still feel twinges of nostalgia for Saks, Tripler, Brooks Brothers, Bonwit Teller, and Tiffanys, of course, with its fantastic fairyland windows designed by Gene Moore.

Bloomingdales, where I worked as a mail clerk for a few weeks, is a good illustration of my disappointment in the degeneration of these fine stores today. In the old days, I was proud to be a menial at Bloomingdales because of the quality of its merchandise and the aristocratic ambiance that pervaded it. The gentlemen and ladies who served the public were well-dressed and spoke courteously in perfect English. One could almost ignore the muffled roar of the Lexington Avenue subways and imagine one was in Harrods. What whiz kid, I wonder, came in and threw out all the old-fashioned charm and dignity and put in blinking surrealistic lights, scads of mirrors, girls in mini-skirts, and lots of high-decibel Muzak?

52nd Street

The apartment I lived in during those halcyon days was almost as close to Carnegie Hall as that of Anita Loos, who lived directly across the street from it. I lived two blocks from it, four blocks from Central Park, and a block or two more from the two most famous delicatessens in Manhattan, the Stage and the Carnegie. Another temptation was 52nd Street, or "Swing Street" as it was called. I usually dined at home, and how easy it was after supper to wander three blocks south and start sampling the delights of the best jazz in the world. What a joy it was to be able to drift over to the Onyx or the Famous Door! If you walked along 52nd Street, marvelous jazz spilled out of the clubs to the sidewalk—no cover charge.

What fun to have enchanting neighbors (they seemed like neighbors), such brilliant performers as Maxine Sullivan, Louis Prima, Mildred Bailey, Teddy Wilson, Peggy Lee, and Billie Holiday!

> *In the shank of the night,*
> *When the doin's are right,*
> *You can tell 'em I'll be there!* [1]
> *(Thank you, Johnny Mercer)*

55th Street

It was Ralph's girlfriend, Sue Read, who got me into the hallowed halls of 145 West 55th Street, my first really desirable Manhattan residence. Sixty dollars a month put me only two blocks away from such landmarks as 57th Street, which was almost as posh as Fifth Avenue. I was only four blocks from beautiful St. Thomas's Cathedral with its gorgeous stained glass windows and great music. The New York City Center was almost next door to me, and the 55th St. Playhouse was across the street. There was a kind of tea-room half a block away in what used to be the stables of John D. Rockefeller, Sr. Frances Bell, who presided over it, loved indigent show folk, and many a dinner or lunch check was blithely torn up if Frances took a fancy to you.

---

1 Mercer, Johnny, and Hoagy Carmichael. "In the Cool, Cool, Cool of the Evening." Famous Music Corporation, 1951.

For those who were working and in the chips, there was the fabled Jane Davies Restaurant, right in the lobby of my building. Marvelous food, and we all adored it. Not just peasants like me, but also lots of celebrities. Jack Benny, George Burns, and Mary Martin dined there, as well as such stars of tomorrow as Gene Kelly and Van Johnson.

This magic block was a special little colony, autonomous, an island within the island. I believe it boasted gifted actors, directors, singers, and writers as prodigally as all of Greenwich Village, though I'm admittedly biased. It was a golden era, bursting at the seams with golden boys and girls. I lived there for thirty years and I savored every moment.

By the time I deserted the East Coast for the West in 1970, I had learned to love not just Broadway and environs, but the whole of Manhattan. Riverside Drive, the churches and museums, Chelsea, Harlem—all had their charms and still do. I suspect I'll always be a New Yorker at heart.

Don't Shoot the Piano Player

The only thing that took the edge off those halcyon days was the fact that the only jobs I could get were in saloons. If you really care a lot about music, playing saloon piano is probably not your dream job. Heaven knows it was wonderful to have a job at all in those depression days. But I felt trapped being a barroom pianist, and longed to express myself, to feel I was making some progress, no matter how tiny.

I took my fair share of flak with those jobs. For example, if the guests got noisy, whom did the bar manager yell bawl out? Not the guests, the pianist, that's who. The bar manager would come to my piano and say something like, "For Pete's sake, don't play that Prokofiev piece again. People don't come here for classical music. Play 'Melancholy Baby!'"

Even so, there were serendipities. I was playing the piano one slow night in the bar of the (then) Park Central Hotel on Seventh Avenue between 54th and 55th Streets in west Manhattan. A waiter came to the piano with a note for me. I read with disbelieving eyes: "Would you like to have a drink with me?" The note was signed, "D.W. Griffith."

The waiter pointed to a table in the shadows where a kingly looking older man sat alone. I approached him timidly because I recalled a time when he *was* Hollywood, a giant artistically, the director of *The Birth of a Nation, Orphans of the Storm,* and Broken *Blossoms.* He had discovered and mentored Dorothy and Lillian Gish, and Richard Barthelmess, three mythical heroes of mine.

He was as timid as I—probably, as I learned later from a Griffith biography, because he had been rejected by the town he had created. He was a broken and desperately lonely man. He told me he loved my playing and tipped me twenty-five dollars, not a paltry sum in those days.

My mother once told me that the only time she ever felt sure she was looking at genius was one night when Richard Strauss conducted a concert in Birmingham. Ellie Gordon was working backstage that night, and saw the maestro, after he had conducted one of his tone poems, leaning against a wall in the wings, sweating profusely.

I thought of Mother that night, as I sat with D.W. Griffith at a table in the shadowy Park Central bar. I never saw him again, but—like Ellie Gordon—I knew I was in the presence of genius, and I felt blest by the brief crossing of our paths.

I suppose we all have laundry lists of missed opportunities that we never forgive ourselves for. I suspect my list is longer than most. On my list is not having followed through with my meeting with Mr. Griffith, and not because I wanted anything from him. On the contrary, I think I had something to give him. If I am to believe his biographers, everyone, including his wife and dearest friends, had turned their backs on this titan. I wish I had called him the next day, invited him to lunch, taken him to a museum or a concert, and tried to persuade him that people, even as young as I, realized his greatness.

Chapter 9

I Like the Theater, But Never Come Late

When I first arrived in New York in the 1930s, the theater was startlingly alive and well. We had, to name a few, Eugene O'Neill, Clifford Odets, Philip Barry, Noël Coward, Bernard Shaw, Chekhov, Sidney Kingsley, Ibsen, and Maxwell Anderson—no mean refreshment. Also, a special favorite of mine, Thornton Wilder.

And our producers—like George Abbott, Max Gordon, Herman Shumlin, Dwight D. Wiman, Florenz Ziegfeld, The Theatre Guild, and many others—were dedicated men and women who passionately loved the theater and gave their lives to promoting her welfare. I must not omit Jed Harris who, in 1937, gave us Thornton Wilder's *Our Town*—in my opinion the greatest American play.

The musicals—even more miraculous! There have been golden ages of playwriting and production in the past, but nothing like the dazzling, innovative proliferation of great musicals that illuminated the stages during this era. At least not since Gilbert and Sullivan were doing their thing.

The Gershwin brothers knocked us all for a loop with *Of Thee I Sing,* and Ira took home a Pulitzer Prize in the process. Rodgers and Hart opened some new doors with *On Your Toes,* the first time that ballet advanced the plot instead of interrupting it. Irving Berlin and Moss Hart raised the standard of revue so high that *As Thousands Cheers* has still not been topped. Cole Porter raised the flag of hedonism over a series of naughty little entertainments so brilliantly fashioned that he made us all forget the foolish librettos.

But the father of us all was and is Jerome Kern. He never felt the need to take the trailblazing style of *Show Boat* into new, uncharted fields. Evidently he didn't have an overwhelming desire to break new ground after that. I think he felt that he and Oscar Hammerstein II had pushed the limits of unconventionality just far enough.

Mr. Kern had a rich and elegant lady friend upon whom he relied as a sort of mentor. "Jerry," she once casually remarked to him, "don't ever take on a project that doesn't have a little of the fragrance of sachet clinging to it." How astute of her. She blessed us all with that simple admonition, that led to *Sweet Adeline, Music in the Air, The Cat and the Fiddle,* and *Very Warm for May,* all of which have more than a little of the fragrance of sachet clinging to them.

But what makes Kern "numero uno," at least for me, is that he seemed unable to write a bad song. This can be very irritating to us lesser mortals who turn out at least two mediocre songs for every good one. We songwriters scratch our heads in wonder.

Chapter 10

Hooray for What!

I HAD MY THEATRICAL BAPTISM in a Shubert musical launched in 1937. The show was *Hooray for What!*, the brainchild of E.Y. (Yip) Harburg, always a strong crusader for world peace and brotherly love. Yip was trying his wings with this ingenious fable about a mad peacenik named "Chuckles," who almost succeeds in bringing all the nations of the world to the peace table. I believe *Hooray for What!* might have been a great show if sensitive producers had understood Yip's dream and brought it to the stage of the Winter Garden as he had conceived it. At least the Shuberts gave him a star worthy of the project.

Ed Wynn played the zany "Chuckles" to perfection. At every performance, eight times a week, two shadowy figures huddled in the wings. One of them was a very young Keenan Wynn. Keenan was determined to be a fine comedian in his own right, and heaven knows he succeeded. His training began in the wings watching every flicker on the face of his remarkable father. There was plenty to watch; no two performances by Mr. Wynn were alike. He was always experimenting, always trying to stay one step ahead of the audience, who knew nothing of the meticulous, exquisite care that went into each Ed Wynn performance. But for Ed Wynn, I would never have experienced the magic of watching a great clown hone his craft, for I was the other shadowy figure huddling close to Keenan so as not to get thrown out by our stage manager. Mr. Murray, father of Don Murray, was a sweetheart, but a perfectionist, and we knew that he wouldn't hesitate to give us the boot if we slowed up the tempo.

One thing only was constant at each performance: as "Chuckles" walked off stage at the end of a scene, the happy, cockamamie Ed Wynn face, with every corner turned up, would collapse into a tragic mask. As he walked to his dressing room, Keenan and I would look at each other, sometimes with tears. Keenan longed to see his father smiling as he exited, and I, too, ached to see it. But that joy, during the entire nine months run, was never realized.

Nothing I could tell you about the trials and tribulations of *Hooray for What!* could improve on Agnes de Mille's account of it in her fascinating little volume *Portrait Gallery*.[1] It gives an accurate picture of the goings-on during this show's rocky road to Broadway via Boston and Philadelphia.

How did I get sucked into this carnival called The Shubert Empire? Kay Thompson was the talk of New York show business, winning praise in America via coast-to-coast radio, while the grapevine spread the news that seeing her in person was even more dynamic than simply listening to her sing her unique vocal arrangements.

One of the first to notice Kay's charisma was Harold Arlen. He came one night to watch us do our radio show and came back the following week with Yip Harburg, who immediately joined Harold on the Thompson band wagon. A flurry of phone calls followed: to Lindsay and Crouse, book writers; Vincente Minnelli, director, and, I regret to say, the Shuberts. How I wish the musical could have been launched by a producer with class. I've often wondered why the Shuberts were chosen. My hunch is that they had Ed Wynn under contract and Mr. Wynn was an essential part of the equation.

---

1 De Mille, Agnes. *Portrait Gallery*. New York: Houghton Mifflin, 1990, pg. 314.

Hooray for What!

In all fairness I must admit there was one Shubert with a sense of fairness and courtesy. I have great respect for Johnny Shubert, nephew of Lee, and son of J.J. Our paths crossed later during World War II, and I found him to be an officer and a gentleman.

Kay was engaged for the show and she brought Ralph Blane and me into it with her. Just before we went into rehearsal with *Hooray for What!*, one of Kay's girl singers dropped out. I presumed to ask Kay if she would audition Wynelle Patterson. Wynelle was the girl singer with Harrison Cooper's Orchestra when I went to South America with his band in 1932. She was visiting New York at the time, but Kay's schedule was too formidable for an audition, so she took her on my recommendation. Wynelle's presence in the company turned out happily for everyone. Kay liked her voice, and everyone was impressed with her beauty. Agnes liked her, too, although Wynelle's southern slowness didn't exactly fit Agnes's drill sergeant "snap to it" style of staging. Agnes nicknamed her "Alabama."

"Alabama," Agnes reproved gently, "you're doing fine. But on that downbeat after the change of key, all the girls are supposed to spring up from the kneeling position and be instantly upright on 'two.' Every time this happens, the girls pop up and you come straggling up two beats later."

"Oh, Miss DeMille!" Alabama looked stricken with remorse. "I don't understand it either. I leave the floor at the same time they do."

Rehearsals for *Hooray!* got off to a flying start at the Majestic Theater. The schedule was rigorous; we had no union to protect us, and Minnelli seemed oblivious to our need for food and sleep. Seeing the crumpling effect his rehearsals were having on my fellow gypsies gave me a flash of righteous anger. I tried to rally the "kids," as chorus people seem destined always to be called, into squaring off against Minnelli and his punishing rehearsals by refusing to show up at the ungodly hours he demanded. The revolt fizzled out because my friends desperately needed their jobs and were too frightened to risk losing them.

Ten years later, I found myself facing him across a very large executive desk in his private suite at MGM, and the first thing he said to me was, "I hear you led the rebellion against me in Philly."

"Yes, I did." No use beating around the bush. Confession is good for the soul. No further reference was made to my call for "stouthearted men." I thought that after all those years he might think the whole incident was funny, but he looked very stern indeed.

Pandemonium Li'ble to Come Upon the Scene

Under Minnelli's direction, we rehearsed for six weeks, then loaded onto special train cars geared to transporting the huge cast, scenery, costumes—the whole kit and caboodle—to Boston where we were scheduled to open at the elegant Colonial Theater facing the Boston Commons. I experienced deeper. more intense musical thrills during those six weeks than in all the years of my long career that followed. I had been given no warning that assembling a major Broadway show is the most hypnotic, riveting endeavor so far invented. The climax is always the day that the rinky-dink rehearsal piano is put under wraps and the orchestra, in all its glory, starts exploding with gorgeous sonorities. Suddenly the little tunes we were beginning to tire of become symphonies and rhapsodies. Our orchestra reading took place at the Wilbur Theater, and I will never forget that experience. It was the most exciting day of my entire show biz life.

I had never worn stage make-up before, so I was at a loss. Ralph Blane to the rescue: the only thing we had was the tubes of Max Factor that we got at the drugstore because, way back in 1937 A.D., pancake hadn't been invented yet. The tubes were filled with greasy face paint that was very hard to remove, even with cold cream or Albolene. Ralph experimented with the colors to get the right formula for Hugh Martin. They all had picturesque names; we ended up with Sallow Old Man mixed with Ruddy Youth.

The last few days before the official Boston opening were chaotic. The Shuberts went on a rampage of firing people, which sent Minnelli into a frenzy, trying to fit the new people into the old staging. Someone told him that I was a pianist, and he dropped his resentment of me, begging me for help in setting keys and training the new actors. I jumped into the breach, gave up all my lunch breaks, and worked late into the night.

As a result of doing this favor for Vincente, I was absent from all the chorus rehearsals. So when I walked on the stage of the Colonial on opening night, my first such experience ever, I suddenly realized that since I hadn't been at those rehearsals, I also had no indoctrination on what to do or where to go. I stumbled around the stage clumsily. Some sixty plus years later, I still bless the "gypsies" who instantly sized up the situation and passed me smoothly from person to person in such a clever way that the audience was none the wiser.

Things seemed to be going well during the next few days. We got reasonably favorable notices, and business was good. The crash came with no warning at all. During an evening performance, I was crossing the basement floor to make a costume change when a bloodcurdling scream pierced my ears. Everyone froze. It had come from Kay Thompson's dressing room and was followed by heart-wrenching sobs from my beloved benefactor. Within minutes, it seemed, the whole company was aware that the Shuberts had fired Kay. We couldn't believe our ears. We had seen her stop the show night after night; we had heard the thunderous applause for her, and watched the slick way she played second banana to Ed Wynn. Fired? Impossible!

Agnes de Mille had also been purged. I'm so glad both Agnes and Kay were vindicated by successes in other media soon after the debacle. Agnes, bless her, was a tough and marvelous lady. She suffered the humiliation but rolled over it. Kay was more vulnerable. She rolled *under* it and it crushed her. She was well on her way to being the next Ethel Merman, but the benighted Shuberts broke her spirit. She never appeared again in a legitimate Broadway show. I wish she could have known then what tremendous success she would receive one day as an author. It's hard to bring the two Kay Thompsons together because they're so different: Kay Thompson, singing star, musician de luxe, and at the same time, Kay Thompson, author extraordinaire of the classic children's series of *Eloise* books written around an irrepressible, adorable little six-year-old brat who stood the Plaza Hotel on its head.

We in Kay's singing group were stunned. *Hooray for What!* was more to us than just another job. It was a musical we cherished deeply. It was a fraternity, a sorority, a club, almost an alma mater or a church.

Our first impulse was to walk out en masse before the Broadway opening previews, but Kay wouldn't let us do it. We begged to be allowed to demonstrate our loyalty to her, but she said, "You kids need this job. Why should you give it up to people who haven't sweated for it the way you have? Stay! And by staying you'll be helping to protect our good work."

Almost before we realized it, Kay was gone, though far from forgotten. Why did the Shuberts fire Kay? The reason was pathetically simple. Overlooking her unique and phenomenal gifts, they decided she did not have enough sex appeal, so she was expendable. The order went out, "Get a blonde with curves!" The blonde they got was Vivian Vance. Viv was an excellent comedienne and a sweet person. She would become famous in the fifties as Ethel Mertz in *I Love Lucy*, but Kay's shoes were impossible to fill. Vivian fought valiantly against replacing her. Like all of us, she adored Kay. But the Shubert mill ground exceedingly fine. The glory was gone; the show ran a decent nine months on Broadway, but oh, what a classic it could have been with Kay Thompson.

The Gutsiest Woman I've Ever Known

Agnes DeMille's vindication came shortly after the *Hooray!* firing thanks to Richard Rodgers and *Oklahoma!* I was only a chorus boy in *Hooray!*, but Agnes was wonderfully kind to me. She took me to lunch at Sardi's, a hitherto mythical venue reserved for the brightest and the best. When I asked questions regarding theatrical costumes and their changes through the centuries, she delved into her personal library, pulled out priceless books on the subject, and lent them to me, to be returned under pain of death. She even stuck me into two of her ballets in the show and gave me movements so easy that even I could master them. I loved her, especially her devastating yet compassionate wit. She wrote like a dream and her books on dancing are outstanding.

She had more guts than almost anyone I've ever known. After her massive stroke in 1975, which would have left most people incapacitated, she fashioned ballets that could hold their own with her master works choreographed before her stroke. She continued to write to her friends—not via dictation, no, she learned to write with her left hand. I treasure those clumsy-looking letters, difficult to read but symbolic of her indomitable spirit.

A Fateful Decision

During the turbulent run of *Hooray!,* a seemingly unimportant thing happened that in retrospect was very important indeed. Arthur Freed, the best producer of Hollywood musicals who ever lived, attended a performance. He was in the throes of trying to decide who should write the score for a pet project of his, *The Wizard Oz.* One of the songs he heard that night caught his attention. It was "In the Shade of the New Apple Tree." Arthur felt it possessed the tone that he was looking for in his forthcoming *The Wizard of Oz.* "Old-fashioned yet swingy," was how he described it. Listening that night at the Winter Garden, he found the solution to one of his biggest problems, and a few days later gave the assignment to *Hooray for What!'s* composer, Harold Arlen, and its lyricist, Yip Harburg. I heard this fascinating story from Laura Lynn Broadhurst, who wrote to me for information she needed for a doctoral dissertation.

What made my ears perk up was the realization that the "Apple Tree" number is old-fashioned sounding if you play the sheet music as written. It sounds rather like a minuet, but it's not at all swingy.

However, enter a brash, ambitious young chorus boy named Hugh Martin. They had fired Kay Thompson, and they wanted the third chorus to be a vocal arrangement of the song for male quartet, of which I was a member. I demurred out of respect for my adored mentor, Kay, but Kay urged me to do it.

"If the songs sound good they will help all of us, even me," she said, so I chose three of the singers, combined them with me, and made a Modernaires-type vocal arrangement for four boys that sounded less like a minuet and more like Glenn Miller.

Could my little arrangement possibly have been the catalyst that pushed Freed irrevocably into the Arlen-Harburg choice? I have a tendency to be my own press agent at times, so when asked about the authenticity of this story, I just smile inscrutably.

Chapter 11

Sing for Your Supper

MY FRIENDS SUPPOSED AND HOPED that after the hijinks and dirty tricks of *Hooray for What!*, I would regain my right mind and return to storming the gates of NBC and CBS. I knew they were probably right, and I half-heartedly made the rounds of the radio networks. NBC asked me to be a page. I accepted the offer because I needed a good weekly paycheck, but at the last minute I didn't show up. The theater bug had bitten me and I was hooked. During the six-months run of *Hooray for What!*, *Our Town* had opened a few blocks away from the Winter Garden, and many from our company flocked to see their Thursday matinee whenever we could. (Our matinee was on Wednesday; the Henry Miller Theater had a Thursday matinee.) The beauty of *Our Town* overwhelmed my fellow performers and me, and probably played a part in inspiring a lot of us to consider the acting profession.

I began to make the rounds of the theater agents in the Broadway area, with precious little encouragement. One or two liked my looks, but when I confessed to zero acting experience, it was usually "Sayonara." A young agent, Eve Gincher, was the exception. Eve liked me, was touched by my love for the theater, and tentatively sent me to a few producers.

She arranged a movie audition as well. I was asked to show up at David Selznick's plush offices on Park Avenue to read for *Gone with the Wind*. They gave me a scene for Charles Hamilton who was Melanie's brother and Scarlett's first husband. The folks at the casting table complimented my authentic southern accent, and they thought I looked right. Well, almost. When they turned me down, they explained, "You don't look robust enough to threaten Clark Gable." I couldn't argue with that!

In the midst of all this rejection, I had a compulsion to write a letter to Richard Rodgers, a hero of mine. I had never seen, much less met him. I don't remember where I sent the letter—possibly in care of ASCAP, since I hadn't the foggiest notion where he lived. Nor do I have the foggiest notion why I took it into my head to write him. I'm glad I did, though, because it changed my life. As nearly as I can remember, the gist of the letter was as follows:

Dear Mr. Rodgers:

Before explaining the purpose of this presumptuous letter, may I try to tell you what a tremendous impact your music and the lyrics of your partner, Lorenz Hart, have had on this aspiring twenty-four-year-old musician.

It is precisely because your songs are so great that I dare to ask this question: why do I never hear anything resembling a vocal arrangement when I go to see a Broadway musical? I certainly hear the most wonderful songs being written anywhere in the world today. But I feel cheated when I hear nothing more imaginative than a verse and two choruses—or at best an interlude or a patter of some kind. When I go to the movies, I hear all sorts of inventive treatments that seem to me to enhance the quality of the songs. The songs themselves are seldom as good as the Broadway material—nothing that could inspire the least envy of you and Mr. Hart, or the Gershwins, or Jerome Kern, or Irving Berlin; but sometimes I have more fun at the movies because I find that I enjoy the surprises that musical movies give me when they elaborate on the simple verse and two chorus routines.

I realize I have a heck of a nerve writing such seemingly critical thoughts to a giant like you, but honestly, Mr. Rodgers, I am simply asking for information, not in a spirit of criticism.

Your grateful admirer,
Hugh Martin

After I posted the letter, I thought, "Why in the world did I do that? Who am I to tell Richard Rodgers how to present his glorious music? Maybe Mae West was right and I really am crazy."

Well, *au contraire.* A few days later I received a phone call from a pianist friend of mine named Joe Moon.

Joe: Can you come down to the Alvin Theater right away? Dick Rodgers wants to talk to you. (pause) Hugh, are you there? Were we cut off?

Hugh (weakly): No, I'm here.

Joe: Well, when can you get yourself down here?

Hugh (gulp): Now. Where is it?

Joe: The Alvin? It's on 52nd Street between Broadway and Eighth Avenue. Come to the stage door and ask for me.

I did. Joe took me to Mr. Rodgers somewhere in the ropes and cables of the theater's wings. Rodgers greeted me warmly, thanked me for my letter, and remarked that it had arrived at an opportune time.

Rodgers: We are in rehearsal here with a new musical called *The Boys from Syracuse.* It is based loosely on Shakespeare's *Comedy of Errors.*

I tried to look intelligent.

Rodgers: There's a critical number right at the end of the show. You might call it "the eleven o'clock spot." You've heard that expression?

I hadn't but said I had.

Rodgers: It's called *Sing for Your Supper,* and Larry [Lorenz Hart] and I want to make it a trio composed of our three leading ladies, Marcy Wescott, Muriel Angelus, and Wynn Murray. We thought it would be amusing if they sang it like one of the girl trios that are so popular nowadays. You've heard of the Dolly Sisters?

I hadn't but said I had.

Rodgers: Here's the song.

He handed me a production copy of "Sing for Your Supper."

Rodgers: Take it home and play it—fool around with it and come back here tomorrow and let me know what you think of it.

I did as I was told. I went home, played it on my rented upright piano, sang it, and fell in love with it. I was probably one of the first to hear it, but seventy years have flown by since my first impression and thousands of Rodgers and Hart buffs have since confirmed my humble seal of approval.

"What a wonderful song!" I thought. And being fairly egocentric then, my subconscious added, "and what a break for me!"

I sat at the piano for a couple of hours fooling around with it as Mr. Rodgers had suggested. I also prayed hard. I desperately wanted to make this wonderful song more wonderful.

Early the following day I reported to Mr. Rodgers. Mr. Hart remained invisible through all this, seeming to prefer to let his partner mastermind the unconventional treatment being planned.

There is a manager's office one floor above the stage door at the Alvin, spacious enough (or so it seemed in 1938) for a baby grand piano and a dozen or so people to surround it. Mr. Rodgers took me there, and I was certain he would ask me to sing what I had written. I was vastly relieved when he told me instead to sit tight while he attempted to spring his three leading ladies from their various rehearsals.

"I'll be right back," he said cheerily.

I was not so cheery—terrified was more like it—but the adventurer in me overcame my anxieties. I knew I had written a gangbusters arrangement, and I wanted to know whether it would sound as good in the throats of three top-notch Broadway stars as it did in my head.

About a quarter of an hour later, the door opened and in walked Mr. Rodgers with Marcy, Muriel, and Wynn in tow. I was prepared for the Botticelli-like Marcy to knock my eyes out. I had seen her in *The Two Bouquets* with Alfred Drake, and I knew she was a dazzler. But Muriel was beautiful, too—an English redhead with a peaches and cream complexion like Greer Garson's, who came on the scene ten years later. And even Wynn, though her comic stock in trade was her weight (about 250 pounds), had a pretty and vivacious face. It was a formidable trio of thrushes.

"This young man has made a trio arrangement of 'Sing for Your Supper,' and we're all anxious to find out what he's done," explained Mr. Rodgers. He introduced the young ladies to me and started for the door. "Come and get me when you're ready to let me hear it." Off he went, leaving me with three gorgeous and gifted women. I was nonplussed but suddenly ready for the challenge.

"It's a verse and three choruses," I said in a weak voice. "Mr. Rodgers told me the voice ranges of each of you, but please holler if I've put you too high or too low." They smiled and nodded. Photocopying machines were non-existent in 1938, so we all four huddled around the single copy on the piano.

The verse was a snap, no problems there. Each of the ladies seemed comfortable with the keys. The first chorus was a cinch, too—alternating solos, no fancy stuff. Then after many repetitions, we came to the third chorus, the zinger, where most of my novel ideas were packed. That chorus was what brought on the bombshell. A cloud passed over Wynn Murray's plump face.

Wynn: Is this harmony?

Hugh: Well, yes. It's a trio. Trios sing harmony.

Wynn: I can't sing harmony.

Marcy: Oh, Wynn, of course you can sing harmony.

Muriel: We'll help you, darling.

Marcy: Hugh will be very patient. Won't you, Hugh?

Wynn: I really can't sing harmony. I used to try when we sang songs at school. They always gave up and let me sing melody.

Hugh: That shouldn't be a problem. Ninety percent of the time you are on melody, but there *are* a few little spots when three-part harmony will really make people smile. I don't think it's ever been done in a Broadway musical.

Wynn looked threatened. Her big eyes looked as if they might spill over with tears. "I'll try."

Marcy: Atta girl!

Muriel: Good show!

Hugh: Bless you!

We pitched in and started the hackwork of getting the harmony parts in their necks. To my great relief, Marcy and Muriel were conservatory trained and read like a streak. Wynn was a natural belter who had never been asked to do anything else, so she had never learned. But look at her! She was red in the face, straining every muscle, eyebrows knit in intense concentration. I loved her! I loved all three of them!

And they loved me. I think they sensed my desperate desire to get my foot in the door, and they felt sorry for me. Many years later, I saw *The Odd Couple* on screen, and the high spot was the scene with the Pigeon Sisters. Their struggle to buck up Jack Lemmon conjured up my struggle to teach Wynn harmony, and the way Marcy and Muriel strove to save the day for me. Even the British accents were there to make it all come together.

Back at the piano, harmony was going well until the process was halted by a loud shriek from Wynn, "I can't do it!"

I was mute, seeing my big chance fly out the window in the key of G flat. But Marcy and Muriel, my own precious Pigeon Sisters, had not given up. One of them left hurriedly to fetch coffee; the other mopped Wynn's brow and fanned her with a magazine.

The session appeared to have ended in defeat. But wait, Wynn said she would get a good night's sleep and try again the next day. Cheers from the Pigeons and a petrified me. We hugged goodbye, practically brother and sisters by now, and I went down to the stage to find Mr. Rodgers and tell him the tragic news. I was startled when he roared with laughter.

Rodgers: Don't worry, Hugh. I've gone through many a crisis with actresses who think they've been pushed beyond their abilities.

I think Wynn will get it eventually. She's very musical, you know, and quite intelligent in her own peculiar way. Be patient."

I promised him I would, but I must have looked so woebegone that I could still hear him laughing as I stumbled through the stage door onto 52nd Street.

The next day we all came back to the scene of the crime. Mr. Rodgers had scheduled two hours for the afternoon ordeal. Wynn came in bravely, said she was feeling fit, and ready to lick her demons. We took off our coats, ties, scarves, rolled up our sleeves, and went at it.

It was maddening. Wynn would get her teeth into the harmony part, send it vibrating merrily into the air, then *zoink*, she would slip over into Muriel's part or perhaps Marcy's. Many tears were shed, and it looked for a while as if we were a lost cause. Then it happened. The two girls exchanged meaningful glances with me as I sat pounding away at the piano. Wynn was holding on for dear life to her harmony part, and it sounded terrific. We roared through the whole trick third chorus, and except for a few minor glitches we crossed the line in a photo finish! Such cheers! Such hugs! Such tears, but happy ones!

"Go get Mr. Rodgers," said Muriel.

"No!" screamed Wynn, "what if I can't do it again?"

"Wynn is right," said level-headed Marcy. "Let her get one more good night's sleep and one more rehearsal. Then nothing will knock her off that harmony. She'll have it right here," she said, and rapped on Wynn's head. We all agreed that was good thinking, and when we assembled the third day it was there, nice and solid.

We were ready at last for Mr. Rodgers to join us. He came. He heard. We conquered.

Never one for hyperbole, he said simply, "That is remarkable, just what I hoped for. I have a feeling it will work."

After a couple of run-throughs, Mr. Rodgers said I could turn it all over to the specialists now, the choreographer in particular, and that I was welcome to attend rehearsals any time I wished, but that if I wanted to get on with other jobs, I was free to do so.

"No, wait," he added, "there's one more person you should meet before you leave us. I'd like you to have a session with Hans Spialek who will orchestrate your arrangement."

I knew Spialek's work and loved it. Hans was an exemplary musician, and I had been thrilled by his work in previous Rodgers and Hart shows. An effervescent but quiet gentleman from Czechoslovakia, Hans was always referred to by Mr. Rodgers as "the bouncing Czech."

It still moves me that Mr. Rodgers, who was at the top of his game, treated me with complete respect right from the start rather than with the rejection, indifference, and even derision I had encountered so frequently from others. He then patiently mentored me, a Johnny-come-lately who had never written a single song. Always the gentleman, he dressed conservatively, but made us laugh with risqué but tasteful jokes.

The Lonely Lyricist

A couple of years after *The Boys from Syracuse,* Rodgers and Hart did another show with George Abbott, *Too Many Girls.* The first day of rehearsals, a smiling Dick Rodgers handed me a production copy of "I Like to Recognize the Tune." He said, "Your arrangement of 'Sing for Your Supper' gave us the idea for this song. I think it's right up your alley."

I was speechless. I never thought I would trigger a Rodgers and Hart song. I think Dick enjoyed my confusion as much as I treasured the moment, and I felt very close to him.

Lorenz "Larry" Hart created the finest lyrics about loneliness ever written. The reason is pretty obvious; he was monumentally lonely. He had dozens of friends who praised and adored him, but there was never that "someone" as in "Make Someone Happy." And he wanted that more than he wanted to be rich and famous.

I realize I am being presumptuous to do this two-bit analysis of a very great man. I wouldn't risk it if I didn't feel it was common knowledge. We all loved Larry, and felt we knew what made him tick. Show people have a sixth sense about these things. We knew when Judy Garland married Vincente Minnelli that, though they were both brilliant and loving human beings, and produced a daughter of enormous ability and charm, something was not quite right. We couldn't explain it but we knew it. We understood about Larry, too, and prayed for an epiphany that never came.

In "A Ship without a Sail," he wrote:

Still alone, still at sea.
Still there's no one to care for me.
When there's no hand to hold my hand,
Life is a loveless tale
For a ship without a sail.

In "Spring Is Here," he wrote,
Spring is here,
Why doesn't the breeze delight me?
Stars appear!
Why doesn't the night invite me?
Maybe it's because nobody loves me.
Spring is here, I hear.

I found his lyrics heartbreaking, joyous, bitter-sweet, funny, and rousing to a degree I felt other lyricists never quite attained. I wonder if anyone could have touched hearts as deeply? I think not.

In spite of his innate sweetness, sometimes Larry behaved outrageously. There were violent outbursts, often about nothing at all; he could be profane and loud and rude. He went on drunken benders that took him to God-knows-where and lasted for long periods, sometimes right in the middle of rehearsals for a big budget musical. Professional to his fingertips, though, by opening night he made sure the lyrics were there and perfect. I admired Dick Rodgers' commitment to Larry. Dick and Dorothy loved the man and did everything possible to make him a "member of the wedding."

Dick resolutely turned down any offer that left Larry out, and tried to please him, even when Larry was in one of his unreasonable cycles. For instance, Larry had an unfortunate propensity for breaking up rehearsals when he drank too much. Sometimes he erupted with laughter; other times with rage. An example of the former was when he asked the drummer for "Too Many Girls" what his name was. When the man said "Jesus," it sent Larry into a laughing jag from which the rehearsal never recovered.

An example of his fits of rage happened at the same rehearsal. When the chorus girls made their first entrance wearing stunning costumes designed by Raoul Pène du Bois, Larry screamed, "Is he crazy? They look better than the principals. Throw them out! He's got to make our leading ladies look great!"

By the end of the work session, he had calmed down enough that I dared to speak to him. I told him that one of the top orchestras of the day had already recorded the featured ballad of the show, "I Didn't Know What Time It Was."

Larry reacted like a man shot out of a cannon. " Gotta hear it!" he cried. "Gotta hear it tonight!" I told him I knew a music store that was open until midnight, and he asked me to take him there. He spurned my offer of a taxi, and off we went on foot. My friends at the Colony were impressed, and Larry liked the recording. Those ten minutes with Larry, between the Imperial Theater and the Colony Music Store were the only ten minutes I ever spent one-on-one with the great man, but I learned a lot about him in a roundabout way.

Chapter 12

It Was a Very Good Year

*1*939 WAS A VERY GOOD YEAR, not just for me. but in all areas of entertainment: movies, theater, and radio. Hollywood outdid itself, churn-
ing out one film classic after another. As a movie-goer imagine having
the luxury of choosing from such films as *Gone With the Wind, The
Wizard of OZ, Ninotchka, The Women, Beau Geste, Love Affair, Of Mice
and Men, Wuthering Heights, Babes in Arms, Goodbye Mr. Chips, The
Grapes of Wrath, Dark Victory, The Hunchback of Notre Dame, The Story
of Vernon and Irene Castle, Snow White and the Seven Dwarfs,* and *Mr.
Smith Goes to Washington*!

"Vocal Arrangements by _____"

It was a also the year that sprang me from obscurity. I had made a
wish, in my letter to Richard Rodgers, that Broadway musicals would
start utilizing embellishments that vocal arranging could bring to
the art of musical comedy. My *Sing for Your Supper* made such a hit,
that suddenly "Vocal Arrangements by _____" was beginning
to appear on the programs of new musicals. And sometimes those

arrangements were by me! The first person to jump on this band-wagon was Joshua Logan. He was an intimate friend and colleague of Rodgers, so it was a natural connection.

My second experience in this new genre couldn't have been more exciting. Mr. Logan summoned me to the big old Majestic Theater where I had been clapping my hands with Kay Thompson and friends two years earlier. He was busy getting a new musical launched for producer Dwight Deere Wiman, but he took a coffee break when I showed up, frightened to my armpits.

Mr. Logan sized me up immediately and said, "Sit there," pointing to a piano bench in front of a rickety upright piano. "Don't move," he continued. "I'll be back as soon as I can find Ethel and Jimmy." He returned with Merman and Durante in tow and handed me a production copy of a song by Dorothy Fields and Arthur Schwartz called "It's All Yours." After introductions all around, he asked me to play it. "None of us has ever heard it," he said. "It's a duet for Ethel and Jimmy that comes late in the second act."

Oops, I thought, another eleven o'clock number. I hope I don't drop the ball. I played it and we all sang. It registered big, and I could feel myself already itching to tailor it for these two show biz icons.

Just then a whistle blew somewhere and they all jumped up and left me. "Wait!" I cried. Mr. Logan came back.

"Oh, sorry," he said, "I did forget to set it up. Ethel does the verse and first chorus; then mix it up between the two of them in the second chorus. And what I need from you most of all is a typical Durante tag. You know the way Jimmy struts on his exits?"

I knew exactly. I had seen him do it more than once and loved it every time. Already a silly little jingle was forming in my brain. "Thank you, Mr. Logan. Sorry I detained you. What is the name of this show?"

"*Stars In Your Eyes,*" he said and was gone.

I came back the next day with a complete duet arrangement for two of Broadway's brightest. When I sang it for them, the reception was polite. But when it found its way into the Merman-Durante throats, Josh whooped and hollered. He tracked down Dorothy Fields and Arthur Schwartz and forced them to listen. They whooped and hollered. Opening night at about eleven o'clock on a cold February evening, the audience whooped and hollered and made them repeat the tag two or three times. I had been up to bat twice now and had hit a home run both times. I was on a roll! I was profoundly grateful and, wouldn't you know, still scared to death.

Teeter Totter Tessie

About this time the columnists, especially Dorothy Kilgallen, were giving me such a nice push I never needed to hire a press agent. And though I was being referred to as a kind of wunderkind, a sleight-of-hand artist who could bring rabbits out of the hats of songwriters and producers, I was in no danger of becoming conceited because of my never-ending bouts with feelings of inferiority. In any event, my next job, *One for the Money*, was to be a classic exercise in humiliation that would have fended off any tendency to arrogance.

This intimate revue was, to my mind, a masterpiece of the genre. The music by Morgan Lewis was good, and Nancy Hamilton's lyrics and sketches were scintillating. They assembled a first-rate group of young performers, seven women and seven men, many of them stars of tomorrow. Pre-*Oklahoma* Alfred Drake, for instance, pre-*Pal Joey* Gene Kelly for another, and pre-MGM Keenan Wynn.

The producers had failed to provide salaries for professional understudies in the budget, so they came up with a chintzy little subterfuge to satisfy Equity. "Why don't we make Hugh Martin understudy for all the men and say that the salary we're paying him as vocal arranger and rehearsal pianist covers understudying as well?" It was a dirty trick on me. Unfortunately, Keenan came down with flu quite suddenly and I was required to go on for him at literally a moment's notice. No one had taken me seriously as an understudy, so no one had bothered to give me a single rehearsal. I had, however, studiously learned Keenan's lines and watched his skits every performance. I thought, *What have I got to lose?* and I took my place in front of Keenan's dressing-room table and started making up.

Ralph Blane happened to have a ticket for the performance, and later was able to give me a blow-by-blow description of how it all looked from the balcony of the Booth Theater. As Ralph confirmed the following day, I did surprisingly well in the First Act: I showed up punctually on cue, remembered my lines for the most part, didn't bump into anything or anyone. At intermission, I was feeling my oats and ready to top myself in Act Two.

I topped myself all right: Act Two opened with the seven boys and seven girls on seven seesaws singing a little ditty called "Teeter Totter Tessie." Seven seesaws were placed perpendicular to the footlights with the boys on the front end of the big props nearer the audience and the girls back of them on the opposite end, all fourteen facing front and singing lustily. My teeter totter partner was the dancer, Maxine Barrett. Maxine was not overweight by any stretch of the imagination, but I was *really* skinny, some forty pounds lighter than Keenan, who was the usual occupant of that seat. Maxine was accustomed to being gracefully lifted upward by Keenan's ample weight.

As the song began, we seven boys were up and the girls were down. Eight bars later, we were supposed to reverse: girls float up, boys float down. I floated down on cue, big smile on my face, but as soon as my seesaw touched the floor, I began to float up again because I didn't have the necessary poundage to hoist Maxine. I could hear her huffing, puffing, grunting behind me trying to soar heavenward with the other girls, but to no avail. The audience's laughter was becoming uncontrollable, and it increased as they saw my big stage smile fading into suppressed terror. By then, I was grunting, too, and Maxine was sweating heavily. There were plenty of people, however, who were having as much fun as we were having travail. The musicians, for instance, were dropping out like flies. The string players kept scratching away, and piano and percussion were making half-hearted attempts to keep the music going; but the brass and reed players were too broken up to be able to blow so they just put their instruments in their laps and enjoyed the circus.

It was no circus for Maxine and me, believe me. We were a wreck by the time the stage manager, who was at a total loss to cope with this peculiar situation, finally shouted, "Ring down the curtain!" The curtain came down suddenly before any more chaos could occur, and there was a five-minute unplanned intermission to allow the actors and the audience to recover. When Ralph later described the pandemonium from the vantage point of the balcony, he said that at first the audience assumed they were watching a planned comedy routine, but gradually they realized that that poor skinny son of a gun on teeter-totter No.3 was really fighting for his theatrical life, and that his toothpaste smile was fading every eight bars into panic because he *was* in panic. Ralph told me people laughed so hard that many cried real tears, and total strangers embraced each other as they shook with laughter.

Backstage during the five-minute hiatus, Gene Kelly tried to keep me from going to pieces. "Hugh!" he cried, giving me that famous Kelly grin and a bear hug to go with it, "Hugh, you were a smash! They oughta keep it in the show!"

"Not with me," I said, and fled to the privacy of the lavatory.

An Ace in the Hole

During the weeks that ensued, I feared that my disgrace at the Booth Theater might have cost me jobs. For a few weeks, I was the laughing stock of the town, at least the part of town I cared about.

I had made a fool of myself in front of about 300 people. But people—most of us—forget so quickly. It wasn't long before my phone began to ring again. A new syndrome was beginning; singers and would-be singers seemed to think I had a magic formula to put them on top vocally. I didn't. What I tried to do was very like Mr. Logan's style of directing actors.

Josh was something new on Broadway. Dwight Wiman gave him his first big opportunity to show his directorial talents with *On Borrowed Time;* then he worked with Rodgers and Hart on a second Wiman show, *I Married an Angel.* His work on *Angel* encouraged Dick Rodgers to further Josh's career in musicals; they collaborated on *Higher and Higher, By Jupiter, South Pacific,* and *Annie Get Your Gun.*

The Broadway Theater was loaded with men who subscribed to the theory that the director must browbeat his actors into doing it *his* way—until a fresh Louisiana breeze by the name of Josh Logan blew into town.

Josh's approach to direction was simple but revolutionary. He knew that most of the time "less is more." He loved people, especially actors, and was fascinated by that mystical, ephemeral, God-given thing, personality. He cast his shows with performers whom he found fascinating—funny, or sexy, or quirky, or musical or whatever—and started finding their pluses and building them up. By the same token, he uncovered their minuses and soft-pedaled them. None of this tyrannical, playing God stuff, so popular with the current wunderkinds of Broadway.

I tried to do a very similar thing for singers. As you can imagine, there was great diversity among the performers who asked me for lessons. Gene Kelly, for instance, had a small, pleasant voice and had never done any singing. A consummate dancer, he was wise enough to know that a bit of vocal polish would enhance his value. He couldn't afford to pay me for vocal coaching, so he offered to give me dancing lessons in exchange. In the middle of one of our tap-dancing sessions, he shook his head sadly and said, "Hugh, you don't look good even when you get it right." It was the last dancing lesson I ever took.

Alfred Drake, on the other hand, possessed one of the greatest voices ever to grace musical comedy. Alfred came to me because he felt ill at ease singing "up" numbers. He thought he sounded square, and asked me to help him bring off rhythm songs, perhaps even some jazz and blues.

Vivian Vance, who replaced Kay Thompson in *Hooray for What!*, was in awe of Kay and ideally would have wanted Kay to coach her. But in the light of all the suffering Kay had endured at the hands of the Shuberts, it was out of the question. So I was second choice and pleased to oblige. Her singing was less than impressive, but she had charm and a gift for comedy, so I thoroughly enjoyed working with her.

My best pupil was the man who was to become my writing partner, Ralph Blane. I was surprised when he asked me to coach him in his singing, just as I was when Alfred Drake made the same request, because both men possessed glorious God-given voices, so glorious that one would not expect them to ask for help. However, it was clever of them to do it, as musical theater requires so much more than a beautiful voice.

Ralph was studying with Estelle Liebling, who lived in the building at 145 West 55th Street where I kept an apartment for twenty-nine years. Then in her seventies, she had been a famous diva and was considered the best voice teacher in town. One of Miss Liebling's protegées was "Bubbles" Silverman whose mother had the chutzpah to ask Miss Liebling for lessons for her daughter. "Bubbles" was a child entertainer on the Horn and Hardart Hour, a radio show advertising the Automat chain of cafeterias. Miss Liebling sensed the child's potential and helped her become a diva in her own right ... Miss Beverly Sills.

Miss Liebling's other favorite was Ralph. I met Miss Liebling a few years later and loved her. But as Ralph and I rehearsed together, I was appalled! I struggled time and again to excise the operatic overtones she had introduced to his singing.

"No! No!" I cried. "It's not Wagner, Ralph, it's Gershwin. Just sing it naturally, as if you were singing it face to face to a beloved person. Do not declaim it from an imaginary podium."

Ralph's eyes, like those of a stricken antelope, would grow misty. "I don't understand," he would protest, "Miss Liebling says I have a beautiful voice."

"No doubt about it; you do have a *beautiful* voice. Now would you pretend for a moment that you don't know you have a beautiful voice and just tell me, in song, what you think Ira Gershwin's lyrics are saying to your young lady."

Like Eliza Doolittle, the day arrived when intelligence suddenly broke through, and he did it, so tenderly and sweetly that between goose bumps, I was reaching for a Kleenex. And like 'Enry 'Iggins, I felt like hollering, "By George, he's got it!"

I hollered a lot at Ralph during those exciting weeks during which he was born again as a Broadway singer because I wasn't getting through to him. I so much wanted his victory, and felt utterly frustrated, so I would holler. But there was another reason I yelled at Ralph, and I can hardly bring myself to write about it. I was intensely jealous of him—not of him, exactly, but of his singing voice. It was a mesmerizing, utterly beguiling voice, and I wanted *me* to have it, not him. If I could have found a Dr. Frankenstein with the ability to remove his larynx surgically and implant it into *my* throat, I can't promise I would have made the moral choice. It took years of maturing for me to get to the point where I could honestly say I was content for Ralph to have a sensational voice, one mine would never equal, much less surpass.

I don't know how to describe Ralph's sound; it was not like that of any other singer. It was right on the cusp between tenor and baritone, a lovely, lyrical, lullaby of a voice that was uniquely his.

However, it was not always a lullaby. It could be a battle cry; not the brassy, flat-out trumpet that characterized Merman, but more of a Teagarden trombone coming out of a jazz joint on Bourbon Street. When Ralph reached his zenith, there was nothing he couldn't sing, not a note that wouldn't make you either cry into your beer or rush out to enlist in the Army.

Y' Wanna Bet?

I was busy, but still didn't know who I was or where I belonged. Was I a pianist? An arranger? A singer? A coach? A jack-of-all-trades and master of none? One thing I knew I *wasn't* was a dancer, but that didn't stop me from auditioning for Robert Alton, who was, in the spring of 1939, choosing sixteen boys and girls for *The Streets of Paris,* a Continental-style revue produced by my old nemeses, J. J. and Lee Shubert.

To make a long story short, Bob Alton chose me as one of his dancers, not because I was good (I wasn't), but because he remembered from *Hooray for What!* how helpful I had been coaching principals when they were suddenly replaced by the Shuberts. In other words, he picked me for my talented fingers, not because of my two left feet.

My favorite memory of *The Streets of Paris* was of a dancer named Freddy Ney. Something he told me about his mother still makes me smile seventy years after I first heard it. He said that when he left home to try his luck in the Big City, his mother had only one bit of advice for him. "Freddy," she told him, "only be in hit shows." This story became so legendary that Comden and Green used it in *The Band Wagon.*

At rehearsals Bob Alton occasionally came over to sit with me during breaks. He ribbed me unmercifully about having two left feet, but he did it in such a way that I knew he hadn't regretted hiring me. I asked him who the principals would be. "It's mostly comedy and girls," he told me. "Do the names Abbott and Costello mean anything to you?"

I confessed ignorance.

Alton: They will after this show, I think. Very funny fellows. Nice guys, too. I enjoy working with them. Jean Sablon?

Hugh: Oh, sure; I know Sablon from his recordings. I love his voice.

Alton: There's one other star, but they're keeping her under wraps. They want her to be a big surprise opening night. Lee Shubert saw her in Brazil and went crazy for her.

Hugh: What's her name?

Alton: Carmen Miranda.

Hugh: Carmen Miranda!?

Alton: Don't tell me you've heard of her.

Hugh: Heard of her? Bob, I've seen her! She's the absolute living end!

I told him how I went to South America for a few weeks as boy singer for an American dance band. I told him how we used to broadcast in a large room next to a smaller one in which Carmen Miranda did her solo show. And how I had watched her, spellbound, through a peep-hole in the door and she had taken my breath away.

Not only did Lee Shubert protect her from journalists and photographers but even from us, the cast, crew, and orchestra. She didn't need our orchestra, she had been allowed to bring her own— six good Brazilian instrumentalists. Their leader appeared to be her manager and was constantly at her side, so none of us ever got a glimpse of the Carmen Miranda I had seen in South America until opening night. Even at the final dress rehearsal, she walked through the scenes with nary a smile and a minimum of body movement.

I expressed my surprise to Alton, but he had more showsmarts than I. "Don't fool yourself, Buster," he said. "That gal is shrewd. They've billed her as the Brazilian Bombshell and she wants to make sure the bomb doesn't explode until opening night."

I shared a make-up table with Gower Champion, still a long way from being the genius of Broadway director-choreographers. In *The Streets of Paris,* he was half of a ballroom team called Gower and Jeanne.

I told Gower what I thought would occur when Miranda turned on the steam opening night. He laughed at me. "She's no bombshell, she's a bomb. And the bomb won't explode opening night, it'll lay there like a big piece of lead."

I was incensed. You would have thought she was my protegée, not Lee Shubert's; I saw her first! "Y' wanna bet?" I said, so aggressively that Gower blinked.

"Sure. How much?"

"Five dollars?"

"Agreed." We smiled and shook hands.

Opening night, June 19, 1939, was a hot, humid evening. In spite of the lack of air conditioning in the Broadhurst Theater, the show was going well: Abbott and Costello were scoring big, and Jean Sablon had charmed everyone with his romantic chansons.

Suddenly it was time for the finale of Act One, a moment designed to launch Miss Miranda into orbit. The black tie audience at the Broadhurst Theater knew nothing about Carmen Miranda, so they were totally unprepared for the beautiful young woman who suddenly appeared and wriggled her way down to center stage on platform sandals. Her orchestra of Brazilian guitarists gently plinked and plunked—Latin melodies and rhythms that set the stage for something new and exotic. Gone was the stone-faced, ordinary-looking woman we had seen at dress rehearsal. She smiled and shimmered and undulated. The music smiled and shimmered and undulated. The audience seemed to smile and shimmer and undulate.

The theater grew quiet except for the very soft guitars. She wore plumage that moved with her, playing hide and seek with her graceful legs. Upon her head was a turban, flaming with vivid colors, sporting a variety of fruits and flowers. She wore it like a crown.

We all held our breath for a few seconds, and then she began to sing notes so seductive that the Portuguese lyrics she was crooning took on double and triple and quadruple meanings. At the end of the first song the roof of the Broadhurst almost came off. She sang three more songs in Portuguese, then concluded with "The 'Souse' American Way." The curtain fell and she walked to her dressing room with the show neatly wrapped up in her pocket.

I walked off to my dressing room, also, and when I got there, I found a five-dollar bill on my table. Next to it was a piece of scratch paper with these words written in eyebrow pencil: "You win, Hugh." It was signed "Gower."

The Martins Quartet performing during the Fred Allen radio show, 1940.

Chapter 13

The Martins

I DON'T RECALL WHAT PHYLLIS AND JO JEAN ROGERS were wearing that fateful day in 1939 when Ralph introduced them to me. We were in a little cubbyhole in the offices of Ager, Yellen, and Bornstein, a music publishing firm in Manhattan. Since the two girls were fresh from Frederick, Oklahoma, they were short on chic and long on girlish innocence. The innocence was real, no phoniness in these two sisters. During the three brief but joyous years that they sang with Ralph Blane and me in The Martins Quartet, never did a word, action, or an inflection of theirs ever dispel that first impression of naïve sweetness.

God paved the way for us in a most wonderful way. Our first job came after only two months of rehearsing and we couldn't have had a more auspicious beginning. *The Wizard of Oz* was slated to open at Manhattan's Capitol Theater in August, its world premiere. To promote the occasion, MGM sent Judy Garland east for a personal appearance and, as an extra added attraction, they sent Mickey Rooney with her. Roger Edens, that most sensitive and gifted of movie maestros, headed the support team, and Georgie Stoll, an MGM veteran conductor of many films, came with them to line up a large on-stage orchestra.

The Martins.

Fred, our manager, got wind of a plan to augment the orchestra with a vocal group of some kind. We were all familiar with the superb Arlen-Harburg score because Ralph had been granted permission to sing the songs in the piano bar at One Fifth Avenue.

Alas, when Fred went through channels for an audition, he was told that they had listened to every group in New York, had been unimpressed with all of them, and decided to get along with the orchestra only. Freddie pulled out all the stops, and he must have done a good selling job because they relented and agreed to hear us if we could locate a piano. It was after business hours by the time we reached Mr. Edens and Mr. Stoll. Freddie thought fast and said, "We can do it in the lounge of One Fifth Avenue; when could you come down?"

So there, in the room just outside the bar where I had started my show biz life in 1937 as a cocktail pianist, the four of us, with me at the piano, sang "Ding Dong, the Witch Is Dead," and "The Merry Old Land of Oz" for Roger Edens and Georgie Stoll.

Mitzi Green, Ted Gary, and the Martins Quartet singing
"Ooh, What You Said!" from Three After Three, *1939.*

"Well, of course," said Roger. "That's exactly what we want. Don't you think so, Georgie?"

Georgie thought so. We dispersed, leaving Freddie to make the deal. It was a modest one, but *quel* prestige! Also, Georgie said I could be the pianist in his orchestra, which upped my salary considerably. I recalled my instant flop with Kostelanetz and resolved not to get caught off base this time. The five of us were already beginning to feel somewhat like a family with Freddie as Big Daddy, even if he *was* only five feet tall.

The Wizard of Oz

We were assigned the two songs with which we had auditioned; we were to sing them as part of the razzle-dazzle overture. It was a break not to have to learn new material inasmuch as opening day was less than a week away. Two days before the big day, we all assembled on stage and in the wings of the enormous Capitol Theater at 51st Street and Broadway.

Ralph Blane, Jo Jean Rogers, Judy Garland, Phyllis Rogers, and me.
Backstage at Capitol Theatre, New York, 1939.

The orchestra, with frightened (as usual) Hughie at the piano, filed onto the mammoth stage. We had not yet met our two juvenile stars and we were bedazzled fans as we got our first glimpse of them.

"So tiny!" was everyone's first reaction to Mickey and Judy. Indeed, Judy, adorable in a simple schoolgirl type frock, looked no bigger than a Munchkin herself. I didn't know it then, but she told me years later that she, too, had been terrified. But one would never have known it as she walked with dignity down to the footlights at 9 A.M., August 15, 1939. A technician high above spotlighted her, all alone in front of a microphone on the stage of the cavernous theater. The MGM orchestra, lush and sonorous, began to play Ravel, of all things. I recognized it as "*Pavane Pour Une Infante Defunte,*" a gorgeous composition, though I didn't quite see how it came together with Judy Garland at the Capitol. I had not been aware that there was a Tin Pan Alley version of it recently published. The orchestra seemed to turn into the Philharmonic, and little, long-haired Georgie Stoll became Toscanini.

Judy began to sing. No one who was present that day will ever be able to speak of it without a lump in the throat. The auditorium melted and now the Capitol Theater became St. Patrick's Cathedral. Yes, though it seems hyperbolic to say so, it was a religious experience for all except Judy; for her, it was a shattering ordeal. But there was no trace of fear in the sounds that were coming from her throat. I've never heard anything more pure, more full of tremulous feeling than Judy's voice that morning, rich as a pipe organ yet full of childlike simplicity. There was a hint of tears in the sweet sound, but no tears appeared on her face—the only face in the theater, I suspect, that could make that claim.

There was something a bit surrealistic about the following five weeks, the first two with Mickey and Judy, and the following three with Judy, Bert Lahr, and Ray Bolger, who were Dorothy, the Cowardly Lion, and the Scarecrow in *The Wizard*. Mickey had a commitment at MGM, so he had to return to Hollywood after the first two weeks. The whole engagement could have been prolonged indefinitely in light of the extraordinary attendance. Ralph and I, in our tiny dressing rooms, and Phyllis and Jo in theirs, would peek out of our dirty windows to see an intimidating sight. The line of people four abreast waiting to buy tickets extended entirely around the long Manhattan block and met itself coming back, so to speak. The sea of humanity out there looked like an advancing army. These people, a large percentage of them very young, were determined to see Rooney and Garland, and very little short of a typhoid epidemic was going to stop them. Billy Phelan, an eager fifteen-year old who later became the founder and president of The Martins Fan Club, told us that he would get in line at 4 A.M. every other day in order to secure a seat in the front row, where he would stay until the theater went dark. Fortunately the month was August; otherwise I'm afraid the New York school system might have been hit by an outbreak of absenteeism.

Only when we watched the milling throng on the street through the curtains of our dressing rooms did we feel we were on planet earth. Inside, all was Oz. We never saw Judy except on stage, which was almost continuous since management, sensing a bonanza, slapped five shows a day on us.

Ralph Blane, Jo Jean Rogers, Mickey Rooney, Judy Garland, Phyllis Rogers, and me.
Backstage at Capitol Theatre, New York, 1939.

Garland, even at this tender age, was subject to spells of mysterious illness, so when she wasn't on stage or back at her hotel, she was horizontal on a cot in her dressing room where her mother, Ethel Gumm, brought her soup and sandwiches. It wasn't a healthful situation for a teenage young lady. She should have been walking down a country lane or swimming at the beach. This unnatural way of life was an exacerbation of a downward spiral of health problems that began when she signed with Metro. If she could have had a normal adolescence, we, her public, would have been poorer, but, oh, what riches would have accrued to this God-touched creature.

The same brouhaha that felled Judy seemed to cause Mickey to burgeon. He was in and out of everyone's dressing room like a dragonfly, one that was always welcome because he left a trail of laughter and friendliness and lust for life in his wake. Mickey Rooney, intuitive Puck that he was, had the world on a string and he was going to enjoy it. I once asked him how he had prevented the non-stop stimulation in his life from causing burnout. His answer was instantaneous and, I believe, spontaneous: "I think like a child."

Chapter 14

On A Roll

THE TINY SUCCESS THE MARTINS HAD WON with our first attempt at staging the act led Freddie to start thinking about a Broadway show for The Martins. For the third time I landed under the aegis of the brothers Shubert. I still hated the organization, but the show *Three After Three* had many agreeable features, not the least of which was the team of songwriters who had turned in a knockout score. They were Hoagy Charmichael and Johnny Mercer, not only powerhouses individually but powerfully well suited to write with each other. Johnny hailed from Savannah, Georgia, and dripped with Southern charm. Hoagy came from back home in Indiana, but he spoke almost the same lingo as Mercer, as their latest string of hits in Hollywood testified. Their senses of humor, both lyrically and musically, were engagingly congenial. I've always suspected that for *Three After Three* they wrote more songs separately, each writing words and music, than they did in collaboration. One bit of evidence pointing in that direction was my accidental discovery of production copies of two songs for our show bearing the same title, "Wait Till You See Me in the Morning." I suspect one was entirely by Johnny and one by Hoagy.

The two men were delightful company. Both were unpreten-
tious and laid back. They were generous about other writers; also
seemingly devoid of any petty jealousy. I once heard Pearl Bailey discussing jealousy among show people, and she said something that
I had often thought and felt but had never heard anyone express as
openly as Pearl did that night on a TV talk show.

"When I go on the road with a show," said Pearlie May, "I
usually don't hang out with the actors. Too much gossip and
backbiting. I love to go out with the pit musicians or the songwriters. There's something about people who make music in
one form or another; maybe I'm being unfair, but they just seem
nicer than the others. No sir, I'll take the fellas that fiddle and
toot and play pianos and beat drums and write songs. They're
more fun and they don't go around cuttin' other people down
so much."

Pearl was overgeneralizing a bit, but there was a lot of truth in
her assessment of our colleagues. Certainly Hoagy and Johnny were
way above average when it came to niceness and being regular guys,
and in praising and encouraging their peers.

The cast was interesting, too. Top billing went to Simone
Simon, a young French beauty, already an important Hollywood
star. *Three After Three* was designed as a vehicle for her, but a clever
youngster named Mitzi Green rather pulled the rug out from under
her. Simone's looks, and her voice, were delicate, better suited to
the screen with its giant close-ups and amplified sound than to that
exposed and cruel area, the stage.

For Mitzi, it was just the reverse. Her bold, strong face and her
loud, satisfying contralto were just the qualities that appealed to
audiences who wanted to hear every syllable of dialogue and lyrics.
It was the era before microphones began to invade footlights, lapels
of men's jackets, and the bosoms of leading ladies.

Mitzi was a showstopper and we, The Martins, had the good
fortune to help her stop it. Lucinda Ballard had dressed Mitzi and

our two girls in stylish gray and yellow chambermaid costumes; Ted Gary and Ralph and I wore bellhop costumes to match. J. J. Shubert hated the song, which was called "Ooh, What You Said!," and when we scored big with it opening night in New Haven, J. J. was overheard muttering, "Who would ever dream *that* would stop the show? I must be getting old!"

Ellie Gordon

No one was more stimulated by our foray into musical comedy than my mother. Even as a child, I was aware of her passion for New York shows. Now that her son was a principal (well, almost) in a real, live Broadway show, I would have made a scene if anyone had challenged her right to be at the rehearsal because I cherished her and was prepared to stand up to anyone who offended her.

She would get past the stage doorman on my arm; when we entered the auditorium, she would instantly find the least conspicuous spot and sit there, riveted, missing nothing. My mother dressed extremely well, which helped, but by now her figure had lost its youthful slenderness, and in spite of her chic clothes, she looked like the middle-aged suburban ladies that Helen Hokinson drew for *The New Yorker*.

In addition to our own quartet numbers, I had been asked to put together some vocal arrangements for the stars of the show. One spot, particularly, was an attempt to repeat the success of "Sing for Your Supper," a trio for the musical's three leading ladies. One afternoon, shortly before opening night in New Haven, our director, Edward Clarke Lilley, unexpectedly announced a run-through of the first act, including the new trio arrangement.

I protested vehemently. "They don't know the notes yet. We've only been at it two days. We need at least one more day before they can even stumble through it."

Mr. Lilley was adamant. "It doesn't have to be perfect. You must give me *some* idea of what we've got."

He prevailed and the poor girls made an unholy mess of what I had tried to teach them. Sitting in a box in the auditorium, I suffered in silence, head in hands. The episode probably would have blown over without major confrontation if J.J. Shubert hadn't put his two cents in. He suddenly jumped up from his seat in the third row and cried, "The key is too damn high. What is he doing to these ladies?"

It was a red flag to my bull-headedness. Even then I knew I had a knack for setting keys and out the window went my self-control.

"It is not too high, Mr. Shubert," I boomed. I didn't know I *could* boom. It startled everyone including me. "The reason it sounds too high is that they don't know the notes yet so they're reaching for them. They should not have been asked to sing this number until they had learned it."

"Who the hell do you think you are?" cried Mr. Shubert. I suspect no one had dared contradict him for years, certainly not someone in my lowly position.

"I'm not anybody at all, Mr. Shubert. I just know what I know and I know how to set keys."

The auditorium was full of actors waiting for their next scene. They looked stunned. The stage was full of grips and electricians. *They* looked stunned. But no one was as stunned as I was because did I see what I thought I saw? Was that my mother running down the center aisle clutching her purse? My darling, mild little mom whose desire of desires was to be invisible? She was not only very visible, every eye was upon her by now. And she was extremely audible, as well.

"He's right, Hugh!" she shrieked with a volume I had never heard emanate from her up-until-now dulcet Southern throat. "It is too high, Hugh! He's right! He's right!"

I was licked. My own mother had betrayed me. Actually, I wasn't licked. Stubborn to the end, I wangled a rehearsal next day for the three intimidated actresses. God bless them, they had a kind of blind trust in me. They learned the notes and remembered them. At the next run-through, they performed the arrangement confidently, letter perfect, and on pitch. In my key.

I think the whole cast, staff, and crew thought that after New Haven, *Three After Three* would hit Boston and Philadelphia and roll back to New York, be a big hit, and run for months. Oh, the dreams of show people, like whom there are no people according to Irving Berlin. Irving was right. We are a breed apart and a fairly happy breed at that. It's not an easy life, full of rejections and disappointments and burst bubbles. But we live on our dreams, and who is to say dreams are inferior to the world of reality?

The Shuberts, possibly because they owned so many theaters and needed shows to occupy them, sent the show up and down the whole eastern seaboard and then Westward Ho. We got as far west as Chicago, where we got a rave review from Claudia Cassidy, the queen bee there among critics. To get a favorable notice from Claudia in Chicago was like getting one from Elliott Norton in Boston or from Brooks Atkinson in New York. Our bosses made the most of the Cassidy rave, and on the basis of it we stayed for a couple of months. But, except for Chicago, it was single weeks and split weeks, which would have been tiresome if we hadn't been so young and ready for anything. Even fifty-ish Freddie Steele, our manager, seemed young, and he never seemed to tire, so caught up in his zeal to put the quartet on the map was he. He put us on the map all right, or rather the Shuberts did, quite a large hunk of it and all by rail, still the standard transportation for theatrical troupes in 1939. We rattled and jiggled and bounced to Pittsburgh, Providence, Indianapolis, Cincinnati, Columbus, Baltimore, *ad infinitum*. I've never enjoyed flying. The railways and the seaways are what suit me, so I was riding high, even though a lot of soot went in my eyes and the terminals all began to look alike. But railway food was still good then, and there were many serendipities, such as Johnny Mercer, sitting across the aisle from me, engrossed in setting words to a Hoagy Carmichael melody, suddenly calling out, "Hey, Hugh, come sit by me and help me write this lyric. I need some fresh ideas."

Together we wrote a little gem called "Put Music in the Barn," which Johnny and I loved and everyone else hated. Never mind. I had written my first song, and in collaboration with Johnny Mercer, no less, and I was in Tin Pan Heaven. Justifiably I received no credit for the Barn song but at that point in my career, who cared?

The big number for the quartet was "Ooh, What You Said," and we sang and danced it with Mitzi Green and Ted Gary. While we were rehearsing it, Johnny Mercer somewhat sheepishly called me over into a corner and sang to me a little jingle he thought I might like. It went like this:

> Jeep, jeep, I'm a jeep from Jersey.
> Jeep, jeep, I'm a jeep from Jersey.
> 'Lizabeth, Englewood, Weehawken,
> Hackensack, Paterson, Hoboken.

I worked it into my arrangement of the song, and much to everybody's surprise, we stopped the show with it.

Our dream of making our Broadway debut in *Three After Three* was never realized. Near the close of that grinding tour of many months, the show began to fall apart. We were all physically tired by then; most of the dates came during the winter months and the eastern half of the U.S.A. was frozen over. Worst of all, everyone's performance began very slowly to lose its luster. There was one exception: Mitzi Green. For Mitzi, a matinee in Kalamazoo was as important as opening night in New York. But Mitzi could not, single-handedly, keep the electricity going for two acts. Our producers and directors seemed to have lost interest in us; Hoagy and Johnny had been conspicuous by their absence for weeks. We felt like poor little lambs who had lost their way. Baa! Baa! Baa! The grapevine began to circulate rumors that we might close out of town.

Then a more hopeful rumor made the rounds that a new producer, Ruth Selwyn, had caught a performance in Chicago, when we still had zing, and felt we deserved a chance to succeed. We closed out of town and went home wondering what lay in store for *Three After Three.* We had been home for a couple of weeks when Freddie got a phone call from Mrs. Selwyn. Yes, she had taken over the show from the Shuberts and, yes, she planned to go into rehearsal soon with an updated script and some new songs from Carmichael and Mercer.

But no contract was offered, and Freddie got nervous. "I think we should keep auditioning," he told us, "the whole deal sounds very 'iffy' to me."

A new Irving Berlin musical, *Louisiana Purchase,* was getting ready to hit Broadway, and Freddie was an old friend of its producer, B. G. "Buddy" DeSylva. Mr. DeSylva said, sure he'd like to hear the new quartet in town, and we sang for him and Irving Berlin. They offered us a contract on the spot; it was a prestigious opportunity and Freddie grabbed it. I am positive he wouldn't have done so if he had made any commitment with Ruth Selwyn, but he had not.

Freddie felt that she should be alerted about our withdrawal as soon as possible, so he called Mrs. Selwyn and we were invited to her apartment. "Apartment" is not quite the word—"palace" might suffice, "mansion" at the very least. Mrs. Selwyn greeted us graciously until she learned she was losing us. The temperature dropped to below freezing during the shocked silence that followed a declaration of our intention to accept the offer from *Louisiana Purchase.*

She didn't waste time reacting to our information. "Show these people to the door," she said to her butler in an imperious tone that reminded us that Ruth Selwyn had started as an actress before marrying the millionaire impresario, Edgar Selwyn, for whom one of New York's nicest theaters was named. One moment we were sitting on gilded chairs and sofas drinking tea; five minutes later we were on the street—Park Avenue to be specific.

None of us knew what to say; it had happened so fast. I broke the stunned silence by commenting, "Gee, I didn't know Ruth Selwyn was so rich."

"Oh yes," Ralph said matter-of-factly. "Ruth Selwyn is one of the richest Jews in Christendom."

Chapter 15

The 1940s

---

*A*FTER ALL THE FLAPPING AROUND I did in the thirties, I finally surfaced into the forties. Until the second year of that extraordinary decade, I hadn't the foggiest notion of who I was. In 1941, my total blindness about my persona became a glimmer. As the glimmer began to widen, I got a glimpse of what I was not. I hadn't a patriotic bone in my body for one thing. Even Pearl Harbor didn't make much of a dent in my unswerving absorption with myself. I was the center of the universe—shallow, ambitious, insensitive, foolish, and monumentally selfish.

Elaine once remarked to Ralph that she wished she had met me earlier, when I was young.

"Honey," he leveled, "you met Hugh Martin at the right time. Don't waste time regretting the lost years. You wouldn't have liked him."

Nor did I like myself very much. I was beginning to achieve some of the things I thought would guarantee my happiness, but a funny thing happened on the way to success: I loved to travel and was beginning to have enough money to do it, but no matter how exciting my ports of call were, I had to bring myself along, and that spoiled it.

The best antidote to my self involvement was The Martins. The quartet was a godsend to me because the girls and Freddie and Ralph accepted me as an equal. If I occasionally had an urge to throw my weight around, I soon learned to count to ten. I was musically the best educated of the five, so there was a temptation there, but I didn't yield to it for a very self-protective reason; since leaving my family I hadn't really loved anyone, or been loved, and that was many lonely years ago. Now I had a second family, a home away from home, and my one decent virtue at that time was a sincere effort on my part to deserve the affections of Phyllis, Jo Jean, Ralph, and Freddie. It was a successful effort all around. We were a functional family for three wonderful years, a happy little quintet.

Our next show was as big a hit as *Three After Three* had been a flop. It was called *Louisiana Purchase,* and had a long run at the Imperial Theater in the early 1940s. The score was written by Irving Berlin.

Irving Berlin

I knew full well the position he occupied in the hierarchy of American Popular Song. "Irving Berlin is American Popular Song," Jerome Kern had once told a journalist.

But the wonderful songwriters I had been working with on their musicals had almost convinced me that I was wonderful, too. So far there had been Rodgers and Hart, Hoagy Carmichael, Johnny Mercer, Cole Porter, and Jimmy McHugh, all prestigious. They had all but rolled out the red carpet; Cole Porter treated me like visiting royalty. (I did the vocal arrangements for only one of his shows, *Du Barry Was a Lady.*) I didn't realize it, but they had flattered me into perfect condition for Irving Berlin to come in and squash me. This he did, it seemed to me, with a little more gusto than was necessary.

Because I had been so spoiled by Irving's predecessors, I didn't feel I had to approach his throne as if he were a king. I had been given two arrangements to submit to him, "You Can't Brush Me Off" and "I'd Love to Be Shot from a Cannon with You." After a week of preparation, I approached the mighty man. When he asked me to sing the first one, I did so without too much apprehension.

"That's not bad," he commented, "but there are lyrics in there that I didn't write."

I was surprised. "They're not part of your song, Mr. Berlin. They're part of the arrangement. Very insignificant, usually just a transition or a modulation to get back to the song itself."

Berlin: Listen to me, my young friend. When people come to the Imperial Theater to buy tickets for this show, what does the marquee tell them about who wrote the lyrics?

Hugh: Why, Irving Berlin, of course.

Berlin: Then those customers are entitled to hear lyrics by Irving Berlin, not Hugh Martin.

Hugh: Do you want me to throw out the arrangement and have the quartet sing the song without any embellishments?

Berlin: No. Just give me what you've done and I'll write the lyrics you need for those extra bars.

I was chagrined. None of my other heroes had suggested anything like that. They had accepted my lyrics without a murmur. But of course I did as he asked. He wrote the necessary lyrics, and they fit the music perfectly. In fact, they were better than the ones I had written, which really bugged me.

A few days later, he asked to hear my second arrangement. I launched into "I'd Love to Be Shot from a Cannon with You" a little more tentatively than I had sung arrangement number one. I thought I had planned it well, but the little skirmish with Mister American Popular Song had eroded my confidence a millimeter or two. I was swinging along about halfway through the second chorus when he interrupted me.

"Shall I tell you what you wrote for the tag?" he asked me slyly.
"If you'd like to," I said.

I braced myself for something—I wasn't sure what—but it didn't seem probable to me that he could have read my mind.

He had, though. He told me, in advance, what I had worked out for my big surprise ending, and I felt like a sunken soufflé. I hated Irving Berlin at that moment. Actually, of course, I was hating myself for not having had enough creative ingenuity to fool the old bastard—I mean, the old master.

I felt a little better when Michael Feinstein, years later, informed me that my feelings are shared by quite a few of Irving's peers. He told me a story about a famous remark Harry Warren made in 1945 when a friend of Harry's greeted him thusly: "Hi, Harry! Have you heard the good news? They bombed Berlin."

Harry shot him a dark look. "They bombed the wrong Berlin," he muttered.

People who love Irving have told me that my take on him is very biased. It could well be because in those days I was ridiculously oversensitive. But he seemed to me to be a breaker-downer, not a builder-upper. He was a curmudgeon of the first water, and he deflated me with the same skill with which he wrote "Always," "Suppertime," and "There's No Business Like Show Business." Anyone who can write songs like that can be forgiven anything.

Cabin in the Sky

In the fall of 1940, Vernon Duke started writing *Cabin in the Sky* for Ethel Waters and, to my surprise, he asked me to work with Miss Waters. I say to my surprise because I had somehow gotten the impression that Mr. Duke was a musical snob. I accepted the assignment with excitement (two icons for the price of one) but reluctantly, inasmuch as I had a gut feeling he would cut me down worse even than Irving Berlin had done.

Happily, I couldn't have been more wrong. He made me feel I had something to bring to this project of his, a project that I now know was especially dear to him.

It was a project that was especially dear to me, also. I find no sound more exciting than the singing of black people, especially black women. It probably has something to do with my childhood in Alabama, the black nurses that took care of me even before I learned to talk, and the black churches that I always preferred to the white ones because of the unbelievably exciting music that emanated from my friends there.

I had many favorite singers of that genre, but none of them affected me as viscerally as Ethel Waters. There is little doubt in my mind that the greatest singer of pop songs in my lifetime, and possibly in anyone's lifetime, is Judy Garland. But I have to confess that of all the singers I ever heard, the actual sound that caused my endorphins to flow the fastest was the voice of Ethel Waters. I saw her first when I was in high school. I went to the Strand Theater in Birmingham to see an early talkie, a musical revue called *On with the Show*. Ethel sang "Am I Blue?" (great song and she did it superbly) and "Birmingham Bertha" (pretty wonderful, too). I saw her on stage in 1933 in *As Thousands Cheer,* and her renditions of "Heat Wave" and "Suppertime" and "Harlem on My Mind" moved me profoundly. She received a salary of a thousand dollars a week in that masterful revue and, at that time, was the highest paid woman performer on Broadway.

Like Judy Garland, she totally changed personalities in middle age. At Billy Graham's invitation, she became part of his inimitable evangelistic team. Ironically, she had practically lost her voice by then, but the soul was still there and the expressive eyes and the wonderful Waters phrasing. How she managed to move us all so much with that wrecked voice is a mystery, but thousands of people will testify to the fact that hearing her sing "His Eye Is On the Sparrow" and other hymns brought them to God. It was about the time she joined Billy that she came up with one of her classic remarks, still quoted by Waters fans. She was a guest on a New York radio show the night before one of Graham's Madison Square Garden meetings. The empty-headed male talk show host said, "Ethel, do you expect this event to be a success?"

She replied, "God don't sponsor no flops."

Ethel Waters was a child of rape. Just think what the world would have lost if her mother had opted for abortion.

Miss Waters had two important spots in *Cabin in the Sky*. "Takin' a Chance on Love" was as solid in a front-of-the-curtain showstopper as I've ever seen. Ethel did it marvelously, but Vernon longed for lightning to strike twice, and he threw me the challenge of fashioning the title song, "Cabin in the Sky," appealingly enough that it could hold its head up against "Takin' a Chance on Love."

I was very nervous about it and kept putting it off almost hoping it would go away. Then Ethel, who could be a juggernaut, nailed me one afternoon.

Ethel: Hey, are you the fella who is supposed to set my key in the"Cabin" song?

Hugh: Why, yes, Miss Waters. I think Mr. Duke expects me to do that, plus a special arrangement of some kind.

Ethel: Well, where is it?

Good question—and I was caught red-handed.

Hugh: I . . . er . . . actually I was planning to work on it tonight and start teaching it to you tomorrow.

Ethel: You don't have to work on it tonight. What's wrong with now?

My blood went cold.

Hugh: I . . . I . . . if I don't figure it out ahead of time, my mind will just go blank, Miss Waters. You see, you're a great heroine of mine, and frankly I'm so scared of you that if you're right there looking at me, well, nothing will happen, nothing at all.

Ethel: Oh, I wouldn't say that. We'll make this little arrangement together, just the two of us.

I was terrified, my normal state, but Ethel outweighed me and managed to strong-arm me up a flight of stairs to the mezzanine of the Martin Beck lobby. Before I knew it, I was seated at a grand piano, and she was in a chair two feet away. Good grief!

We ran the song a couple of times and agreed that her key should be "D." All the time she was singing I was silently praying that my guardian angel would show up P.D.Q. and save me from writer's block, and to my great relief that's exactly what happened.

I knew that Ethel, as Petunia, would have a small choir of singers harmonizing behind her. How would it be, I wondered silently, if, in the second chorus, the choir sang Mr. Duke's beautiful melody and Ethel sang an obbligato against it? When the choir sang a rising cadence, Ethel would descend and vice versa. I finished the arrangement in my head and sang it to Ethel. She loved it and learned it with great facility, adding a few embellishments of her own. As we parted, she said, "Man, you throw my voice around like toilet paper."

I was still concerned that Mr. Duke would feel I had taken too many liberties with his song. I needn't have worried. Vernon was a far cry from Irving Berlin who would never have allowed such license. Vernon was captivated by my arrangement and made me feel like a St. Bernard that had arrived in the nick of time. "Cabin in the Sky" became one of Ethel's signature tunes. Many impersonators were "doing" Ethel in 1940 and some of them used that song, incorporating my countermelody to conjure up the Waters persona. I'm glad that this gratifying little inspiration made so many people happy, especially me.

Incidentally, Ethel Waters wrote a memoir called *His Eye Is on the Sparrow.*[1] I have read it twice and find it very remarkable. In my opinion, it is perhaps the best autobiography I have ever read.

1 Waters, Ethel. *His Eye Is on the Sparrow.* New York: Doubleday & Company, Inc. 1951.

Chapter 16

Pre-Howard Hughes RKO

I DON'T KNOW WHAT RKO PICTURES WAS LIKE after Howard Hughes bought it. I suspect that, like the proverbial policeman's life, it was not a happy lot. But in the early months of 1940, when George Abbott invited me to accompany him to Hollywood, it was a most endearing little city within a city. Each movie studio seems a bit like that of an Army facility: the Mess Hall (or commissary), the Post Offices, First Aid Stations, Archives, etc. My return address during this first Hollywood baptism was the RKO Music Department, and I couldn't wait to shoot out letters to my friends in New York and Birmingham because I thought it sounded so impressive.

Mr. Abbott had liked my contributions to his two hit musicals, *The Boys from Syracuse,* and *Too Many Girls.* He had not liked, in fact had detested, the film of the former that Universal released earlier that year. He decided to fight back by selling *Too Many Girls* to RKO, provided he could come west and direct the movie himself. He brought with him only three principals from the Broadway cast, and me, the vocal arranger. But I had managed to follow up the "Sing for Your Supper" arrangement in *The Boys from Syracuse* with one for a Rodgers and Hart song called "I Like to Recognize the Tune" in *Too Many Girls*. Both had stopped the show for Mr. Abbott, and there are few things nicer one can give a producer than a couple of show-stoppers. Mr. Abbott rewarded me by giving me my first Hollywood assignment, coaching his principals and backing them up with a great 24-voice mixed vocal ensemble, of which one member was Nanette Fabray, seven years before she made a big hit in New York in *High Button Shoes*.

The morning I reported for work on my first film I was attacked by a flock of rather largish birds. I don't use the word "attacked" loosely; these critters seemed to be going for my eyes. RKO had a big open square in the middle of its executive buildings and sound stages, and I was halfway across it, walking alone and feeling very unprotected indeed. I remember thinking, "What on earth is going on here? What kind of ditzy place is this? Somebody please put me on the Super Chief *right now,* and point me toward Times Square."

I survived the blitz and my mood changed within minutes when I reported to the Music Department. Pre-Howard Hughes RKO was as delightful as any Ivy League campus. Since *Too Many Girls* is a college musical, I found myself in the same atmosphere whether I was on the Pottawatamie set (the name of our mythical college), in the Music Department, on a sound stage, or in the editing room splicing "takes." It was a very different ballgame from Broadway, and the strangeness of it was exciting.

The cast was exciting, too. From the original New York production, Mr. Abbott brought Eddie Bracken, Desi Arnaz, and Hal LeRoy, plus a handful of chorus girls, and one chorus boy, a fellow by the name of Van Johnson. Mr. Abbott stuck Van right in the middle of the screen in all the dance numbers, because Mr. A, with his uncanny flair for spotting talent, believed Van would make it big in Hollywood, and he wanted to give him a good send-off.

The young ladies of the dancing ensemble were, not at all coincidentally, the ones he sensed would be good dancing partners for himself. One of Mr. Abbott's passions was dancing, especially the rumba. His greatest passion, of course, was women. I suspect he chose *Too Many Girls* for the Abbott treatment, primarily because the locale was just across the border from Mexico, so there was a great emphasis on Latin-American rhythms.

He found an after-hours spot in Hollywood that perfectly suited his inclinations. This merry old soul was compulsively drawn every night to Club Zarape which had a great rumba band. There he would reserve a table for himself and four lovelies from his New York chorus line, and they would dance the night away. The girls had to be on the set, made up, bright and early, and many times I would observe a trace of fatigue in their faces when they reported to work. But the around-the-clock routine didn't seem to faze old Mr. Abbott, who remained bright as a button during my six weeks on salary. He had so much energy in his lifetime that it didn't surprise me at all that he eventually died at the age of 106!

To his chosen few, he added Lucille Ball, Ann Miller, Frances Langford, and Richard Carlson, excellent performers all. One day during our first week of preparation, Mr. Abbott set up appointments for me to hear these luminaries sing. He asked me to separate the sheep from the goats, vocally speaking, which made me nervous as all get out. They were for the most part first-rate talents, while I was, by comparison, a total neophyte with not a major credit to my name. But Mr. Abbott had a kind of blind faith in me, and I devoutly wanted to justify it. In they came all day long, one every half-hour, and I would put them through their paces. I made a major mistake right off the bat when I decided to dub Lucille Ball instead of letting her sing for herself. Rodgers and Hart had written only one new song for the film, an exquisite ballad called "You're Nearer," one of their finest. I was afraid Dick Rodgers would have a fit if I entrusted it to Lucy's rough vocal equipment. But I was dead wrong. Later in my years of working with Dick, he taught me the value of voices that possessed character rather than finesse.

(Yul Brynner for instance.) Perfect intonation and trained vocal production should never take preference over that compelling something that a towering personality can bring to a song. Those of us who heard Walter Huston sing "September Song" in *Knickerbocker Holiday* in a quavery whisper can testify that he cast a spell that dozens of high-powered singers might envy.

There was no question about Abbott's Broadway actors using their own voices, nor that of Frances Langford, who had the most velvety, lush voice of any girl singer ever. I did engage a dub for Richard Carlson at his request. His solo was a Rodgers and Hart classic, "I Didn't Know What Time It Was," and he knew the song was over his head vocally.

My last appointment of that glamorous day was Ann Miller, who thoroughly bowled me over. Mr. Abbott didn't know she could sing. The Music Department didn't know she could sing. Her agent didn't know she could sing. *She* didn't know she could sing. She was rather startled by my reaction, and wondered, as she told me decades later when we did *Sugar Babies,* whether I might be another Hollywood phony shooting her a line. I was not. I was genuinely thrilled by the vitality, the vibrancy, the zing of her singing. I couldn't wait to tell Mr. Abbott about this serendipity, and together we reworked the running order of the music so that Annie could sing in a couple of spots.

Next Door to Orson

My office was small, bare, unprepossessing. Next door was an identical one except that I had a piano and my neighbor did not. The name on my neighbor's door was Orson Welles. We were both fresh out of New York.

We were both youngsters—I, twenty-four, and Orson twenty-five. When I went back East, I can safely say that I hadn't made a dent in Hollywood. Orson made a monument. I happen not to admire *Citizen Kane,* but one can't deny that it's a masterpiece of film-making. My objection rests partly on the fact that Susan Alexander is portrayed as a no-talent appendage to the Hearst dynasty. Her character is obviously based on Marion Davies. However, anyone who lived in the 1920s and early 1930s was aware that Marion Davies was an authentic movie star, beautiful and the possessor of a great comedic talent. Since Miss Alexander is portrayed as totally devoid of talent, I find the comparison between her and Miss Davies to be inaccurate and insulting. To hang the Susan Alexander image on this gifted actress has always struck me as being a very low blow.

I rehearsed my 24-voice choir daily during my tenure at RKO, and my spies told me that Orson was frequently on the sound stage, invisible in the shadows, watching and listening for hours at a time. Thinking of how much of his valuable time he spent with us, I confess to a feeling of humble pride, if that's not an oxymoron. We never met.

Too Many Girls didn't win any awards, is not spoken of reverently by movie buffs, did not revolutionize the film musical, and did not launch George Abbott as a new creative force in the industry. Just as a matter of personal opinion, however, I liked it. I confess a weakness for old-fashioned musicals with lightweight plots and heavyweight scores. Not heavyweight as in *Les Miserables* or *The Phantom of the Opera*; heavyweight in the sense that they are heavy with glorious American theater songs, shows with scores along the lines of *Anything Goes* and *Annie Get Your Gun* and *South Pacific,* where every song is one to hum and whistle and remember. And I'm not restricting my partiality to huge hits such as those I've just mentioned. Harold Arlen's *House of Flowers* written with Truman Capote, is such a show. Every musical moment is a finely polished jewel.

But I descend from my soapbox to remind us that *Too Many Girls* is remembered today for only one reason—it provided the occasion for Lucy to meet Desi for the first time.

Comparing Theater to Film

When I started my job at RKO one thought was uppermost in my mind—this is my first foray into working with film. How will it feel compared to working in live theater? I soon discovered there are many appealing features about dealing with sound tracks as opposed to theater acoustics. The latter are very variable; many times I had gotten great sounds from my singers, say, at the Colonial Theater in Boston, only to have my hopes dashed when we moved to the Forrest Theater in Philadelphia.

Here, in Hollywood, on the other hand, if I got a really good take on the sound stage it would probably sound as good in Podunk as in New York. Even more exciting for me, I learned I could make three girls sound like thirty; I could make the boys and girls sound like Munchkins or like a choir of Russian bassos, according to my desire. One of the worst hazards of theater is getting a proper balance. Here in Hollywood, one could make the principals, the chorus singers, and the orchestra as loud or soft as one liked. All that was needed was state of the art recording equipment and a sound engineer who understood the nature of the music being recorded. The equipment was almost always superb; the men who operated it were variable.

At RKO, our long weeks of rehearsal were canceled out by a sound man who mixed our numbers in such a way that we, the choir, sounded as if we were in another room. Four years later, at MGM, the sound department enhanced all the musical numbers tremendously, simply by proper mixing.

Let me jump forward three years. The most fun I ever had electronically was recording "The Three B's" at MGM with June Allyson, Nancy Walker, Gloria De Haven, and Harry James and his orchestra. The MGM sound men were wizards. They looked at my arrangement on paper and blinked.

"You want all that?" they said with some disbelief.

"Oh, I know I can't have it," I demurred. "It's just musical wishful thinking. I'll settle for half of it."

"Hold on," said Mac. I don't remember Mac's full name, but I will salute him the rest of my life. The time I loved him most came the following year when he mixed the sound for Judy Garland singing "Have Yourself a Merry Little Christmas." Mac had trouble seeing the panel because his tears got in the way.

But going back to "The Three B's": the three sound men reckoned as how they probably *could* get it on film.

"Let's give it a try," they suggested. They not only tried, they succeeded brilliantly. They got everything I had asked for, plus a couple of little deals the Harry James arranger had added. I was astounded when I heard the final mix. Astounded and almost convinced that sound stages were my natural habitat. Almost, but not quite.

In order to compare the two media, I ask myself, "Of all the charms theater has to offer, which one eclipses movies?" The answer to that, of course, is that tidal wave that occasionally flows from audience to actors, drenching some lucky performer with unconditional love. I've seen it happen to Jeanne Eagels and Walter Hampden and Anna Pavlova and Ethel Waters and Édith Piaf and Laurette Taylor and Maurice Chevalier and Judy Holliday and Mary Martin. I never had the privilege of seeing it happen to Helen Morgan, but Josh Logan described it to me so vividly that I *feel* as if I saw it. However, I saw it happen to Judy Garland at the Palace in 1951, and held her trembling hand in my own after the performance as she tried to return to earth.

Never, however, did I see it occur more spectacularly than on the night of September 25, 1952, at London's Saville Theatre. It was the opening night of a new show Timothy Gray and I had written with Eric Maschwitz, *Love From Judy*. What made the evening almost unbearably moving was the exchange that took place between a sophisticated West End audience and a young Scottish lassie named Jean Carson. One reason there was love at first sight that night and it was so powerful was that no one had ever heard of this young lady before. She was a total surprise. Watching what happened there forever assured me that no amount of film, no parade of zeroes at the end of a salary check, and no array of Oscars would ever convince me that anything other than living actors performing for a live audience could give me the high that I live for and love.

Chapter 17

Best Foot Forward

I WAS HAPPY IN THE DAYS when I was singing with Phyllis and Jo Jean and Ralph. I suppose it was natural for a twenty-five year old musician to wonder whether it was wrong just to stay in the little niche that had opened up for him, or whether he should be yearning for higher ground.

I didn't have any desire for higher ground. I loved the plateau on which I found myself at the beginning of the 1940s. The only higher ground that interested me was new opportunities for The Martins. I had never enjoyed anything as much as blending with the sweet voices of *les soeurs* Rogers plus the superlative instrument God put in the throat of Ralph Blane. I knew I was the weakest vocally of the four, but I made up for it, I hoped, with my vocal arrangements. I can't describe the exhilaration of joining with the other three in a really good American pop song, especially when our orchestration was top notch. It was the most fun I had ever had and I was happy. I recall remarking one day to Ralph that it would take nothing short of a bomb to bust me loose from the euphoria I was experiencing as a member of The Martins.

The bomb came in the form of a show called *Best Foot Forward*. Ralph was living at that time (1940) in a modest one-room apartment at 101 West 55th Street in midtown Manhattan. A neighbor of his in the same building, same floor, a few doors down the hall, was young Van Johnson, currently giving his all in the chorus of *Pal Joey*. It was a George Abbott show and Mr. Abbott always offered Van a job, predicting that he would make that difficult hop-skip-and-jump to featured player and then to stardom, all of which he did in a few short years.

One day Van and Ralph met in the hall of 101, and Van passed on an item from the grapevine that eventually set off my bomb.

Van: Say, Ralph, some guy in my dressing room told me Mr. Abbott has a new script.

Ralph: Musical?

Van: Yes, it is. He says he doesn't want Rodgers and Hart this time, or any of the big guys. He wants little guys—a new, fresh team of songwriters—because the play is young, about prep school kids, I think he said. Why don't you do an audition?

Ralph: With what? I've never written a song in my life.

Van: Write one. Write two or three. You might get the job. Stranger things have happened.

Ralph: You must be crazy. I can't even write a scale.

Van: Why don't you ask Hugh to help you? Hey, maybe you and Hugh could team up and write a few songs.

To make it brief, Ralph and Hugh did team up and did write a few songs. Actually, we never collaborated; Ralph wrote "Shady Lady Bird," and I wrote "Ev'ry Time." When we did that, with one or two exceptions, we set the pattern for the rest of the score of *Best Foot Forward* and all our future work. Ralph would write a song, music, and lyrics, and I would do the same thing. He would critique my work, I would critique his, we would put both our names on it and, eureka!, a new team was in the running. Thank you, Van Johnson.

A date was set for us to perform our songs for two of the most prestigious gentlemen in the musical theater at that time, George Abbott and Richard Rodgers. We had worked with both before, so we were treated a little more personally than some of the other candidates. Mr. Abbott spoke briefly to us in the auditorium before we walked the last mile up the steps leading to the stage of the Ethel Barrymore Theater.

"Boys, I asked Dick to help me choose my songwriting team, because I'm so ignorant about music. He's agreed to help me out with a few opinions."

Mr. Abbott was not being entirely truthful, but there was a very valid reason for his remarks, inaccurate though they were. Dick's partner, Lorenz Hart, had reached a point of no return in his alcoholism. Dick loved Larry and found it almost impossible to participate in a project without him after those golden years. So when Mr. Abbott asked Rodgers to co-produce this as yet untitled prep school musical, Dick sadly declined in order not to hurt Larry. Then Dick came up with the idea of being a silent partner. It seemed a perfect solution, so he and Mr. Abbott co-produced the show and no one was aware of the partnership until years later after Hart's death.

We walked to center stage, I to the piano, Ralph leaning on it. If he hadn't leaned on it, he would have fallen on the floor. We were both rigid with fright. We did "Shady Lady Bird" first because it's easier and warmed us up enough to get us through "Ev'ry Time."

They thanked us politely and we went home, grateful that we had performed acceptably and relieved that the ordeal was over. We felt quite certain that that was that. So I was startled to get a call three days later from Celia Linder, Mr. Abbott's personal secretary.

"Mr. Abbott wonders if you and Ralph would like to come over to his room at the St. Regis to sign your contracts. I believe Ralph doesn't have a phone. Could you contact him?"

My voice seemed to come from someone else's body as I managed to say, "Why, yes, Celia. What's Mr. Abbott's room number?"

When we got there, Mr. Abbott was very businesslike. He explained how the royalties were to be divided and when he hoped to go into rehearsal, but there was a note of wariness in his voice.

Abbott: This contract is a little one-sided, fellas. You can't get out of it, but I can. Mr. Rodgers and I liked your audition, but two songs doth not a musical make. You've got your work cut out for you, and we have every confidence that you will come through. If the next few songs are of the caliber of the two we heard, I'll proceed. If not, I'll have to drop you.

We gulped.

Abbott: Here are two scripts of *A Young Man's Fancy*. It's only the first draft. You'll get revisions as Cecil turns them out.

"Cecil" was John Cecil Holm, author of one of Mr. Abbott's previous comedies, *Three Men On a Horse*. *A Young Man's Fancy* was Cecil's original title for the new project, eventually to be re-titled *Best Foot Forward*.

Ralph and I signed the contracts, thanked our benefactor, and departed, somewhat in a daze. We reached the lobby, managed to get past the King Cole Bar, emerged into the sunlight, and returned to our separate residences without saying more than a few words.

There were two questions I asked my reflection in the mirror several times a day for the next few weeks, questions to which I never received a reply. One was, "Is this really happening to me?" And the other was, "Golly, can we bring it off?"

Labor Pains

Ralph had a rich friend, a pleasant middle-aged retiree in Palm Beach, Florida. Dorothea loved the theater and had invited Ralph several times to be her guest. He had always been too busy, but now an idea struck him. Her house was huge, so perhaps she would let the two of us hole up there and try to get the show written. We tried out the idea first on Mr. Abbott who thought it a practical idea.

"Yes, go down there and get away from the telephones and the unexpected visitors and all the temptations of New York and go to work. You're not under the gun. No impossible deadlines. We'll be casting in about six months, rehearsing shortly after that, and Dick and I are hitting for an opening shortly after Labor Day, 1941."

Off we went to Palm Beach, where Dorothea showed us to our rooms, quite grand. It was a good set-up for two neophytes who had just had the living daylights scared out of them—providing, of course, they had the talent. I was convinced we did not. Dear, wonderful, ebullient Ralph was convinced that we did.

A familiar scenario was about to unfold: the insecure artist thought a little drinky now and then might ease his fears and give him the confidence he lacked. I've forgotten what my little drinky was in 1940, probably martinis—an unfortunate choice for someone as unstable as Hugh Martin, who really did not hold his liquor very well. It was a problem that was getting ready to present itself to Ralph, to my gracious hostess—most of all, to myself. I'm grateful for my inability to handle alcohol because that's where my rescue lay. When I was drinking, I was not being creative or productive; all I was being was sick—sick physically and sick emotionally. Luckily, I admitted it to myself right away and stopped drinking, cold turkey, but I was still a problem because I was still scared to death so I tried to cop out of the whole project.

Then Ralph, out of the blue, wrote "Buckle Down Tioga" (the name "Winsocki" had not surfaced yet), and I was totally bowled over by it. I remember the first time he sang it to me. He had written the whole thing, words and music. I said, "O.K., that's it. I'm quitting this job. I can't compete with talent like yours. You've really got it, Ralph. Let me just bow out gracefully, dear friend. Mr. Abbott will understand. And if you need someone to write your piano parts or make your vocal arrangements or cheer for you, I'll be on tap."

Ralph looked at me with the expression usually reserved for small children who have done or said something especially weird. After a pause, he said, "Have you gone totally off your rocker?"

I didn't reply. He continued, "I couldn't write a Broadway musical if my life depended on it. I'm not even sure *you* could. But together, don't you see, we'll never get a chance like this again. It could take us out of all the humiliation we've had to put up with from people like Ruth Selwyn and Irving Berlin."

I blinked but said nothing. Ralph said, "Now go upstairs like a good boy. Not by way of the bar, thank you. Don't set the clock, sleep eight, nine, ten hours until you feel sane. Then we'll talk about this again. But keep in mind, if you quit, I quit."

I did as I was told, quite meekly. I did feel differently the next morning, no hangover for a change. And Ralph's breezy confidence had begun to "contage" itself to me.

After a bit of breakfast with Ralph, I crept over to Dorothea's piano and sat down. I looked at it and it looked at me. That was the day I began the loose pattern of songwriting that I still employ.

At Schirmer's in New York, before I took the Florida Special, I had bought a dozen notebooks of manuscript paper. I had written only two or three songs in my life, yet I fell into my writing pattern as naturally and immediately as if I had been practicing it for years. Notebook on piano, pens at the ready, room empty and silent. I had read the script several times and knew it well— the general thrust of it, that is. I sat there, waited for a feeling of repose, then began to play meditatively. I would also sing, usually using the cliché sounds singers use when they've forgotten the lyrics. Or never knew them in the first place. Or, in my case, hadn't written them yet.

Lyrics! What a whole new world writing lyrics opened up to me. It was like stepping through the looking-glass. This analogy is most appropriate since I'm told my lyrics reveal much more of me than I do personally.

"What a field day for a psychologist," remarked the friend of mine who knows me best. "Look at these lines," she demanded.

You are for loving and loving and loving
By someone just as wonderful as you
And so I guess I'll never do.

And this one:

How's my brain?
Well, it's insane but kind of quick.

And look at the title of this one: "I'm Not So Bright."

No wonder I love writing lyrics; very often I can pour out my insecurities. Certainly Larry Hart did. How many times thousands of us have blended our broken hearts with Larry's as he poured out his emotions and matched them to Dick Rodgers' haunting melodies.

I was miles away from Larry or Dick when I took my first baby steps on Dorothea's piano. But, like learning to swim, sometimes there comes a moment when you feel, "Yes, I think I can master this. Something in my blood is telling me to keep doing it."

I kept doing it. What came out was a whole lot of very bad songs. Songs that were so awful that even Ralph, dear encourager that he was, was forced to say sweetly, "Hugh, you can do better."

Then, much to my surprise, I began doing better.

And Ralph, too, was sparking, surprising me every few days with a nifty lyric like "Three Men On a Date." This was almost the only song we ever actually collaborated on in the conventional "Mr. Words" and "Mr. Music" manner. Ralph handed me the lyric one day, and I had the good fortune of finding a suitable tune for it within minutes.

Ralph, like Irving Berlin and others, couldn't read or write music. But he heard it in his head, which was the important thing, and I got it onto manuscript paper. He called me his "flags and dots man." Berlin could play only in one key, F sharp. Ralph couldn't play in any key, but with a voice like his, who cared?

Thumbs Up

The day came when we felt we had put together enough material to show it to Messrs. Abbott and Rodgers. Dick was the critical factor in the equation. Abbott admittedly was not an educated judge of music. That was why he had wanted so much to have Richard Rodgers for a partner, even if a silent one. Ralph and I knew that if Dick's thumb went skyward we were in; if it went the other way, we would be out before we ever got a foot in the proverbial door. So after our return to New York, we made a date with the King, and with fear and trembling presented ourselves at the Rodgers apartment in the Hotel Carlyle at 50 East 77th Street.

Mrs. Rodgers greeted us at the door. Instantly she made us feel expected, wanted, and special. I have remembered her with devotion through the years for the way she put us at ease. If she hadn't, Ralph would have cracked on his high notes, and I would have hit a mass of clinkers.

Dorothy Rodgers was a very attractive woman. She always reminded me of Zorina. Certainly she and Brigitta (Miss Zorina asked me to call her by her real name) had several endowments in common: ash blonde hair, medium height, the figure of a fashion model and wardrobe to match, a low, velvety speaking voice, elegance, and charm galore.

After tea was served, we went through our paces at the grand piano with Dick by our side cheering us on. The Rodgers were the epitome of gracious hospitality. But Dick was in a difficult spot.

Out of loyalty to Abbott and John Cecil Holm, and from sheer business acumen, he had to be gracious to a point, but if the goods weren't there he had to throw us out in the nicest possible way.

It was apparent almost from the first few bars that Dick was slowly being seduced by what he heard. The Rodgers' facial expression can become the "Great Stone Face," as I was to experience on several occasions down the pike. But Dick was happy that day and his face showed it. So did his feet, tapping away during the "up" numbers, and his hands, almost unnoticeably beating time to Ralph's march.

It was the march that won the day. Dick liked some, hated others, but he obviously loved "Buckle Down . . . ," still pre-Winsocki, hence "Buckle Down Tioga." Dorothy loved it, too, and even the children forgot their games and did a little marching. One of the kids was Mary, of course, and nineteen years later I would be marching to *her* drumbeat. In 1959 she was to write, for Mr. Abbott, one of my favorite musicals, *Once Upon a Mattress*, with brilliant lyrics by Marshall Barer and music to match by Mary Rodgers.

When we left the Rodgers' apartment, we were in quite a different state of mind from the one we were in after signing our not very impressive contracts. Then we were shell-shocked; this day, we were euphoric, although I, always the negative one, reminded Ralph that we still had a few gauntlets to run.

Thanks, Dick Rodgers!

George Abbott knew that in Ralph Blane and me he had two unknown quantities. He knew, also, that the fate of his new musical was riding precariously on our ability to turn out a score that could stand comparison with Rodgers & Hart, Cole Porter, Jerome Kern, and Harold Arlen. He had brought in Dick

Rodgers, confident he would get tough with us if necessary. Dick never got tough. He pulled a good score out of us with kindness, encouragement, and courtesy. It was fortunate he did. Any display of ridicule or panic would have instantly melted down what little courage or creative juices we possessed.

Dick took the high road and it worked. With his smiles and tapping feet and praise, we tried harder, and, thanks to Dick, plus excellent work from Abbott, Cecil, and a first-rate cast of youngsters, we came out on top.

Rodgers taught me, trained me, corrected me, encouraged me, drove me, deflated me, mentored me, and brought out all that was good in me. He did it with tremendous warmth, even love. It is not hyperbole to say that Dick Rodgers cared for me like a father.

It's Susan I'm Choosin'

Summer was a-comin' in and Mr. Abbott was swinging into the casting mode. Ralph and I didn't expect to be consulted very frequently and we weren't. Fortunately, our two producers made wonderful choices. All of them delighted us. Probably the major ones were made by Mr. Abbott himself. His gift for casting was legendary along "the street." His first move was to sign a movie star to play the movie star. He had admired Rosemary Lane (beautiful face and figure and a fine singer) in several Warner Bros. musicals, and wasted no time in offering her the key role of Gale Joy, a publicity-seeking starlet on the move. Good start.

Mr. Abbott went to see *Panama Hattie,* and the night he attended, Betty Hutton, featured player, was out of the cast. Her understudy, a hitherto unknown song and dance girl, went on in the Hutton role and captivated Mr. Abbott. It was a kind Providence that furnished this opportunity for a young Miss June Allyson and for all of us.

Ezra Stone was sent around the country by the Abbott office on a talent search for the part of "Helen Schlessinger," the hapless fifteen-year-old victim of Gale Joy's publicity. He came back to us with a trophy: Maureen Cannon, who filled the bill in every way and became a star.

I wrongly fought against casting Maureen as Helen. Mr. Abbott and Ralph and Dick were crazy about her, and if I had had any sense, I would have been too, because she turned out to be one of our greatest assets. The moment I realized I had goofed in this matter took place at the first orchestral reading of the score. Don Walker had done a lovely orchestration of "Ev'ry Time," and after Maureen stepped on stage to put her voice with the orchestra for the very first time, everyone was moved, even the musicians. Without exception, each instrumentalist spontaneously put down his fiddle or his horn or his drumsticks and applauded! It is something that seldom happens at an orchestral reading and there is no sweeter sound in the world.

Ah, Nancy Walker! What a bonanza her discovery was because this young lady possessed genuine comic genius. Her casting was one of those flukes. She had been rejected by every casting director in town, but she was so persistent that she was finally allowed to audition for Abbott and Rodgers. Ralph and I were not present that fateful day, but apparently what occurred was that dear Nancy sang a torch song and sang it perfectly straight. Some quirk in her unique personality shone through the mediocre material, and that smart old eagle, Mr. Abbott, who also had a streak of genius, had to stuff a handkerchief in his mouth to keep from laughing and hurting the poor kid's feelings. At the same time, the wheels in his theater-wise brain started clicking, so after she sang, he asked her please to wait. He and Dick and Cecil went into a huddle and Abbott suggested that Cecil insert a new character into his story, that of a plain, awkward young girl who was attending the school prom as a blind date. Everyone loved the idea and, to her utter amazement, she was signed on the spot. Mr. Abbott's hunch paid off big. He would have the satisfaction on opening night of seeing her walk away with the show.

If at First You Don't Succeed . . .

Everything was happening so fast that my life seemed to be flashing by on speeded up film. This world I was entering, almost against my will, was so new and confusing. Not at all as it had been in my fantasies when I had occasionally dared to dream. For one thing, I had never dared to dream at all of being a songwriter. If I had, I would have fancied myself collaborating with an experienced lyric writer. But writing lyrics? Are you kidding? I wouldn't know how to start. But I *had* started, and the two top men of the Broadway musical theater seemed to like what was coming from my pen.

The last few pages of my working notebook I keep divided into "Lyrics," "Titles," and "Music." When a viable idea in a category hits me, I quickly get it on paper before it flies away. I also have pages devoted only to words or phrases I especially like that might prove useful. The rest of the manuscript notebook, the whole front part, is where I wrestle with the resolution of ideas and snippets of melody into a completed song.

When I'm in the thick of a project, or even just working on a song that needs urgent attention, I keep a small "composer's notebook" in my pocket when I walk, which is whenever I can escape the house, one reason California suits me so well. I have bitter memories of Manhattan and trying to get a musical idea down while trudging in the snow. Do I take off the gloves and get frostbite, or do I attempt the impossible, getting those itty-bitty notes onto those itty bitty lines while wearing gloves?

On with the Show

There was, obviously, still a great deal of work to be done on our score. It was thrilling that much of what we had done had pleased our bosses, but they knew, and we knew, that the surface had hardly been scratched. Incredibly, with this plum assignment in our laps, neither of us owned a piano. It didn't seem too bright to buy one; musicals have been known to fold pretty quickly. For the same reason, we didn't cut our ties with Phyllis and Jo Jean. Who knew whether the team of Martin and Blane would hit the mark or die aborning? Wait and see, we told ourselves, so Freddie Steele booked us into a vaudeville theater in Washington, D.C. Our opening day was to be October 3, 1941, two days after our first trial by fire with *Best Foot Forward*.

So where were we to write? A friend of Ralph's at Ager, Yellen and Bornstein, music publishers, took pity on us and gave us a key to their offices, which were full of pianos. We needed two rooms, inasmuch as we didn't collaborate, but only one piano because Ralph worked strictly out of his head.

Although our benefactor had loaned us his extra key, we still felt like burglars as we sneaked into the building late at night. Ralph would go into his little cubbyhole and I would go into mine, and we would click the door shut between us. The walls were thin so we both felt slightly eavesdropped on, but we were grateful for a little spot of our own where we could get on with it. I had lost some of my self-doubt and Ralph never had any, so we were beginning to have a little fun. The most fun was when we'd finish a song and get it approved by Dick Rodgers. We could then invite the youngster who was to sing the song in the show over to hear it. When I close my eyes today, nearly seventy years later, I can still see the eager faces and the shining eyes. We sang Ralph's football anthem, "Buckle Down Winsocki," for a pink-cheeked, diminutive Tommy Dix. Another night Nancy Walker came up to the mysterious third floor to hear the songs I had written for her: "Just a Little Joint with a Juke Box" and "The Three B's." Marty May, who played the movie star's sleazy press agent, came up to hear the song Ralph had written for him: "Where Do You Travel?" Maureen Cannon had already heard her two songs: Ralph's "Shady Lady Bird" and my "Ev'ry Time," as had our star, Rosemary Lane, when we sang my "That's How I Love the Blues" for her.

But the best night of all was June Allyson's night. She was still dancing in the chorus over at the 46th Street Theater where *Panama Hattie* was running, but she ran over after the show one night and burst into our Seventh Avenue cubicle, make-up still on that adorable face. "Do it!" she commanded. "Sing it! Sing *my* song! Nobody ever wrote a song for me and they probably never will again." She plopped down on a hard chair and tried to catch her breath. I had written a very corny little song for her which I had been sure Dick would toss out, but he hadn't. We sang a verse and two choruses of "What Do You Think I Am?" for her and she squealed like a bobby soxer.

"Do it again! Do it again!" she pleaded, and we did it again. And again. And again. It must have had a dozen encores before she let us stop, but it was no chore, not with that sunshiny Allyson face smiling at us, looking like Tiny Tim when Bob Cratchit brought in the plum pudding.

Hey, Let's Put On a Show!

Casting was finished and the first drafts of the songs were approved, so we went into rehearsal on a torrid day in the summer of 1941. Even without air conditioning, spirits were high and there was a feeling of expectancy. Cecil's script was funny and real, at least we thought so. Who knew whether we could crack the solemn faces of those hard-boiled critics in Manhattan's newspapers?

How exciting for Ralph and me to look up on the stage of the Ethel Barrymore Theater and see our little brain children coming to life in the persons of a good-looking and talented cast and chorus. But hold everything! Something was strangely wrong. The choreography being taught to these young people was somehow false. It wasn't in harmony with the script or the songs or the spirit of the show. I went first, of course, to my partner. Ralph thought I was being nervous and over-critical. Maybe so, I thought. A day of rehearsals went by, then another, and another.

Now I *was* getting nervous, and *very* critical. I bypassed Ralph this time, and since I was scared to death of Mr. Abbott, I went to Dick Rodgers. Dick watched patiently for a few minutes, never one to do anything precipitously, then said, "Hugh, this is your first show as a songwriter and I think you're just overanxious. And I know how disappointed you were when we couldn't get Bob Alton. I think when you look up there on the stage and don't see what you imagine Alton would do, you feel a little frustrated."

I sat alone in the darkened auditorium and became increasingly miserable. The show just wasn't jelling, and I couldn't put my finger on why. By now I had developed confidence in my work; I'd always had confidence in Ralph's. Cecil's script was felicitous, and Abbott's direction was as smooth as ever. But the choreography . . . it didn't fit. I went back to Dick. "What kind of contract does this guy have? Is there a certain date before which he can be replaced?" Dick shook his head.

Rodgers: No, Hugh. We would have to buy him off. But if you're really unhappy . . .

Hugh: Oh, no. I wouldn't do that to the budget.

Rodgers: Don't worry about the budget. I'm beginning to see what you mean. Let me talk to George.

He talked to George. George said that if Dick and I were in accord, he would feel out Mr. X and let us know. It turned out to be not too expensive to be feasible. The man also said that he himself had some misgivings about his suitability for this particular project.

"O.K." said Mr. Abbott to me, "You got your wish. Now where do we go from here?"

Hugh: Are you sure you can't get Bob Alton?

Abbott: Impossible. Forget it.

Hugh: May I sleep on it?

Abbott: Yes, but sleep fast. We only get five weeks' rehearsal and we've lost three days.

A Touch of the Irish

I was not a praying man at that age (just twenty-seven) but I had developed a habit of sitting in churches for an hour or two and just waiting. It had worked for me before. Please let it work again.

One of the most beautiful cathedrals in Manhattan is St. Thomas's, 53rd Street and Fifth Avenue, a half hour's walk from the Ethel Barrymore Theater. I went. I sat. I waited. And I was rewarded. But was I? The idea was so audacious, so utterly impractical that even if it was good, no one would buy it. I scurried back to the theater and tracked down Ralph.

Hugh: Ralph, can you come over here—in the corner where we can't be heard?

Ralph: What on earth?

Hugh: I think I know who should choreograph our show!

Ralph: Who?

Hugh: Gene Kelly.

Ralph: Gene Kelly?!!

Hugh: Gene Kelly.

Ralph gave me the same withering "you weird child" look that he had given me in Palm Beach.

Ralph: You're off your rocker.

Hugh: I wish you'd stop saying that. At least phrase it differently; it makes me nervous.

Gene Kelly.
He signed this photograph for me at MGM in 1943, but it was in 1941, when he
agreed to choreograph my first show, Best Foot Forward, *that he changed my life.*
I am convinced that without his contribution, the show would have failed,
and I would have had no career whatsoever.

Ralph: Gene Kelly is appearing eight times a week at the Shubert Theater two blocks away.

Hugh: I know.

Ralph: How can he do both?

Hugh: He probably can't, but I have to talk to him.

Pal Joey had made Gene a big star. However, I knew he liked me, and I thought he would see me, even though he was in the middle of a matinée. I was right.

Gene: Hugh, you old stinker, come on in my dressing room. Good timing. Intermission just started. Want a Coke?

I did not want a Coke. I wanted to throw my insane idea at him before I passed out or became incoherent. I laid my cards on the table and waited for the guillotine to drop. Gene looked perplexed.

Gene: Who told you I wanted to do choreography?

Hugh: Well, no one. I don't even know whether you do that or not. (pause) Do you?

Gene: Yes! I want it more than anything. Much more than performing. What made you think of me?

Hugh: I'll be honest. Bob Alton was my first choice, but he had another commitment. I was searching around in my head for the one guy who would have that touch.

Gene: How do you know that I have that—that touch?

Hugh: I don't know how I know. I just know.

Gene: Hmm. Clairvoyant yet. Well, kid, I've got news for you. I do have that touch. And I've been hankering for a long time to prove it. Listen, I've got a four-week vacation coming up. Mr. Abbott has promised me a month's break from *Joey*. Maybe I could stage your show then. That would be better than a vacation for me.

Hugh: Oh, Gene!

I couldn't think of anything sensible to say. I raced back to the theater, dodging the late afternoon traffic rush. I went straight to Dick and told him the story. God bless him, he looked almost as excited as I!

Rodgers: I don't know if you can convince the boss, though. He's got a lot of loot tied up in Kelly. Of course, I do, too, come to think of it.

We found Abbott and cornered him. I repeated my implausible conversation with Gene.

Abbott: You're off your rocker, Hugh.

Hugh: That's what Ralph said.

Abbott: He's right. Take him away. Lock him up.

Rodgers: George, Hugh is not entirely crazy. He loves this show. He just wants every department to be first class.

Mr. Abbott slightly lost his cool, something he seldom did.

Abbott: Can't it be first class without robbing me of my star? *Joey* is our biggest hit yet, Dick. If it ain't broke, let's not fix it.

Rodgers: Calm down, George. Kelly says he'll give up his vacation and knock this off in the four weeks you promised him.

Abbott: Wait a minute, you two. How the devil do you know this man has any gift for choreography? Have you ever seen any of his choreography?

Hugh: Nothing big time. He did Billy Rose's *Diamond Horseshoe*, but that didn't give him a chance to show what he could do.

Abbott: Then how the . . . how the . . . .

He was becoming inarticulate, probably for the first time in his life.

Hugh: I don't *know* how. I just know.

Abbott: You're off your rocker.

Rodgers: This is where we came in.

Abbott: Everybody go away. Go home. I've got some thinking to do.

The meeting broke up without smiles or small talk. The next morning Mr. Rodgers and Ralph and I were alerted via telephone that Mr. Abbott wanted us to roar over to his office at 630 Fifth Avenue. It's the building fronted by a massive statue of a nude man encircled by a floating metal ribbon, known lovingly by the locals as the Bronze Fart.

None of us was late because those who work with Mr. Abbott learn quickly that one does not keep him waiting. He is a kind and gentle soul, but his gentleness does not extend to tardiness. Promptly at 9:00 A.M. we were ushered into Mr. Abbott's office.

Abbott: I think I'm a pretty good judge of character, Hugh, but I perceived you as a lamb and now I find out you're a bulldog.

I couldn't think of anything to say so I didn't say anything. Dick and Ralph laughed because they knew how right he was. I laughed, too, but not as heartily because I was wondering what in the world this canny entrepreneur was up to. He didn't waste time making me guess.

Abbott: I dropped by the Shubert last night and I had a little talk with Gene Kelly. Hugh, this idea of yours could be a brilliant idea or a fiasco. Gene is on your side.

I perked up.

Abbott: He insists that he's a choreographer at heart. Before he came here, he and his brother, Fred, ran a dance studio for kids in Pittsburgh. To make a long story short, I made a deal with him, and he starts work next Monday.

"Hallelujah!" I said softly. Dick said nothing but I could tell he was pleased.

Abbott: Before you utter too many hallelujahs, I hope you will ponder the frightening thought that we only have five weeks rehearsal time and we've lost one whole week.

But he couldn't fool me. My beloved patriarch was, like Dick and Ralph and me, excited. I started counting the minutes until the fateful Monday morning.

Monday morning came and our actors assembled on stage in rehearsal clothes. Gene Kelly arrived promptly in time for proceedings to begin at 10:00 A.M. There was electricity in the air. Gene was perhaps one of the brightest stars currently on Broadway, and our "children" felt a certain awe. Although most of our performers had not reached twenty, I'm inclined to retract the word "children" as I recall the amorous goings-on backstage during the months to come. Mr. Abbott, usually unflappable, was startled and put off by it, and he swore never to do another show with a cast of "children."

It is a wondrous thing to walk into a darkened theater and find a bunch of gifted people dancing to melodies that until now had only been heard in one's head. As I wandered in on Kelly's first work day, the song that was coming out of the upright piano on stage was "Don't Sell the Night Short," my least good contribution to the show. But behold! In Gene's hands (and feet), it was turning into something quite interesting. One reason I fought so hard for a good choreographer is that by now I had watched a few shows floundering on the road before coming into New York, and I had learned how totally dependent the songwriter is on the dance director. If the latter gives life and humor to the number, it makes a huge difference as to how it is received. A great score can lay an egg if the show is ineptly staged. Vincent Youmans' *Great Day* was, I'm told, such a show. On the other hand, a show with a moderately good score can seem like an absolute gem if the opposite is true. *High Button Shoes* comes to mind.

Being so aware of the power of choreography, I felt my morale zooming into outer space as I watched Gene Kelly turning my mediocre song into a snappy opening number. My fantasies were interrupted by a gesture from Mr. Abbott; the eagle's talon was beckoning me to the back of the theater. I positioned myself against the wall because I had a feeling I was going to need it to lean on. I didn't want to look at Abbott's face, but he was about three feet away and there was no way I could avoid it. His height had increased from 6 feet 3 inches to about 7 feet 6 inches. The expression on his face reminded me of Moses just before he smashed the tablets of stone at the foot of Mount Sinai.

Abbott: I thought you told me Gene Kelly was going to be good for this show.

I summoned up the guts to look straight into those cold blue eyes.

Hugh: Yes, I did. And he will be.

Mr. Abbott fixed me with a look Rasputin might have envied and replied, "Well, I just thought you might like to know that (pause) you're right."

I went down like a telescope being folded up. Mr. Abbott looked down at me in my kneeling position. I looked like an idiot savant without the savant. He laughed so loudly that the kids on stage stopped dancing. He had had his fun with me, probably to rap my knuckles for the week-long torment I had inflicted on him. He was happy, and so, Heaven knows, was I!

One of the qualities I'm guessing that he noticed about Gene was his rapport with his dancers. Their eyes were bright, their limbs seemed supercharged, and there was more than a little laughter. Gene had borrowed from Bob Alton the trick of giving nicknames to his gypsies. Bob had in turn borrowed the idea from John Murray Anderson, that irascible old showman from England; Murray's nicknames were outrageous and both feared and treasured. He called Ralph "The Blockbuster," and he called me "The Birdseed." When I introduced him to my sister, he looked at her intently for a few seconds and then decreed, "Yes, definitely of the seed variety."

There were numerous meetings. They are a necessary evil, but no one has come up with a better plan for bringing together the minds of very diverse and sometimes temperamental craftsmen. One meeting settled the question of what to call the show, hitherto entitled *A Young Man's Fancy*. I've forgotten who came up with *Best Foot Forward*, but I've always suspected that Mr. Abbott's pleasure with what Gene Kelly was fashioning might have predisposed him to accept a title in the mode of dance.

Another meeting was for the purpose of finding a name for the mythical prep school our characters inhabited. Everyone was hooked on Ralph's wonderful and highly original "Buckle Down Tioga." Tioga was a name Ralph used simply because he ran across it in John Cecil Holm's script, but Cecil never intended it to be the title of the school. Abbott asked the four of us for ideas. Cecil said it should have "win" in the name somehow, and Dick Rodgers said, "It should have 'sock.'" Ralph said, "How about 'Winsocki?'"

Right on, Ralph!

What a great song it is! Mr. Abbott told me later that at intermission opening night he wasn't sure as to the fate of the show, whether it would hit or miss. "It was 'Winsocki' that made the difference," he said. "The curtain went up on the second act, and two minutes later little Tommy Dix was belting out 'Winsocki' and suddenly I knew we were in."

The time has come when I have to confess my hang-up with "Buckle Down Winsocki." My Walter Mitty fantasy had not included a Ralph Blane song wrapping everything up and being the show-stopper of the evening. I should have been on my knees with gratitude, and part of me was, but human nature being what it is, I was jealous! I'm reminded of Berenice in *The Member of the Wedding* teasing Frankie: "Look here at me. You jealous! Go and behold yourself in the mirror. It is a known truth that gray-eyed people is jealous." Well, my eyes were not gray but if Ralph was as smart as I'm convinced he was, he probably took a good look at me and said to himself, "Hugh, you is jealous."

Rehearsals were hectic and left little time for going out occasionally to wind down, something we all sorely needed. The emotional intensity of being involved in the genesis of a new musical headed for Broadway is hard to describe. It takes over every waking moment and even invades one's dream life. I very much needed to share a few quiet moments with someone congenial, and I asked Nancy Walker for a date. I didn't know that she had an adolescent crush on me.

Nancy and I were a couple of babes in the woods. She was a total stranger to the world of romantic relationships. I was scarcely more experienced than she; we were both shy, clumsy, insecure, inarticulate. In spite of our naiveté, we had a great time together for quite a while.

Her gifts had been a revelation to us in rehearsals. Her comic genius stemmed partly from a delivery that seemed never to be trying for a laugh. When June Allyson, as Minerva, said to Nancy,

"It looks like we've got a lot in common," and Nancy replied, "If it's common, we've got it," it sent cast, crew, and staff, and eventually audiences, into stitches. Her face was a combination of Buster Keaton-like deadpan mixed with sensitive mobility. While not what you'd call a "looker," she possessed a kind of offbeat attractiveness. I've noticed that many comediennes who are required to play women who are perceived as less than lovely have an aura, a kind of angelic spirit hovering over them, making them seem beautiful, i.e. Martha Raye, Fanny Brice, Ethel Waters.

Nancy was wildly profane but somehow never offensive. I make this statement entirely by hearsay because whenever she saw that I was in the room, the four-letter words ceased. Even Mr. Abbott's presence didn't curb the flow, but mine did. God bless you, dear, wonderful Nancy!

Try-out in New Haven

A popular cliché in my racket is that "shows are not written, they're rewritten." Generally speaking, the saying is true, as I would discover and rediscover during the labor pains of my subsequent shows. But *Best Foot Forward* seemed to lead a charmed life. After the usual five-week rehearsal period in New York, we packed our suitcases and took a short trek up to New Haven, where we opened without much advance hoopla. Our show was full of delectable young girls, and New Haven was full of Yale boys who liked delectable young girls, so we had a head start even before the curtain went up. When our collegiate audience discovered that our young ladies had talents that matched their sex appeal, we had a built-in support group. The New Haven newspaper liked it, too, and so did *Variety*. There was a bright expectancy in the crisp autumn air, and when Mr. Abbott called a production meeting, he looked ten years younger than he had looked in New York. As the meeting broke up, he suddenly cried out, "Wait a minute, gentlemen. Before we disband, I'd like to request all of us to express a vote of thanks to Hugh Martin. This guy is probably the stubbornest character in the world. But when he locked horns with me and importuned me to engage Gene Kelly to choreograph our little opus, he probably saved the show." Cheers. Applause. And a blush or two from me.

Another Openin', Another Show

Opening night on Broadway finally arrived and it was a time of fear and trembling for Martin and Blane. Everyone knew we were totally inexperienced and rather expected we would fall on our faces. About 8: 30 I perched on the top steps leading down to the lounge. Ralph had enough courage to sit in an actual seat in the auditorium, but the feeling of nausea in my belly made it clear that *that* was not the way to go for me. A pretty young usherette offered me a program. It might have been Lauren Bacall because, I'm told, she was employed at that time by the Ethel Barrymore Theater to serve in that capacity.

I tried to read the program but my eyes refused to focus. I wasn't sure I'd be able to see the actors on the stage. The orchestra under Archie Bleyer was now playing the Overture, and the songs sounded vaguely familiar, though I had no sense of having written them.

Someone pushed a sheaf of telegrams into my clammy hand. The two I remember vividly were, understandably, the ones from Cole Porter and Vernon Duke. The encouraging things they said via Western Union seemed totally unreal to me. The whole situation seemed totally unreal: the loud orchestra blaring away, the black-tie and tails and evening dresses (audiences used to put on their own show in those days), the sense of impending disaster. It was a Kafka nightmare from which I wanted to escape but couldn't.

I mustered enough courage to go backstage at intermission. There were flurries inside of caucuses surrounded by huddles. Were we clicking? Did they like it? Would we be a hit?

The Entr'acte started up and each one of us scurried to wherever we belonged. Me, of course, sitting on the steps, trying to convince myself that I was breathing.

The curtain rose on Act Two, and after about six or eight innocuous lines of dialogue, pint-sized Tommy Dix began to sing "Buckle Down Winsocki," backed up by the entire cast, plus a rousing orchestration. It was a great moment for all of us because "Winsocki" neatly wrapped up the show and put it in the smash category. For Ralph, it must have been an impossible dream come true, because "Winsocki" is and always was his personal brainchild. We were all winners together, but the special heroes that night were Tommy Dix, singing Ralph's marvelous and very original song, Gene Kelly's ingenious and lively dances, and the adorable Nancy Walker.

There was a cast party after the curtain fell, but I can't tell you about it because I wasn't there. Nancy and I went to a little joint with a juke box and had our own party. A very sweet one it was. We had a couple of beers, but we were thoroughly intoxicated long before the mugs touched our lips.

Chapter 18

Three Bombs

I WOKE UP EARLY on Thursday, October 2, 1941, trying to believe what had occurred the previous night. I was thankful that Nancy and I had drunk so little alcohol on our date because a jam-packed day awaited me. A reporter from *The New Yorker* phoned during breakfast and requested an interview that afternoon with Martin and Blane. *The New Yorker*! Wow!

Friends and family had heard reports of the rave reviews of *Best Foot . . .* and phoned us to express astonishment and delight. They were not a whit more astonished than I, I told them. When the two girls of The Martins Quartet called, they were with Freddie. They said they were thrilled for Ralph and me, but it didn't take a psychologist to interpret the note of anxiety in their voices. They had resigned themselves to our breaking up the act, and I hastened to renounce the idea.

"No way, fellas. There's nothing that can compete with The Martins. It's the best part of my life. And I know Ralph feels the same way."

Their voices perked up a bit, but it was obvious they thought we were trying to let them down easy. I wasn't, though, and I don't think Ralph was. Our thinking was, if *Best Foot . . .* really takes off, it could be the break the quartet needed. I had told them once, quite sincerely, that it

151

would take a very large bomb to break up The Martins. One bomb had exploded and we were still in place. But two more were on the way.

The Second Bomb

The second bomb was an invitation for me to sign a seven-year contract with Metro-Goldwyn-Mayer. I got a kick out of being pursued by the biggest and best of all the Hollywood studios, especially in the realm of musicals, but I didn't at first consider accepting their offer for two very good reasons.

First, they were looking for a vocal arranger, not a songwriter. I certainly had not become so grand that I now considered arranging beneath me, but *Best Foot Forward* was a hot ticket on Broadway, and to ignore totally the fact that Ralph and I had written it made me wonder if MGM was playing games.

The second reason I vetoed it was that the invitation was made to me alone with no mention of Ralph. In turning it down, I mentioned both of these points and, presto, a second offer was made, one that included Ralph and requested our services as songwriters. I was stunned, especially when they named a salary for me that was exactly twice what they were willing to pay Ralph. "Why on earth?" I asked myself. Ralph said he thought it was because they intended to load me down with heavy duty, wall-to-wall vocal arranging, hence I would be working twice as hard as he. Of course his feelings were somewhat hurt by the discrepancy in the salaries offered to us, but Ralph was a businessman, something I never was and probably never will be. He had the vision to foresee what working in the Arthur Freed Unit, the *sanctum sanctorum* of MGM musicals, could mean for this "born yesterday" team of beginners. I spent a week or two with indigestion and insomnia before finally caving in and signing the contract.

About this time, Pearl Harbor happened, and all of our lives were turned topsy-turvy. The draft had begun even before the bombing, and

Mr. Abbott began to wonder whether he would lose a platoon of young males from his cast of teenagers. Ralph and I were eligible for service also, but we had served our purpose, so Mr. Abbott didn't worry about us. Ralph's physical came first, and he was rejected. He was happy that the war wouldn't interfere with the many wonderful things that were opening up for him. Then it was time for my physical, and I didn't impress my examiners any more than Ralph had, and was classified 4-F for being underweight.

I had mixed feelings about that label. All kinds of thoughts swam in my brain when I received that verdict. What will my parents think? My brother had been accepted and they were very proud of him. Will they love him more than me? I felt pulled in many different ways.

The draft problem having been temporarily resolved, we faced another problem head on. With our new MGM contracts we realized that we had to disband The Martins. It wasn't easy to tell Freddie and the girls, but they were magnanimous. "You've got to do it!" they insisted. "This is an opportunity you can't turn down. Don't worry about us."

I did worry about them. They came down to Pennsylvania Station the morning Ralph and I boarded the train, the plush Twentieth Century Limited, which was the ultimate in luxury at that time. It was a gorgeous spring morning in Manhattan, and a pesky little voice in my ear kept whispering, "What are you doing now to screw up your life?"

Phyllis and Jo Jean and Freddie were on the platform as we got on the train, and there were tears in all our eyes. I cracked a joke or two that fell painfully flat. Soon my three beloved friends were fading from view, and Ralph and I were sitting in Compartment C watching slums and smokestacks roll past our unbreakable glass windows.

"Could you use a drink?" I asked Ralph. He said he could, and we stumbled down the rocking corridors, touching levers that sprang heavy doors leading to other huge cars and eventually to the dining car. It was between meals so we were handed a menu of drinks. I felt like downing all of them but we both settled on dry Martinis.

Ralph stopped after one but I didn't, unfortunately. I've always been prone to becoming a lush, and narrowly missed it many times. Guilt had been building up inside me, along with remorse and a bad case of the wibber jibbers. I began to get misty, which I thought would embarrass Ralph, but he calmed my fears. "There's hardly anybody here but waiters," he said cheerily. "Go ahead and cry. It'll get the demons out."

He was going to regret that "go ahead and cry." I didn't get noisy about it, fortunately, but gradually the floodgates opened and I was losing control. I had not quite comprehended what a very important part of my life the girls and Freddie were. I wept silently for hours and didn't sleep much the first night. However, the following day I was to have an even more wrenching emotional experience.

The Third Bomb

I had finally regained my composure and decided to go to the club car and rejoin the human race. I picked up a copy of *Life* magazine and thumbed through its pages. The cover was a horrifying photo about the sufferings of a segment of our military. There were graphic pictures of wounded G.I.'s, scores of them. The captions stated that many were bleeding to death because there weren't enough medics to fill the need. If I hadn't been in a vulnerable state from yesterday's crying jag, I think I would have reacted as most of *Life's* readers probably did: I would have felt concern for their plight, concern for America, and anxiety about the outcome of the war. Instead, I was suddenly, violently, overwhelmed with guilt. I had my physical before signing with MGM, and had been turned down, something that, at the time, had been a source of relief. Now, suddenly, I was aghast at the realization that these young men were going through the jaws of hell for people like me, a decadent musician about to embark on seven years of soft labor at a movie studio.

In a single flash, I knew that my priority was to volunteer and pass the next physical, to take a chance with life and limb in the greatest war in history. It was an obsession that was to consume me for the next two years.

Chapter 19

California, Here We Come!

I was reasonably cheerful during the second and third days of the three-day journey to Los Angeles. But after we crossed the mountains and desert, we chugged through miles of orange groves, and I became restless again. I began to wonder what I was doing in this picture-post-card place.

I said to Ralph, "I hate orange trees. I wish I was back walking the dirty old streets of New York."

In retrospect, I deplore the ridiculous trauma I put Ralph through. I certainly didn't do it to torment him, but my emotions had spun out of control.

Our train finally found its way through the last orange grove with me muttering and cursing under my breath. We jammed everything we had into our flimsy suitcases, got brushed off several times, and tipped everyone a little more than we ever had before. After all, weren't we rich and famous writers checking into a great film studio where everyone was breathlessly awaiting us with open arms? Well, no, but we were theater folks, so pretending was right up our alley.

It didn't look like Tinsel Town on the morning of April 19, 1942, when Ralph and I walked behind our luggage cart to the line of taxicabs.

We found Los Angeles Union Station dignified, spacious, and beautiful, evocative of an earlier century. And looking through the windows of our cab en route to Hollywood, we saw nothing at all crummy. Hollywood seemed like a very wholesome, clean, old-fashioned city, almost small townish in personality; gorgeous greenery everywhere; streets filled, but not crowded, with happy natives; no freeways, and, blessedly, no smog. Since it was Sunday, we saw people filing into churches.

When our taxi deposited us at the quaint old Chateau Marmont, it was difficult for me to sustain my bias against Hollywood, because it was a delightful hotel with period furniture, plus a grand piano in the lobby.

We had allowed ourselves a whole week to settle in before reporting to Culver City to meet our new bosses. We did a little sight-seeing, then started thinking about where to live and how to get about. It's not easy to hail a taxicab anywhere in Southern California, and phoning for one, then waiting for it, can be frustrating. Neither of us had a driver's license, since cars are a liability where we came from, but I had done a lot of driving in Alabama and felt reasonably sure it would come back to me, so we rented a car and turned up at the Department of Motor Vehicles with it. Ralph flunked his test, but fortunately I didn't, so we were okay in the wheels department for a few days.

Without Ralph I probably would have done things the easy way and lingered a while at the Marmont, but Ralph, as always, had superior judgment in the areas of business and finance.

"We pay more per week in a hotel than we would per month in a rented house," Ralph told me.

"Of course you're right," I said. "You always are when it comes to money."

We did a little searching and found what we wanted at 123 North Elm Drive. It was in Beverly Hills but not at all posh, and the rent was modest. No swimming pool, but what interested me more was a really nice baby grand that looked and sounded as if it were just waiting for me to come along.

Chapter 20

A Maverick at Metro

---

*T*HE SETTLING IN FLEW BY and suddenly it was Monday, April 27, 1942, the day we were slated to bite the bullet and present ourselves at 10202 Washington Blvd., Culver City. It was fortunate we arrived fairly early, about 9 a.m., because I drove our rented car to the wrong gate. The security guard courteously but firmly informed us that the names Hugh Martin and Ralph Blane meant absolutely nothing to him and that he therefore could not admit us.

Remarkably, and seemingly symbolically, Judy Garland showed up with her mother at that precise moment and precise spot, and said there must be some mistake because Arthur Freed and Roger Edens were expectantly awaiting our arrival and would be extremely disappointed if anything happened to prevent our meeting with them. How like Judy to exaggerate our importance and smooth the way for us! Especially since she was ill and being physically held upright by her mother, Ethel Gumm. Evidently Judy's little bouts with illness had become frequent by then, so when Judy fell sick, she and Mrs. Gumm usually ducked out onto Washington Blvd. through this side gate to avoid being pounced upon by Judy's fans.

We were surprised that Judy and her mother had recognized us, because during those three turbulent weeks at the Capitol Theatre in 1939, we hardly ever saw Judy except when she and Mickey were actually on stage with us doing their non-stop personal appearances. She was too tuckered out to socialize or have visitors in the dressing room; it was sing, eat, sleep, sing for all of us. Now, three years later, standing at an ugly iron portal in Culver City, the four of us exchanged brief hugs, because Judy looked really bad. She was on a different treadmill now. It was sing, dance, eat a bit, and sleep, if possible! Take downers! Show up for work at crack of dawn! Take uppers so the famous Garland eyes will sparkle! And so on. What a merry-go-round for a sweet, normal child. She was nineteen, but she was still a child, or would have been if they had allowed her to be.

It was a curious prelude to my two MGM years. I think my devotion to Judy began at that strange moment, seeing the haunted look in her eyes. I had learned to love her as a performer in *Oz*; now I was beginning to feel connected to her as a person. Through the years the connection became much deeper than either of us expected. We were never romantically involved, but there was an extraordinary bond between us. Her death in 1969 at the shockingly young age of forty-seven devastated me. I thought that the passing of the years would diminish the nearness of her, but the reverse has been true. I still have vivid dreams of her on a regular basis.

The gate I had mistakenly driven to turned out to be miles from the one through which we should have entered, so it was obvious we were going to be late for our first appointment. We were not allowed yet to drive through the gates, so we looked about for some means of transportation. There were angry little shuttle cars everywhere almost knocking down pedestrians. And huge black limousines, heavily shrouded like hearses, so that no one could get a glimpse of who was within. Garbo? Tracy? Hepburn? We had fun wondering.

We looked for a public phone so we could apologize for our tardiness, but we couldn't find one.

"Let's walk," I said and Ralph groaned. It was our usual syndrome, me wanting to walk and Ralph groaning. Several of our friends used to call us Laurel and Hardy.

In retrospect, I'm glad we were able to take in so much of MGM's 163.6 acres right off the bat. It was a miniscule part of the whole but it gave us an overall impression of this "factory" that we never would have gotten if we hadn't bypassed the proper entrance. What met our eyes mainly were masses of edifices that resembled airplane hangars. These, we learned later, were sound stages. Some of them were for the purpose of filming, some for rehearsals, others for recording. Sound Stage One, the most famous in Hollywood, was where Judy Garland recorded "Over the Rainbow" and "Dear Mr. Gable," and Lena Horne joined forces there with the incomparable MGM orchestra to lay down tracks of "Honeysuckle Rose," "'Deed I Do," and "Just One of Those Things," among others.

In the near distance lay fields of rugged terrain for the Westerns, a small lake, a harbor, a miniature jungle and park, and innumerable full-scale city streets calculated to evoke places from all over the world, including one elaborate complex for the *Andy Hardy* series. We didn't get to see any of these wonders; we were too busy threading our way without a chart to the hub of all the activity, the Irving G. Thalberg Administration Building. Here we could find the high muckety muck himself, Louis B. Mayer, along with all the smaller muckety mucks.

Next in importance to Mr. Mayer was Arthur Freed, who had chosen me and, by proxy, Ralph. He had seen *Best Foot Forward* on one of his talent searches in Manhattan, and eventually bought the show, seven of its young stars of tomorrow, and the two writers who gave them fourteen songs to sing, some good, some—well, not so good.

Evaluation time was at hand, and Mr. Freed and Mr. Edens were about to get a preview of what they had purchased. Would we be the new hotshot *wunderkinder*? Or would we be weighed on the scales and found wanting? Our knees buckled slightly as our destination came into sight. It was like approaching the Emerald City.

Both Mr. Freed and Mr. Edens were to be found in adjacent offices on the second floor. I can't overstate the importance of Roger Edens to Arthur Freed. Both were brilliant but in different ways. Roger was the class, the quality, the patina on Arthur's sturdy furniture. Together they were a formidable team—Arthur making the major decisions, and Roger adding the extra touch of elegance that their projects required.

Arthur was a successful lyricist before switching to the executive branch of the film world. It was his contributions to *The Wizard of Oz* that had been responsible for his status in 1942 as king of the musicals, second in power only to Mr. Mayer himself. Mervyn LeRoy had been the nominal producer of *Oz*, but everyone instinctively knew that it was Arthur's baby, one he had loved and nurtured for years. Judy Garland had come into his life at exactly the right moment, had swept him off his feet and into a decade of superlative musicals that have never been surpassed.

It was time to face the music. We combed our hair, checked our flies, cleared our throats, and opened the door with Arthur Freed's name written on it. An attractive young woman said, "I'm Kathleen and Mr. Freed will be with you in a moment."

Before that moment arrived, Roger Edens turned up, for which we were grateful, because we had come to know and feel comfortable with Roger in New York when he chose The Martins to sing with Judy and Mickey at the Capitol Theater. When we finally entered Mr. Freed's private office, I realized that Arthur, too, was relieved that Roger was nearby to break the ice. In spite of his enormous clout at the studio, Arthur Freed was, I think, a very shy man and somewhat inarticulate, too, a real paradox because although he lacked the poise and *savoir faire* of Roger, he possessed a unique producing ability. His instinct for assembling the cream of artistic talents was unsurpassable, and he blended his ingredients with the skill of a master chef.

Arthur Freed was portly and looked like a businessman. Roger Edens was elegance personified. He was quite tall, perhaps six feet four, and looked like the Southern gentleman he was.

Arthur and Roger pulled out all the stops to make us feel welcome. He put us at once on a first-name basis, and apologized for not having a suitable office ready for us.

Freed: We'll probably release fifty or more feature-length films this year, so we're bustin' at the seams. Roger, maybe we could put the boys in the Little Red Schoolhouse.

Edens: It won't be available 'til June, when school lets out.

Freed: Oh, that's right. Say, do you have a piano where you're living?

Hugh: We do, a first-rate baby grand.

Freed: Well, then, why don't you work at home until something opens up?

Ralph: Great!

Edens: This is a break for you. When I started here, I had to punch a time clock.

Freed: You've met my secretary, Kathleen? Come down the hall and meet Mr. Mayer's secretary. She wields more influence than anybody else in this building.

The two of them took us to an office on the same floor. We met a dear, motherly lady named Ida Koverman, who instantly took us under her wing. When she heard I had spent only six weeks in Hollywood two years ago, and that Ralph had never seen it before, she urged us to call on her if we needed references or help of any kind. Like her boss, Mr. Mayer, Ida was warm and sentimental, a perfect Jewish mother. After we took leave of our two new protectors—three, counting Mrs. Koverman—we relaxed for an hour at the Commissary and lunched on the most famous of its special dishes, chicken soup. The recipe for the soup had come from Mr. Mayer's mother.

The MGM Commissary had happy associations for Ralph and me and one most unhappy one. It was, of course, great fun to watch the MGM stars enjoying their breaks from the stress of shooting on the various sound stages. It was startling to see Boris Karloff wander in in full monster regalia, or a regiment of soldiers from the eighteenth century. Besides, the food was excellent.

I spotted Robert Walker there at lunch time one day and wished that I had the nerve to speak to him and tell him how much I admired his work. Simultaneously, and much to my surprise, he walked over to me and said, "Are you Hugh Martin?"

Hugh: Why, yes. How ever did you know?

Walker: Listen, were you an actor for a time—before you started writing songs?

Hugh: Very briefly. I was not a good actor.

Walker: Well, you were good enough to take a role away from me.

Hugh: What are you talking about?

Walker: Did you play "Phil" in *Where Do We Go From Here?*

Hugh: Yes, I did. Was that the name of the character?

Walker: It certainly was. Ask me how I know.

Hugh: How do you know?

Walker: Because I played "Phil" before you did. They tried the play out here on the West Coast before they took it to New York. They fired me and put you in my part.

We were both breaking up by now.

Hugh: Then they fired *me*!

We sealed the conversation with a quick bear hug, and I blessed him for finally squeezing out the last ounce of bitterness from my long ago failure.

A less felicitous incident occurred in the big dining room a few weeks later. Ralph and I had solved a little musical problem that had been troubling Arthur Freed, and we thought he'd be pleased to hear some good news about it. We walked over to where he was lunching and told him our new idea. There were a couple of empty chairs. We sat down on them. Conversation became very hushed, but we were able to grasp the fact that we had violated the sanctity of The Freed Table. We had committed The Unpardonable Sin.

Ouch! It was the coldest blast of frigid air we ever met up with. Instant winter, as Ralph described it later. I don't remember who the favored apostles were who were seated there that day. Roger, of course, Lena Horne. I've mercifully blocked out the others. But I'll never forget the horror of the sudden realization that sitting down uninvited at The Freed Table is beyond the pale, *de trop*, taboo! We boycotted the Commissary pretty much after that experience unless we were very short of time. We would go outside the gates and look for a sandwich somewhere in Culver City, where they seemed glad to see us.

Historic photograph of the MGM music department in 1944.
On floor: Sammy Cahn, July Styne, me.
Standing: Nat Finston, Johnny Green, Johnny Mercer,
Harry Warren, Ralph Freed, Ralph Blane—last gentleman unknown.
(photo by MGM)

Chapter 21

The Arthur Freed Unit

I HAVE HEARD OF NO ONE in musical films or musical theater who didn't want to be part of the Arthur Freed Unit
at MGM. The exception was me. I know this sounds pretentious and snooty and above it all, but it's the truth. When MGM
offered me a seven-year contract in 1942, my first reaction was
"No way!" I'm not sure what made me cave in. It wasn't the
money; my salary at Metro was well below the norm for working songwriters.

What was it then that possessed me to sign my life away for
seven years? I'm still not sure. It might have been the pressure
brought to bear by friends, more aware than I that the Arthur
Freed Unit was the *crème de la crème*. They were right; I don't
deny for a minute the superiority of King Arthur's Camelot. But
when I got to Hollywood, my overwhelming love for live theater
swept over me and pushed all else aside.

When I get depressed, I stop eating. I don't snack, I just
starve. Period. That's what happened after a few days at MGM.
Ralph would go out for breakfast, lunch, and dinner and try to
coax me to join him.

"Just sit with me, Hugh," he would say. "I don't know a soul in Hollywood, and I get lonely sitting at a table chewing away in silence."

I knew he hoped that if I were in the hustle bustle of Hollywood restaurants, and there were so many great ones, I would forget to be blue and start nibbling. I went with him occasionally, but even seeing and smelling some truly gourmet concoctions, I was never tempted. I must have been terrible company, but Ralph was on a crusade to get me back into the world, partly because my insanity was a threat to his career, but more I think from a genuine concern for my feelings. He knew I was suffering.

My hunger strike broke in an unexpected way. After about ten days of this nonsense, I allowed Ralph to drag me off my bed of starvation and into a neighborhood movie theater. *The Man Who Came to Dinner* was playing. I can't think of many other films so uproariously funny it would jolt me out of my pity party. I started to chuckle when Monty Woolley, as Sheridan Whiteside, slipped in the snow on the doorstep of the hapless Mr. and Mrs. Stanley, utterly unprepared for the invasion they were about to experience. As the marvelous Kaufman-Hart comedy unfolded, I laughed more and more heartily. My breathing became regular, my muscles stopped twitching, and I could almost feel blood filling my veins and strengthening me.

"Ralph," I said as we left the theater, "I'm hungry."

Laughter is a miraculous thing.

Johnny Green

I liked Johnny Green. I liked his exuberance and, of course, the songs he wrote. But Johnny seemed to find me resistible. My acceptance into Broadway circles at age twenty-seven had been effortless and, to Johnny, who had been paying his dues for quite some time, it seemed undeserved. Worse, my success had come about largely through the sponsorship of Richard Rodgers, who was a very close friend of Johnny's.

During my MGM tenure, George Abbott produced on Broadway a Johnny Green musical called *Beat the Band*. Abbott asked MGM to allow me to come to New York for a month to do the vocal arrangements for Johnny's show. Permission was granted, but my work on *Beat the Band* elicited a violent anti-Martin response from Green. He gave Abbott an ultimatum: get rid of Hugh Martin or you lose Johnny Green. Since I was more expendable than the composer, I was sent back to the Dream Factory, feeling banished, which is just what I was.

A few months later, Johnny Green was made head of the MGM Music Department, a prestigious post indeed. Almost immediately, Ralph and I were summoned to his office. He was all smiles and courtesy itself, and when we left, Ralph looked at me in disbelief. "How can you be civil to that man after the way he treated you on *Beat the Band?*"

I looked blank.

"Oh," I said.

"What do you mean, 'Oh'?" said Ralph.

I had to confess I had totally drawn a blank about the whole episode. I don't think Ralph believed me, but I was telling the truth. I wasn't playing the martyr or being The Great Forgiver; I had plain forgotten the whole affair.

If I thought I could win Johnny over by eternal forgiveness, I was mistaken. He always got the last laugh. Just when I congratulated myself on having exorcised all his demons concerning me, he was invited to lecture on American popular song lyrics. He spoke at the De Young Museum in San Francisco's Golden Gate Park.

I had been Johnny's whipping boy so long he couldn't break the cycle. I wasn't present when he gave his lecture, but there is usually some gossipy soul prepared to pass on all the gory details.

Johnny chose one of my songs, "Pass that Peace Pipe," as a perfect example of the worst kind of rhyming. Unfortunately, he was fairly accurate in his finger pointing, but I probably would have winced a bit at the relish with which he pointed. I had written the song with Roger Edens and Ralph, but the bad rhymes were mine and I don't wish to pass the buck to Roger or Ralph. I don't know why I committed those rhyming atrocities. I can't remember whether I had forgotten what Dick Rodgers had taught me, or whether I was impatient to finish the darn thing and so took the easier and less excellent way. At any rate my sins found me out, and Johnny had a marvelous time taking Martin apart glitch by glitch. That's how it was described to me, and I'm afraid, knowing Johnny, the account was probably accurate. If I close my eyes, I can hear the gloat in his voice and see the little smile of victory on his lips. Hoh Yoh Toh Hoh, YOH!

The Sweetest Music this Side of Heaven

The MGM Orchestra was many orchestras, not one. It was four pieces or forty, or even more when the studio wanted to make a big splash. The roster of conductors and orchestrators boasted more wizards than Oz, and they were masters at turning sows' ears into silk purses. With the Freed Unit, this was seldom necessary. Arthur and Roger had exemplary taste. If one of them picked a loser, the other was on tap to pull him back. Between Arthur and Roger, the Johnny Greens, Conrad Salingers, George Bassmans, Leo Arnauds, David Raksins, and other orchestrators usually had quality music to work with that they, in turn, made even better.

Conrad Salinger was the standard bearer. He was a modest, private, sweet gentleman; we all loved him and thrilled to his arrangements, especially those for *Singin' in the Rain, Show Boat, The Band Wagon, Easter Parade, The Pirate,* and *Billy Rose's Jumbo.*

Roger Edens

When I reported to RKO in 1940 for my first Hollywood assignment, I instantly took to almost everyone there, and they seemed to take to me. I had never been called "Hughie," but before I left the studio at the end of my first working day, that was my name, and it stuck right through my tenure on Gower Street.

Two years later when I checked in at MGM for the first time, I half expected to get that old feeling, the friendly ambiance that had so beguiled me at RKO. No such luck. Except for my wonderful stable of state-of-the-art choral singers, all of whom were adorable, the MGM people, from the top echelon executives down to the workers in the Commissary, seemed subtly uptight, even paranoid, but it's perfectly possible that in those swiftly shifting twenty-four months between the two assignments, I had become paranoid, though I don't think so.

I was naïve, yet it was apparent to me that a few of my colleagues were putting me down in various ways, pretending to like me, then laughing behind my back, questioning my taste, my ability, even my truthfulness. Ralph and I were taking home paychecks that were, we discovered much later, about half of what we could have had. At the major studios, our kind of monetary ineptness reaps contempt not sympathy, whereas the manipulators are eulogized and idolized.

The oasis in the midst of all this craziness was Roger Edens. Arthur Freed asked MGM to sign him shortly after he played piano in 1930 for *Girl Crazy* in one of musical comedy's most famous pit orchestras. Many of the greats of jazz had played in the pit orchestra that had enhanced the wonderful Gershwin songs and helped make Ethel Merman and Ginger Rogers sound their best.

It was one of Freed's most felicitous moves. Roger, through his talent and popularity with his singers, gradually became the power behind Arthur's throne. More and more, when faced with a multiplicity of choices, Roger's nearly infallible judgment led him to right ones. His star protegé was Judy Garland. How providential for that little girl to fall into the hands of a kind and wise gentleman like Roger! I shudder to think how her talent, phenomenal yet fragile, would have been hurt by the philistines at Fox or Warner Bros. Do I sound smug about MGM? If I do, it's not without reason. Compare the MGM musicals of the Golden Age with those of their competitors. No contest. The glamour of MGM's big stars, the stature of their stable of fine supporting players, the chic (when appropriate) and razzle-dazzle (ditto) of their costumes, the richness of their décor and, of special interest to me, the excitement and beauty of their orchestras. Except for a few wise insiders, it was not generally realized that much of MGM's superiority could be credited to Roger. His appreciation and support did more to enrich my two years at the studio than any other factor.

When he and Ralph and I wrote "Pass that Peace Pipe," we intended it for *The Ziegfeld Follies,* but it was deleted and ended up in *Good News.* The song "The Joint Is Really Jumpin' Down at Carnegie Hall" bears all three of our names, although it was actually written by Roger alone. Judy sang it with José Iturbi in *Thousands Cheer.* After he finished writing it, he was chagrined to discover it had a rhythm similar to a passage I had written for Nancy Walker as part of "The Three B's," so over Ralph's and my protests, he insisted on adding our names to his on the credits line of the song. Typical Edens generosity.

Chapter 22

Best Foot Forward

(Déjà Vu All Over Again)

JUNE ROLLED AROUND and the famous Little Red Schoolhouse, now empty, became the office of Martin and Blane. Judy Garland had scribbled on its blackboard, as had Mickey Rooney, Elizabeth Taylor, Roddy McDowell, Lana Turner, Freddie Bartholomew, and Ann Rutherford. It was a cute little place, not in a building, but all by itself with grass all around, just like a real schoolhouse, which is what it was. There were two tiny rooms, one where the teacher could grade papers, and a classroom. Ralph loved to play director and chart out production numbers on the blackboard.

There were no vocal arrangements on the assembly line waiting to be done, so they started sending us a few stars for vocal coaching. Our first pupil was Lena Horne. The teachers, in this case, learned more from the pupil than vice versa. Her voice was coconut sweet; we were thrilled by her singing and startled by her beauty.

Our second pupil was Judy Garland, and we learned even more from her. Roger asked us to drive over to her house to demonstrate a song called "Three Cheers for the Yanks." I had written it in New York just before we departed for the West Coast.

We drove to a modest little cottage where Judy was keeping house for her husband of a few months, David Rose. She was alone when we arrived. Ralph and I were very nervous, performing for the queen of the lot, but she was the soul of graciousness and loved the song. It was love at first sound when Judy and Ralph sang for each other; Ralph demonstrated the patriotic song as lustily as Caruso singing "Over There." Judy needed a song for *For Me and My Gal*, the World War I story she was doing with Gene Kelly. I wish our song had been as authentically 1917 as "Over There." Unfortunately it was full of blue notes and jazz phrases that reflected the forties more than the teens.

But Judy liked it so much she begged the studio to let her do it. Everyone tried to talk her out of it, but when she sang it, the impact was so dynamic she got her way. I made a flamboyant vocal arrangement for a large choir, George Bassman did a dazzling orchestration and we were given a time slot to record it. Judy did a magnificent job, and the performance of the sixteen singing boys and girls was not far behind that of the star. But no matter how brilliant the performance was, nothing could disguise the essential wrongness of the song for a movie about World War I. The sequence was dropped after the first preview.

Ralph and I read in the trade papers that Columbia Studios had bought the film rights to *Best Foot Forward*. They announced that they would film it immediately. Lester Cowan would produce it, Rita Hayworth would play the movie star who was invited to the school prom, and Shirley Temple would be the teenage girl who felt threatened by her. We assumed the deal had been finalized, but Arthur Freed did a little snooping and learned it was not too late for MGM to make George Abbott a better offer. Ralph and I did an informal command performance of the score for Freed and Edens, and they decided they wanted it. Whatever MGM wants, MGM gets. They raised the ante, got the property, and we received a telegram from Mr. Abbott, which read simply, "Good work, boys!"

Ralph and I were thrilled, of course, mainly because we thought that having it done at our home studio meant we would have some control over our baby. Wrong! We were able to produce several outstanding soundtracks, some involving principals only, others utilizing large groups of singers with, in some cases, Harry James and his orchestra, others with the fabulous MGM Orchestra. But Ralph and I were totally shut out in every area except songs. We were not consulted about script, director, casting, etc.

Unlike my work in *Too Many Girls,* this time I had sound engineers who really knew how to mix. If the other departments had been as congenial as the sound department, our MGM experience would have been a joy.

When we were total neophytes on Broadway, Dick Rodgers and George Abbott had shown us great respect. They treated us as if we had been writing scores for Broadway musicals for years. At MGM the opposite was true. All artistic choices were presented to us as *faits accomplis.* If we were pleased, "That's nice, boys." If not, "Oh, really? I thought you'd like that, too bad."

Occasionally our polite disagreements drew blood. I read one morning in the *Hollywood Reporter* that Vincente Minnelli had been granted a six-month deferment by his draft board.

"Terrific," I thought, and forgetting that old devil protocol, I grabbed a phone and called my boss.

"Arthur," I said breathlessly, "I just read about Vincente's deferment from the draft. Do you suppose you might consider having him direct *Best Foot . . .* ?" There was a moment of silence, just as there was in the book of *Revelation* before the Seventh Seal was opened. Then, as in the Bible, all the demons and vials of poison, pitchforks, and brimstone (verbally speaking) came pouring out of the receiver of my telephone. I got a tongue-lashing that crackled like a forest fire.

He spoke slowly as if savoring each epithet. "You . . . ignorant . . . stupid . . . moronic . . . presumptuous son of a bitch," intoned my esteemed employer. "How dare you," he thundered, "have the audacity to tell me how to make movies? When I picked you out of that mass of nobodies in New York, you were *nothing*! And if you don't straighten up and fly right, you will very soon be *nothing* again!"

He hung up, I dissolved in tears, then began plotting revenge. Quickly I realized that revenge didn't seem possible, so I switched to escape. There must be some way I could break loose from this reform school for freedom-loving writers. When I cast about for a sympathetic rebel, I discovered I couldn't think of a single one, not even my own partner. Everywhere I looked I saw happy, affluent, obsequious slaves sniveling, driveling, shriveling, and kissing the feet of a few uncouth, illiterate demagogues who carried big sticks. I was furious, but impotent. I was impaled on the horns of a piece of verbose legalese that declared MGM could drop me anytime they so desired but until they did, I was just one more compromiser like all the others; except that I wanted out and they, poor wretches, apparently did not.

I chuckled years later when Freed and Minnelli became an acclaimed team. As in the case of Johnny Green, I've never had a lot of trouble forgiving people. I don't have a whole lot of virtues, but I am pretty good in the forgiveness department. What made it easier in the case of Arthur Freed's unexpected diatribe was that someone who knew him well explained to me that blowing up for apparently no reason was a Freed trademark. It had happened to a humiliated Lucille Ball. Her experience was far worse than mine. I had been alone on a telephone; poor Lucy was excoriated on a huge sound stage in front of a whole mess of stagehands, electricians, cameramen, gofers, and assorted lackeys. She was devastated and unable to work for a few days. Among the insults Arthur chose to hit her with was "When I sack you, you can go back to the streets, which is where you belong."

I don't know how I knew Minnelli was going to become one of the top directors in Hollywood, certainly the top director of musicals. He admitted to me he knew about my rebellion against him way back in the *Hooray for What!* days. I believe he never quite forgave me for the incident. I am sorry he felt that way, because I was, and am, a tremendous fan of his.

During our first few weeks at MGM, Ralph and I took him out to dinner. He was pleasant and interesting and gave no hint of resentment about the *Hooray for What!* mutiny. All I remember about the conversation that night was something he said as he got into his car to drive away, and for some reason I remember it word for word.

"It must be exciting," I said to him, "to know that you can choose to work with any one of those great stars that spark you. Do you have any hunches about which one has the greatest potential?" Vincente's face was very expressive, and I could see him running through the roster in his mind. After a few seconds he said, "I think . . . the little Garland girl."

With Ralph Blane (left) and Harry Warren at MGM, 1946.

(photo by MGM)

Chapter 23

Hooray for Hollywood!

$\mathcal{I}$NCONSISTENT CREATURE THAT I AM, I eventually had to confess that there were certain undeniable charms about the place I had so hastily and unfairly despised on arrival. In 1942 the air was like perfume—no smog, all flowers and ocean breezes. I began to feel foolish remembering some of the sophomoric insults I had paid my new habitat. I comforted myself by recalling that some very bright people had shared my first low opinion of Hollywood. Larry Hart had pleased scads of inveterate New Yorkers when he wrote:

> *Hate California, it's cold and it's damp.*
> *That's why the lady is a tramp.*

And Fred Allen had remarked, "California is a great place to be—if you're an orange."

I was beginning to like living in a house again after years of trying to make everything work in a tiny New York City apartment. I had to admit also that I was enjoying driving again. It was fun, after working hard all week, to jump in the car and go to Knott's Berry Farm, or perhaps one of the beautiful Franciscan missions, or the

177

famous Mission Inn in Riverside, or even Palm Springs, a heavenly spot at that time with a magic of its own.

Since America was at war, gas was rationed, but I had enough coupons to get to the studio. I did the long hauls with friends who bought black market gas, but I never bought any myself. Well, almost never . . .

Locally a major delight was Saturday nights at the Kelly's. Gene and Betsy hosted the informal get-togethers of movie society each weekend—the casual set, you might say, as opposed to the black tie people. There was almost no alcohol, but plenty of Cokes and Seven-Ups and maybe an occasional beer. Ralph and I had a standing invitation to come and play The Game, which was a variation of Charades. Also, we were usually the intermission feature at the Kelly piano, augmented by Lena, Judy, and other musical folks. Funny folks, too, like Phil Silvers, and funnier even than Phil was Elliott Reid. The Kelly's Saturday nights were a time for laughter, and no one made us "forget your troubles, come on, get happy," more than Ted Reid.

Gene and Betsy were probably the most romantic couple in Hollywood. They were newlyweds, almost honeymooners. Gene was dark and handsome, Betsy lovely and graceful, and they were both superb dancers. When Gene was courting Betsy back in New York, he knew hundreds of lovely, graceful young dancers and first-rate actresses. What gave Betsy the edge? It might have been her sharp, rebellious, non-conformist brain. Gene himself was as strong intellectually as he was physically, and it must have intrigued him to meet his match in someone so young.

I, too, found Betsy stimulating, and I became closer to her than I was to Gene. I soon discovered that her philosophy was extremely left wing; in fact she persuaded me to enroll in a course in Dialectical Materialism. I didn't know what it was then and I still don't. I tagged along for months, simply because I found Betsy such delightful company. We two mice had a lot of innocent fun while the cat was away making movies at MGM with Judy Garland and friends.

Betsy's memoir, *The Memory of All That*,[1] revealed a much more complicated woman than I had been aware of in our Hollywood days. After reading it, I realized I hadn't understood Betsy any better than I had Dialectical Materialism.

In my opinion, Gene never quite reached the level of Fred Astaire. His zenith, for me, was the title number of "Singin' in the Rain," and I cherish to this day the memory of a very articulate, intellectual critic who was discussing the "Singin' in the Rain" number on a BBC documentary about Kelly. "It was . . . it was . . . " He was searching for the right words, ". . . unutterably perfect!," and he said it with such gusto that he almost fell off his chair. The funny part is he was right. It *was* unutterably perfect!

Ralph and I occasionally took in one of the flashy, glitzy Hollywood parties, usually not by choice, but because we were expected to entertain. The most glittering one we ever attended was a big bash at Arthur Freed's home with practically every star in Hollywood present. I was happy it coincided with a visit by my mother and sister because I knew it would give them enough material to keep Birmingham buzzing for a long time. When we entered, Ellie Gordon and Ellen and I headed for the darkest corner, practically pulling our shyness over us like a blanket. We undoubtedly would have remained there, invisible, for the duration of the party if it hadn't been for the sharp, sensitive eyes of a very dear MGM contract player named Cyd Charisse. Cyd boldly entered our hiding place, took Ellen's trembling 15-year-old hands into hers, and said cheerfully, "Wouldn't you like to meet some of the guests?" Half of Ellen wanted to and half of her didn't, but Cyd prevailed and off they went.

"Mr. Gable, this is Ellen Martin."

"Ellen, I want you to meet Greer Garson," etc.

---

1 Blair, Betsy. *The Memory of All That*. New York: Alfred A. Knopf, 2003.

It only got better after that because Judy Garland sang, Ralph and I did our thing, and Harold Arlen and Johnny Mercer introduced "Ac-Cent-Chu-Ate the Positive" for the first time in public. It was some enchanted evening!

Trying to Go to War

Among other Hollywood major delights were a couple of aspiring playwrights named Robert E. Lee and Jerome Lawrence. They were sergeants in Armed Forces Radio Network, a morale-building Army unit headed by the lovable and gifted Meredith Willson. The three of them got permission from Freed to do a condensed radio version of *Best Foot* . . . with the MGM cast, to be broadcast to American fighting forces overseas. Ralph and I cooperated with enthusiasm, and during meetings and rehearsals, Bob, Jerry, and I became great friends. All we did was talk—talk, talk, talk, talk, talk incessantly. We were idealists but in such totally different ways that there were innumerable intellectual skirmishes. However the debates were usually amicable. I told them of my eagerness to enlist, and Meredith tried to open doors for me to become part of Armed Forces Radio Network, but the stumbling block of my 4-F classification always torpedoed me.

"Keep getting healthy," they urged me, "and gain some weight."

I was determined to become an active part of the war in any capacity. My first choice was to be a soldier, but the army was not yet desperate enough to draft an underweight, sedentary songwriter. My second choice was the U.S.O. I tried to persuade Judy Garland to go overseas with me. I knew she'd be a sensation with the troops, but she leveled with me.

"Hugh," she said, "I'm going to confess something to you. I'd be too scared to do it. The thought of being near the guns scares the daylights out of me!"

I went to the U.S.O. and applied for a job as accompanist for anyone who might not have one.

(top to bottom) Robert E. Lee and Jerome Lawrence, 1944.

"What do you play?" they asked.

"Piano," I said.

"You won't find any pianos where the shooting is. Can you play the accordion?"

No, but I immediately got a teacher and tried to learn. For some reason, I couldn't. Piano came second nature to me, but I never was able to master the infernal accordion.

I continued to haunt the recruiting centers, and while waiting for a green light, played piano for Virginia O'Brien, Nancy Walker, Cass Daley, and others at the Hollywood Canteen.

With Marsha Hunt, a long-time friend and pupil.
I coached Marsha during our MGM years together, 1942–1944.

(The photo was snapped in April, 2006 by Lynne Brighton)

Chapter 24

More Stars Than There
Are in Heaven

*B*EST *FOOT FORWARD* OPENED AT GRAUMAN'S CHINESE THEATER in Hollywood and simultaneously at the Astor in New York. Ralph and I liked parts of it, especially Lucille Ball as Lucille Ball. Her presence, plus the freshness of the young Broadway stars imported from Abbott's production, saved the project from mediocrity since neither the script nor Eddie Buzzell's direction was on par with the original presentation.

"You should have listened to me, Arthur Freed," I scolded him silently in Walter Mitty fashion. "Some day attention must be paid to songwriters."

Apparently our first movie didn't do too badly, because a few weeks after it opened, the studio gave us a prestigious office of our own. It was a freestanding bungalow almost in the center of the beehive, a desirable little two-room affair that had belonged, for as long as people could remember, to Franz Waxman.

One of the first people to call was a young David Raksin. Ralph and I introduced ourselves and asked him what he was working on. He told us a little about *Laura,* which he was scoring over at Twentieth Century Fox.

Judy Garland signed this picture for me
the night before I reported to the Army for induction, 1944.
(photo by MGM)

"Everyone seems to like the *Laura* theme a lot," he told us. "Johnny Mercer heard it and I'm hoping he'll put a lyric to it."

We told him how fine we thought that would be, and he said, "Would you like to hear it?" He played it for us, and its strange beauty still lingers in my memory.

We began to coach several MGM stars, all women. The male stars seemed to consider singing expendable, but the ladies knew that musicals were riding high in the early forties and they wanted some of the action.

We got a call from L.K. Sidney. "We just signed a swimming champion who thinks she can sing. Will you fellas take her on?"

"Of course," we said. "She should have great breath control."

Esther Williams knocked on the door of our bungalow and for the next hour she had us in stitches. She was a blast, a truly funny and honest gal.

"I just bought some sexy black underwear," she said apropos of nothing. "Wanna see it?" Without waiting for permission, up flew her skirt over her face and head. Then she lowered the flag and giggled uncontrollably when she saw our confusion.

When she got down to the business of singing, we were surprised and pleased by the vivacity of her singing style. She was right on pitch, but there was a major problem. Esther, bless her, was rhythm deaf. She never waited for the "rests," just skipped right over them to the consternation of the orchestra. The only other pupil we came across who had the same problem was Fernando Lamas. Years later they got married, and when Ralph and I heard about it, we looked at each other with a knowing expression and said in unison, "Perfect match!"

Our favorite pupil was Marsha Hunt. Her singing voice was melodious, her intonation and musicianship were far above average, and she was easy on the eyes. But we also loved Marsha for reasons not so obvious. There was a quiet wisdom about her, which seemed strangely mature in one so young. Sixty-two films and six Broadway plays later, Hollywood suddenly felt too small to contain her dreams, and she found herself a citizen of the world. In 1983 she turned her attention and compassion on the homeless, a huge and neglected area of global misery. For twenty years, this was the focus of her drive to make a difference.

Marsha Hunt in an MGM publicity shot, 1944.

But Marsha never totally abandoned her natural milieu, the
world of art and entertainment. She composed fifty songs, words
and music, and still found time to write and assemble a beautiful

coffee-table book[1] comprising hundreds of photographs of fashionable clothes of the thirties and forties and her comments on all. It is in its third printing.

Returning to the 1940s and MGM, another beauty, very different from Marsha Hunt, was Marilyn Maxwell. Her background was the circus, of all things. She was the daring young girl on the flying trapeze, and her parents were acrobats. Her real name, appropriately for a circus performer, was Marvel, and she asked Ralph and me to call her that. She was so gorgeous that all of the wolves in town were chasing her. She had not been endowed with spectacular vocal abilities, but she was too clever and too diligent to let that stop her. This gal was a worker. Consequently, she achieved goals that many less driven women with superior singing voices might have envied. Marilyn plugged away with us as often as the studio would give us time together, and we were all three pleased with the results. Evidently, so was Bing Crosby, because he chose her to sing with him on his Kraft Music Hall for many months. Little did we know that Marilyn was to become a bona fide four-leaf clover for Ralph and me.

1 Hunt, Marsha, *The Way We Wore*. New York: Fallbrook Publishing, Ltd., 1993

ACT TWO

The Road Gets Rougher

Timothy Gray and me rehearsing
High Spirits, *1963.*

Entr'acte

My life has been sprinkled with unusual people, and some of the things they said to or about me, or simply in my presence, often pop into my mind at unexpected times. Here are some samples:

Ralph Blane (to a waiter in New York's Childs' Restaurant, east side of Seventh Avenue at Forty-ninth Street): I'll have the smokery-hicked ham.

Waiter: I'm sorry, sir, we're all out of the—what did you say, sir?

Ralph: Never mind. Just bring me the navy boon seep.

Gore Vidal: People who need people are the unluckiest people in the world.

Gene Kelly (in Childs' Restaurant, west side of Broadway at Forty-sixth Street in 1940, just before he took New York by storm in *Pal Joey*): I've made a decision about my career, Hugh. I've accepted the fact that I'm never gonna make it as a performer. I have hopes for myself as a choreographer or maybe a director, but as for Gene Kelly, performer—never gonna happen.

Mike Todd (to me): You're fired! And don't come messing around the theater; the doormen have instructions to throw you out.

Hugh: But Mr. Todd! (sound of door slamming.)

Hugh: Would you excuse me, Ralph. I have to write a letter.

Ralph: Who toom?

Beatrice Lillie (in Hollywood): Where shall we dine tonight? At the C.O.C.K. and Bull? Or would you prefer the Tail of the C.O.C.K.?

Jerome Kern (to Ralph and me in 1942): I think that was disgracefully unpatriotic of you to write "Buckle Down, Winsocki" when we're at war with Japan.

Joshua Logan: The greatest concentration of magic that I've ever experienced in a theater was Helen Morgan singing "Bill" in *Show Boat.*

Gertrude Stein (trying to describe to me a friend of hers whom I hadn't met): She has no sense of humor at all—she wears purple.

Timothy Gray: I think the only man Princess Margaret ever really loved was Group Peter Captain Townsend.

Hugh: Do you ever read the Bible, Ralph?
Ralph: Oh, yes. It's a *heavenly* book!

Lena Horne (to me): If you'll excuse me, I think I'd just as soon not sing that lyric you wrote about darkies loving cornbread.

Hugh Martin, Sr. (to Mike Todd in the lobby of the Winter Garden during intermission of *As the Girls Go*): I'd like to introduce myself. I'm Hugh Martin's father.
Mike Todd: God help you!

Gore Vidal (to me after Princess Diana's death): Do we really want Elton John to sing at our funerals?

Ralph Blane (on being asked his opinion of a war movie he had just seen); Too many boom shots.
Hugh (incredulous); Too many boom shots?
Ralph: Right.
Hugh: Ralph, do you know what boom shots are?
Ralph: Well, of course I know what they are. Boom!—*Boom!!* BOOM!!!

Judy Garland on the famous trolley in Meet Me in St. Louis,
courtesy George Feltenstein, 1945.

(photo by MGM)

Chapter 25

Meet Me in St. Louis

I AM CONVINCED the plum assignment of *Meet Me in St. Louis* would have gone to Rodgers and Hammerstein had it not been for Marilyn Maxwell. We passed Arthur Freed in the hall one morning and he said, "Boys, how is the little circus girl coming along with her singing?" We did a one-minute commercial for Marilyn Maxwell, and he smiled, saying, "Bring her to my office tomorrow afternoon at two."

Marilyn had twenty-four hours to look her rip-roaring best. When we showed up the next day it was apparent from the moment we walked through the door that she had Arthur's undivided attention. Best of all, he was also impressed by her singing. She sang my arrangement of American folk songs based on the square dance, "Skip to My Lou." The following day Ralph and I received a phone call from our boss telling us he had chosen us to write *Meet Me in St. Louis*.

This new challenge had all the ingredients Ralph and I might have conjured up in our wildest imaginings. Judy Garland was to be the star and Vincente Minnelli the director. We didn't know it at the time, but Judy had fought the project for months. She was a young woman of twenty-one now, and she was determined never to play another teenager. Finally Freed, with the aid of Minnelli, convinced her to let this be her last hurrah in the teenage world, and he promised her some juicy adult roles if she would do him this one last favor.

Arthur cared greatly about this film. It was well known he loved it even more than *The Wizard of Oz,* to which he had been passionately committed. He had wanted to do a musical based on *Life with Father,* and had been greatly disappointed when Jack Warner stole it from under his nose. When he read, in *The New Yorker,* the enchanting pieces by Sally Benson, he knew he had found the property he wanted.

Freed told us at the start he wanted only three new songs because he planned to use old songs from the period of 1904, the year of the St. Louis World's Fair, plus, "Skip to My Lou." We were somewhat disappointed we wouldn't have the opportunity to do an entire score, but Irving Brecher's script was irresistible.

We were allowed to work at home because it was apparent we would get more accomplished without the distractions in the Factory. I worked at the piano in the living room and Ralph holed up in the next room, which happened to be the dining room. This was the way we usually worked since we hardly ever collaborated in the conventional sense. Often we would go to work on the same spot in the script, but we would resolve duplication in an amiable manner.

We had been released from all our other duties. Vocal arrangements, coaching, and other tasks went by the boards. Realizing somehow that this new assignment might be the most important ever to come our way, we plunged into it full steam ahead. Too zealously, as it turned out, since our first efforts were promptly rejected. We asked Arthur and Roger if they had any second thoughts about our suitability for the project. They assured us our slow start was more or less par for the course. We would suddenly hit our stride, perhaps, any day now. We didn't, however, and Ralph got discouraged. We were probably spoiled after the experience we had had on Broadway with *Best Foot Forward.* It had gone so smoothly and only one song had been deleted on the road.

The entire Smith family on the set of Meet Me in St. Louis,
Vincente Minnelli and Arthur Freed flank Judy Garland, rear.

I was discouraged, too, but my discouragement whipped me into trying harder. I became a workaholic for the first time in my life, and it paid off because I soon had a gem in my portfolio, "The Boy Next Door." Ralph had written a song with the same title, but it had been turned down. So when my wandering fingers hit on an unusual and beautiful melody in three-quarter time, Ralph urged me to try my hand at the same title and subject. He also made an invaluable contribution to the song by suggesting I incorporate the addresses of the young lovers in the verse. I did, and it was the first song to be accepted.

Judy Garland played the role of Esther, and we wrote several songs for her to sing in a trolley sequence. All were rejected.

"Boys," said Freed, "these songs you're writing for the trolley spot are not bad songs. I like them all, but I want a song *about* a trolley."

We went home crestfallen because we had drawn a blank on

songs about trolleys. The impasse was causing me anxiety and I stepped up my working hours, hardly ever leaving the piano except to eat or sleep. Ralph, on the other hand, began to work less. When I brought up the subject, I was disappointed by his reply.

"Your salary is twice what they're paying me," he said, "so I don't see anything wrong with you working a little harder."

One morning Ralph left his workroom and came into the living room to ask me a question. "I couldn't help hearing what you've been playing," he said, "and I fell in love with a very sweet melody you were developing yesterday and the day before. Today I was listening for it and you didn't play it. How come?"

"How come," I said to Ralph, "is simply that I tried dozens of ways to resolve the darn thing and never found one I liked."

"Will you do me a favor, Hugh? Will you try another dozen times? I have a funny feeling about that little tune. It sounds like a madrigal."

After he went back to the dining room and closed the door, one word he said stuck in my mind. Madrigal. I picked up the script and leafed to the end and read the Christmas scenes. The phrase *"Have yourself a merry little Christmas"* popped into my head and it fit my melody. Maybe Ralph was right. I went back to the piano and started struggling to make it work.

An hour or so later, I called Ralph in to hear the results. He thought it fit very naturally into the script because Esther is very despondent at that point, so perhaps the lugubrious lyric I had written would be what they all wanted.

We made an appointment to audition the song for Arthur and Roger the following morning and in we went very jauntily. I played the introduction; Ralph loosened his tie and cleared his throat.

Have yourself a merry little Christmas,
It may be your last.
Next year we may all be living in the past.
Have yourself a merry little Christmas,

Pop that champagne cork.
Next year we may all be living in New York.

When we finished the chorus, they laughed. I was shattered. "It's not supposed to be funny," I said.

Roger, still chuckling, said, "I'm sorry. Really I am. It's a gorgeous melody. But it's so desperately sad!"

I said, "I thought Esther was desperately sad in that scene."

Roger was searching for words that wouldn't crush me. He could see I was slightly wounded.

Arthur said, "I really think you're on the track of something good. Please play around with the lyric. It's O.K. for it to be bittersweet and nostalgic, but it shouldn't be a dirge."

Two days later, I ran into Roger at the Commissary. "Hey, Hugh," he said, "I sang your Christmas song for Judy."

I brightened. "What did she say?"

"She said, 'If I sing that lyric to little Margaret O'Brien, the audience will think I'm a monster.'"

"You tell Judy," I said with a touch of hostility, "that if she wants the melody, she's gotta take the lyric. Period!"

It was Tom Drake, who finally broke down my stubbornness. He asked if he could buy me a cup of coffee. Then he nailed me, but not in a mean way. Tom was a good friend who admired my music and didn't want to see me louse myself up.

He looked me straight in the eye.

"Hugh, this is potentially a very great and important song. I feel that in my guts. Now listen to me. Don't be a stubborn idiot. Write a lyric for that beautiful melody that Judy will sing. You'll thank me."

Tom got through to me over a cup of coffee where the big executives had failed. That was sixty-five years ago, but Tom, I do thank you from my heart!

Ellen.

(taken by Moss Photo Service)

Chapter 26

My Sister Ellen

ABOUT THE TIME THAT I WAS BECOMING FOCUSED on leaving Birmingham for more glamorous surroundings, my mother had another baby, this one a daughter. Ellen was 13 years younger than I, but we eventually shared a special bond that transcended our age difference. We were both considered, by our father, to be "out there somewhere"—that is, we seemed to inhabit a fantasy world—a world that was a far cry from the real world.

It was inevitable we should form a special relationship. My mother brought fifteen-year-old Ellen to California at my invitation during my two-year tenure at MGM. I knew somehow those two years would be the glamour segment of my life, and I wanted Ellen and Ellie Gordon to wallow in it a bit with me.

When I did *Too Many Girls* at RKO in 1940, they paid me a visit, but I didn't have the time to entertain them properly. I was determined to make up for that oversight in 1943. We saw and gaped at Rosalind Russell and Henry Fonda at Perino's, Margaret Sullavan at Chasen's, and Madeleine Carroll at Ciro's. To Ellen's amazement, Madeleine Carroll actually gaped at her! Ellen and Ellie Gordon and I were sitting at a little table at Ciro's far from ringside when a waiter came over and handed us a note addressed to my mother. The note read:

Dear Madam,

If this request is an intrusion on your privacy, please feel free to ignore it. I am sitting with three friends just across the dance floor from you. We are all so taken with the young lady at your table that we have made wagers as to her age. Our guesses range from twelve to twenty-five. May we send an emissary to your table to get the correct answer?

It was signed, "Madeleine Carroll."

Mother shyly thanked her, Ellen blushed, and I beamed. "She is almost sixteen," Mother told Miss Carroll, "but she has always looked younger than she is."

Not only did Ellen look young, everything about her was quintessential springtime. She was a zephyr, a dragonfly, a will-o'-the-wisp. The only other person who ever gave me that feeling was Audrey Hepburn.

I watched some home movies of my family recently, quite ordinary until someone pointed a camera (silent, of course) at my sister who was improvising to a Dinah Shore recording of "Buttons and Bows." Suddenly everything changed, like going from a sepia Kansas to a Technicolor "Oz." We heard the music that wasn't there, we seemed to see Dinah in her buttons and bows, and everything came to life through Ellen's subtle movements. Isadora couldn't have done it better!

It took a great dancer to recognize Ellen's special gift. Paul Draper, the famous tap virtuoso, saw Ellen perform and asked her to team up with him. He had never worked with a partner before, always the great classical soloist. He took her on a concert tour that crisscrossed the whole country.

Ellen wanted success but she ran from it at the same time. I've always wondered whether her psychoanalyst (she was in analysis most of her adult life) could have explained to me why she never seemed

Ellen Martin, my sister, at age 25.
(taken by Michael Brown)

Ellen Martin, December 30, 1956.

able to connect with the bluebird of happiness except for her last few years when a good marriage and a beautiful daughter brought her great joy. It seemed such an anomaly to those of us who cherished her that with such an overabundance of qualities that brightened the lives of others, she should be on intimate terms with the blues. Perhaps it was the "laugh clown laugh" syndrome with a variation: "dance ballerina dance."

Something revealing happened once during a Mass we attended at St. Patrick's Cathedral in New York. The Bible reading was from Paul's letter to the Philippians. "Brethren," he wrote, "pray for me. I have poured myself out for you like a libation." As the priest read those words, Ellen grabbed my hand and squeezed it so hard it hurt. Freely translated, that grip was saying to me, "Dear Hughie, do you realize that that is why I'm always so exhausted? I pour myself out like a libation for everyone in my life."

To those who know how full of paradox life is, it will be no surprise to you to learn that Ellen, the essence of all that is lovely, died of breast cancer at age 49.

Chapter 27

Trouble in Paradise

*I*T WAS NOW A SOLID YEAR since I picked up that copy of *Life* in the club car of the *Super Chief* en route to Hollywood. The obsession about wanting to enlist had been festering all this time. Frankly, I don't know, even today, what my true motivation was. Probably part guilt, part wanting to break my contract with MGM, and part wanting to be one of the good guys. Whatever it was, I knew deep down that if I were ever to be able to look at myself in a mirror, or fall asleep with a clear conscience, it might be necessary to get myself P.D.Q. to the nearest recruiting center and try to turn a 4-F into a 1-A. I was a pacifist at heart and still am, but if ever there was a righteous war, it surely was W W II. I thought so then and I think so now.

There were trivial considerations, also, but I hope not as strong as my patriotic urge. Not at all trivial was my constant need to be loved. Who was getting the devotion, the outright adoration of the man in the street—not to mention the girl in the street? Who was getting the hugs, the kisses, the love letters these days? It wasn't the 4-Fs. A woman had screamed at me on the train, "My God! I thought you were my son!," but her face had fallen when she saw I was wearing civvies.

Bette Davis sang a song in *Thank Your Lucky Stars* called "They're Either Too Young or Too Old." I didn't want to be either. I wanted to be wanted, and who was more wanted in 1943 than G.I. Joe? Everybody wanted him and everybody loved him. Hey, wait for Hughie!

It seems like self-deception to say that I'm still not totally clear why I was so determined to enlist before WW II ended. I heard a contemporary pop song recently that had a powerful and moving last line. Listening to it, I felt it held a clue to my hang-up.

And when you get the chance to sit it out or dance,
I hope you dance![1]

I admit to having had ambivalent feelings about MGM. Granted, in the thirties and forties it was the royalty of Hollywood. Their films, under that old tyrant, L.B. Mayer, led all the rest, no denying it. Then why were my two years at The Dream Factory so unhappy?

Betty Hutton

More than half a century after my MGM tenure, I got an insight from a most unlikely source, Betty Hutton. I never had the pleasure of meeting Miss Hutton, but I have a hunch she must have been as sweet a young lady as any star in Hollywood.

I watched with near incredulity as this vulnerable lady poured out her heart to Robert Osborne, Turner Classic Movies' estimable host, shortly before she died. I'm sure no one who viewed it will ever forget that interview. Miss Hutton, evidently liking and trusting Mr. Osborne, tore herself to shreds in front of a vast television audience.

She had chosen a simple, attractive outfit, a lime green jacket with white slacks. I hadn't expected her to be the blonde jitterbug

---

1 "I Hope You Dance," words and music by Tia Sillers and Mark D. Sanders, copyright 2000

who was Paramount's biggest star in the 1940s. But time and trouble had taken more of a toll of her lovely face than usually happens to women of great beauty. I felt a shock, not of disillusion, but of compassion, for someone who had obviously been through so much.

Oh, but her heart! It was as shiny and golden as her tresses had been in those musicals. Betty Hutton was a lover; every word that she spoke testified to that. She told Mr. Osborne how happy she had been at Paramount. Everyone, from "Buddy" De Sylva down, had helped her, encouraged her, praised her.

"Then I went to MGM to make *Annie Get Your Gun*," she continued. "I had always dreamed of doing a picture there some day. And here I was at the top studio, doing *Annie Get Your Gun*, a marvelous show. But the cast was awful to me. They wanted Judy in the part, and I don't blame them. But I was there. And Howard Keel, they were just terrible to me."

Bob: Really?

Betty: Yeah, the crew, everybody. *Annie* was the heartbreak of my life. I wanted that picture so badly, and I had the worst experience, Bob . . . I think MGM has an absolute score for being evil. They were mean, and there is no other word for them. And they were mean to all their stars, but I guess they were used to it. I never "could perform under them."

As I listened, mopping my eyes, I felt a great sense of relief. Then I hadn't just imagined it! All these years, I had accused myself of paranoia, putting myself down as an over-sensitive writer who had expected the red carpet treatment and was sulking because he didn't get it.

Buster Keaton

I fear Betty Hutton was not an isolated case of a gentle soul who had the artistic life squeezed out of her by MGM. If you were tough, like Cecil B. de Mille or Joan Crawford, you fought back, and sometimes you got the victory. But a tender sweetheart of a guy like Buster Keaton could be—and was—demolished by the Mayer-Thalberg juggernaut.

Keaton's style of cinematic comedy was sparked by spontaneity. MGM signed him in 1928 and immediately began forcing him into a mold of structured farces with every gag worked out on paper in laborious detail. Keaton was miserable, but helpless to fight back because he had mismanaged the millions he had made and lost. He was near bankruptcy, so he tried to adapt himself to MGM's way and it didn't work. Keaton's great classics, pre-MGM, were shot in a wildly haphazard way. He and his team would get a funny premise for their movie, they would figure out more or less how they would end it, then improvise what came in between. Buster was never able to resolve the conflict between the two styles, and the result was disaster for everyone. He was simply ground to powder by the MGM monolith.

The Enlistment Bug

I recall vividly a conversation with Arthur Freed in his office. I had requested a private interview with the boss and it had been granted.

"Arthur," I said, getting right to the point, "I feel like a slacker and it's killing me. I want to enlist immediately."

Mr. Freed looked threatened. We were right in the middle of the brouhaha that goes into the making of a big budget musical, and losing one of his team at a critical moment was not in his game plan. I knew from experience that he could turn very ugly when crossed, and in that warm, comfortable room, sitting across the desk from L. B. Mayer's number one producer of musicals, my fingers felt icy.

"Can't you wait until you finish your work on *St. Louis*?" he asked me, reasonably enough.

"No, I can't!" I blurted out. It was the first time I had ever raised my voice when addressing him, and it startled both of us. I continued: "This is 1943 and we've been at war for two years. For some reason I can't explain, I feel I have to be more than a spectator."

My producer looked so troubled that, much to my surprise, I found myself feeling sorry for him. He loved this film. After his death, I heard his daughter on a talk show, and she stated it was his personal favorite of all his films. I could see he was honestly searching for a fair solution to this unexpected roadblock, and he found a most ingenious one.

"Is your mother still in Hollywood?" he asked me. I allowed that she was not.

"If we phoned her," Arthur said, "where would we find her?"

"Birmingham, Alabama."

It's a trick, I thought. I'm not going to let this ruthless, single-minded mogul mastermind me out of my magnificent obsession.

"Oh, she won't want me to wait," I said confidently. "My brother is serving overseas with the 44th Infantry Division and she's so proud of him." That was the truth but not the whole truth. Ellie Gordon *was* proud of my brother Gordon, but not because she was all that concerned with the war effort. Saving face and the honor of the family were the important emblems on *her* flag.

Arthur said, "Don't get me wrong. I'm not against your enlisting." He looked sincere. "I promise you I won't stop you. But don't leave me in the lurch now. You only have a couple of songs to do, and then you can go with my blessing."

I was silent.

"Hugh," Arthur said, "if your mother agrees with me that you should finish writing the songs for *St. Louis* and then enlist, would you do it?"

I felt sick. In a crazy sort of way, I loved this inarticulate, blocked, highly sensitive, crazy craftsman. I knew his reputation for getting his way, but I was so sure that my mother was as anxious to see her son in uniform as I was, I found myself agreeing to his scheme.

Before I could protest, his fingers were dialing my little house in Alabama. "May I speak to Mrs. Martin?"

I was on an extension phone and my heart skipped a beat when I heard that dearest of voices. "This is Mrs. Martin."

"This is Arthur Freed, Mrs. Martin. I met you at my party. Your son, Hugh, is working on a movie for me here at MGM Studios called *Meet Me in St. Louis.* He's doing the best job of his life, but the enlistment bug has bitten him, and he wants to leave us halfway through the project and go into the Army. He has told me you want him to serve, but he has agreed to wait until he finishes the picture if you advise him to do so."

Too late; before she even replied, I suddenly remembered one of my mother's character quirks, and I knew I had lost. My mind raced back to school—grammar school, high school. What had happened whenever there had been some little difference of opinion between teacher and pupil? Why, Sonny had been wrong, that's what happened. She had never taken my side, not one single time. It was going to happen again and it did. Teacher was right and Hugh, Jr. must conform.

"Yes," she told the clever Arthur Freed, "I think you are absolutely right. He must fulfill his obligation to you first. Let me talk to him." Her little birdlike voice was as autocratic as Toscanini's. She was the original steel magnolia.

"Hello, Ellie Gordon," I said sheepishly. In a matter of seconds, my expensive Rodeo Drive-tailored suit had turned into short pants, and I was listening to a little lecture on discipline and promise keeping. I assured her that I would play by the rules. I put down the phone and looked across the table at Mr. Freed. He was smiling.

Halfway through the shooting of *Meet Me in St. Louis,* Ralph and I heard a rumor that made our blood run cold. In typical

Hollywood fashion it reached our ears by the grapevine, not from legitimate sources. The rumor turned out to be true: Freed had bought a song by Rodgers and Hammerstein and planned to use it in "our" movie. We knew that if *Meet Me* had even one song by those masters, it wouldn't be *our* movie, it would be *their* movie. If it had been a mediocre song, we might have shrugged it off, but it was a glorious song. The melody was Dick Rodgers at his freshest and best, and Oscar had written an exquisite lyric, profound yet simple. They called it "Boys and Girls Like You and Me." It had mysteriously been dropped from *Oklahoma*! during its out-of-town tryout, joining the ranks of great lost songs from musicals. The classic example was "The Man I Love" by the Gershwin brothers; similarly "Over the Rainbow" was salvaged at the last moment.

A sequence incorporating "Boys and Girls Like You and Me" was actually filmed. Fortunately for Martin and Blane, the locale was Skinker's Swamp, a less than fetching spot before the Louisiana Purchase Exposition took it over and turned it into a fairyland. Arthur and Roger looked at the rushes and reached for the scissors. In a few precious moments, a Rodgers and Hammerstein masterpiece bit the dust. Ralph and I resumed breathing.

Three Hours that Changed My Life

Fans of *Meet Me in St. Louis* often think of it as possessing a full score, like a full-blown musical film or a Broadway show. Actually, not counting songs of the period, plus "Skip to My Lou," which is a medley of folk songs, there were only three new songs. Now that I had written an upbeat lyric for the Christmas song, two-thirds of the needed material was securely in place because "The Boy Next Door" had passed the test.

One fine Sunday afternoon, I dragged myself back to the piano and continued the search for a song for the trolley sequence. Ralph decided to take the day off and see a movie, but on his way out, he put some research he had done at the Beverly Hills Library on my piano. One item was destined to change my life forever. It was a very old clipping from a St. Louis newspaper circa 1904. There was a cartoon of a trolley car, and underneath it was a caption: "Clang, clang, clang, goes the jolly little trolley."

Something about the rhythm of those three clangs started a little beat in my head and a most amazing thing happened. I sang and played the first sixteen bars of "The Trolley Song" exactly as it would eventually be sung by Judy Garland, not to mention a whole lot of other people. I never had to change a note or a syllable. It survived in all versions of the song, just as I sang it that suddenly happy Sunday afternoon. Best of all, it opened up the remainder of the song. I could then visualize the form of what was to come, all eighty-eight bars of it.

Just then, the doorbell rang. It was Margaret Hayes, a girl Ralph and I had lunched with on the train. She had gone to MGM, had asked for my address from a young receptionist named Ray, and he had dug it up for her. Ray said, "I'm just going off duty, I can drive you to Mr. Martin's house."

They were lovely people and I liked them both but what terrible timing! I wonder why I was so afraid to ask them if we could get together another time, but I thought they wouldn't stay long, and I dreaded hurting the feelings of such nice people. I positioned myself near a notebook into which my trembling fingers would write from time to time words like "bump," and "plop," and "chug."

When they finally left, God bless them, I could start working on what was to become "The Trolley Song." Ralph was gone about three hours, so that's about how long it took for me to write it. After writing, "and it was grand just to stand with his hand holding mine," I needed a zinger for the last line and added the words, "to the end of the line." I will never forget the exhilaration of that moment.

The ink was scarcely dry when Ralph returned from the movies. "You're not going to believe this," I said. "Sit down." I sang the whole thing to him and he sang it back to me in that unique Ralph Blane voice.

A few days later I tackled the verse. I had a crazy idea, picked up the phone and called Irene Sharaff. Irene was an old buddy from my Broadway days and had designed costumes for me to wear in some of my early musicals.

"Irene, I'm sweating over a verse for the song on the trolley. You know the spot. Irene, have you any idea what Judy will be wearing in that scene?"

She said no, she hadn't designed it yet.

"Could you just give me a clue as to what you might put her in?"

Pause, then she said, "Well, a girl of that period might have on a high-starched collar."

I wrote that down. "What else?"

She continued, "Probably high-topped shoes."

I was beginning to click.

"Irene," I said, "is there any possibility that her hair might be piled high upon her head?"

"Oh, yes," she said, "more than a possibility."

"What about Tom Drake," I persisted, "any ideas about his costume?"

"I was thinking of a derby probably, and some kind of a bright tie."

"Thank you, Irene," I said. "I love you!"

The funny thing is that in the movie neither of the young lovers wore anything resembling what Irene had described. But I had my verse!

When I was planning to record "The Trolley Song," we all wanted the ensemble singing back of Judy to sound like a large number of people. Even the experienced sound specialists thought I was nuts when I asked for five girls instead of fifteen. I chose a girls quintet, The Music Maids, instead of a whole big choir of singers and they sounded like a trolley car full of girls. The sound man amplified them and everyone was amazed at the result—even me.

Likewise, when I started coaching singers at MGM, I knew how much they all wanted their voices to sound ample and impressive, so I coached them to put a lot of breath in their lungs and let it rip. After a few months of failure, I had a great revelation. If I wanted one of my pupils to sound more powerful, I would lower the key and have them croon rather than sing. What would then happen was that the sound engineer would adjust the volume control and *presto!* Esther Williams, or Doris Day, or Peggy Lee would sound more sumptuous and full than little Miss Soprano or Contralto who wanted to knock 'em dead. Because the louder the belters sang, the quicker the sound man would reach for his volume control and turn them down.

Whenever something special is afoot, the word always seems to buzz around somehow. Judy and I began to receive a lot of invitations from people who had heard that the songs were out of the ordinary. We didn't really have time to socialize, but when Greer Garson invited the two of us to her house for tea, it felt like a command performance for us two little hicks. Singing the songs for Greer and having Mrs. Miniver herself pour tea for us, turned her modest little bungalow into Buckingham Palace.

I have always been remiss about saving memorabilia: programs, posters, photographs, even recordings, and sheet music of my own songs. So my archives are a sad spectacle, more like Mother Hubbard's cupboard than something you might find in The Library of Congress. Roger Edens, bless him, observed my lack of acquisitiveness and most thoughtfully presented me with a recording of all the *St. Louis* sound tracks. Unfortunately, the song, "Boys and Girls Like You and Me" was still very much in the running when Roger gave me the sound tracks. When I sent the recording to my mother in Alabama, I forgot to disclaim the Rodgers and Hammerstein song. A few days later, I received a letter from her.

I opened it with shaky fingers because Ellie Gordon was far from the stereotypical doting mother. When we wrote our first score for *Best Foot Forward* we got a better notice from Brooks Atkinson in *The New York Times* than I did from my tell-it-like-it-is mom. This latest letter began:

> *Dear Son,*
>
> *As you know I have always leaned over backwards to avoid being one of those dreadful stage mothers who rave about their clever children to every ear they can reach. I prefer to be an honest and constructive critic instead. But today I am forced to lay aside my restraint and confess that you have finally written a great song. "Boys and Girls Like You and Me" is your best work so far.*

Grrrrr!

In Army uniform during WWII.
(photo by Marcus Blechman Studio)

Chapter 28

See Here, Private Martin!

*L*OOKING BACK AT THE MOUNTAIN-TOP EXPERIENCES of my life, there were two that affected me more deeply than the others: four summers as piano accompanist for a beloved and gifted contralto gospel singer, Del Delker, and my Army service. My Army tenure started in June, 1944, the month of the D-Day invasion, and ended shortly after V-J Day, 1945. These were critical years, and it probably isn't hyperbole to say it was a time when the fate of the world hung in the balance. But my experiences during those years were more comic than cosmic. Consequently I was never able to relate to the classic World War II books and films. I'm certainly not one of Irwin Shaw's *Young Lions*. I was in Europe, not the Pacific, so *Tales from the South Pacific* doesn't fill the bill, and I can't relate to those tough young prisoners in *Stalag 17*. I was pretty old for one thing; I turned thirty while taking Basic Training. I never saw combat, although I came within hours of being thrown into the Battle of the Bulge. I won no medals nor performed any acts of heroism.

It took Norman Corwin to trigger my empathetic responses. I listened recently to a rebroadcast of his masterpiece, *On a Note of*

Triumph,[1] a radio drama especially written for the day of victory in Europe, and at last I found a literary expression I could cling to and call my own: "This is it, G.I.! This is it, little guy!" The tears came, and the goose bumps, and I blessed Mr. Corwin for including me. "All the way from Newbury Port to Vladivostok, there's a hunk of rainbow 'round your helmet!"

I blessed God, too, for letting me be a tiny piece of what Tom Brokaw calls *The Greatest Generation.* I had a sinking sensation back in the forties at the thought of being on the sidelines of something so overwhelming. I had desperately wanted to participate, but at my age and weight I knew that I might turn out to be a liability rather than an asset.

One day, just as I had almost given it up, there it was in my mail box, so unobtrusive that I picked up the morning mail and shoved it into my briefcase without really seeing it because I was late for a luncheon appointment with my mother and sister. A few minutes later, we were sitting at the sidewalk table of a little café next door to Martindale's Bookstore in Beverly Hills. I should have checked my mail before giving the waitress my order because, when I discovered I had actually passed my physical and had been accepted, my appetite went out the window, and my avocado and tomato on rye went untouched.

"Greetings," indeed! I had wanted it so passionately; now that I had it, all my doubts and fears took over. I had never been athletic or physical in my adolescence; now, at twenty-nine, I was in really mediocre shape. Writing music, writing in general, is a sedentary affair. *Can I cut it?* I asked myself. Was the whole thing a grandstand play, a reaching out to be loved and admired, a false, hypocritical attempt at patriotism? There in Beverly Hills with the warm California sun falling on our table, there were "icy fingers up and down my spine." (Thank you, Johnny Mercer.)

---

1 *On a Note of Triumph,* a radio drama written by Norman Corwin for CBS.

"What's the matter, Hugh?" Ellen inquired, "You look as if you've seen a ghost."

My mother caught on immediately. "Your induction notice?"

I gulped then nodded. "Yes."

MGM was reluctant to release me, but my chores on *Meet Me in St. Louis* were completed, and Arthur had promised me—and my mother—that he wouldn't stand in my way. Early in 1944 I had moved out of my Beverly Hills home and into a modest apartment next door to Bob Lee and Jerry Lawrence in the Georgian Gardens at Laurel and Fountain. I made this move because I felt fairly sure by now the Army would take me, and my friendship with Bob and Jerry was so enriching I wanted to experience as much of it as I could before going into the service. Several years later we three would write a Broadway musical together.

Jerry and Bob helped me store my few possessions, and Judy Garland invited me to a party the night before I was to report. It would have been more sensible, I suppose, to pass up the party and be wide awake on that "great gittin' up mornin'," but who wants to be sensible on such a night as this? Judy made a fuss over my adventure and asked if I'd like a photograph to remember her by. She ran upstairs and returned with a portrait of herself that is as breathtakingly lovely as any I've ever seen of that unforgettable face. She sat at a table and wrote on it with her delicate left hand:

> *Hugh darling—*
> *If you should ever get lonesome or sad,*
> *look at this picture and know that*
> *I'm thinking of you and missing you.*
> *I won't really enjoy singing again*
> *until we can sit together*
> *on somebody's piano bench*
> *when you come home.*
> *Love always,*
> *Judy*

Roger Edens was there that night and was apprehensive at the vacancy I had created in the vocal arranging department. "Do you know anyone we could get as good as you?"

My reply was ready. It had been ready for eight years, ever since a certain lady from St. Louis, Missouri, had swept me off my feet in 1936.

"Get Kay Thompson, Roger. She's not 'as good as' Hugh Martin, she's 'better than'!" There is a lot of fabulous footage in the MGM vaults to validate my predictions.

Judy's party depleted me a bit, but the memory of it, and of her, carried me through some awful moments just around the corner. Sleep was hard to come by that last night as a civilian. When I get scared, I get very cold, even in the middle of a heat wave. My tiny room at the Georgian Gardens was steam heated during the winter. It was June, but my teeth were chattering from fear, so up went the thermostat right to the top. I had given Bob and Jerry my room key, and asked them to wake me up in case I overslept. When they unlocked my door at 4 A.M., they were immediately drenched in steam.

"Hugh! Hugh! What's happening? Are you there? Are you all right?"

"I'm here," I said sheepishly through the fog, "I'm all right."

My Army career began on a note not of triumph, but of slapstick. Less than two hours after I arrived by bus at Fort MacArthur, a communiqué was shoved into my hand. I opened it and read with disbelief a very official announcement informing me I had been granted a three-month deferment. I stared at it for a few seconds, considered the possibility of slipping it into a trash can and thought better of it. This latest blow was so preposterous that I was filled with Dutch courage. I marched into the waiting room of a general whose name I have forgotten, charged up to the reception desk manned by a PFC, and said boldly, "I must see General So and So."

"Not so fast, buddy. You're not even inducted yet. What makes you think you can demand to see General So and So?"

"Well, that's just it. I *want* to be inducted. I just settled all my affairs and gave away all my clothes and came down here to *be* inducted."

I showed him the unwanted deferment. He roared with laughter.

"This is the first time anybody ever came in here demanding to get in. Usually they're crying to get out. Go sit down. I'll ask the General if he'll see you."

I was admitted almost immediately. The General was larger than life, and sported more ribbons on his chest than any human being I'd ever seen. Bless him, he laughed even louder than his assistant.

General: Didn't Cobina tell you she was working on your case?

Hugh: Cobina?

He didn't ask me to sit down, but all my blood had gone to my feet so I sat involuntarily. The General didn't seem to mind. He said, "Cobina and I are old friends. I got the impression she thought she was doing you a big favor."

I began to stutter like Jimmy Stewart.

Hugh: W-w-w-ell, you see, it's j-j-j-just the opposite. I've been trying to get into the Army for a couple of years, and I sure don't want any deferment.

General: Did Cobina know that?

Hugh: Uh, I don't know. I guess not.

General: Well, now, don't worry. You don't have to take a deferment. I'll push you right through. You can be inducted tomorrow.

The blood flowed back to where it belonged.

Hugh: Thank you, sir.

General: Dismissed.

A word of explanation about Cobina. Cobina Wright was a New York socialite who was as famous in the thirties and forties as Perle Mesta for the lavish, celebrity-attended parties she threw in her Park Avenue apartment. She had a lovely daughter,

Cobina, Jr., who, along with Brenda Frazier, was as well publicized as any debutante who ever marched down the red carpet at the Waldorf. The way I had met them was that the mother wanted the daughter to have singing lessons and someone recommended me. I took her on, fearing she would be useful to me only because she could pay me well. But surprise!, at our first session I discovered her voice was as sweet and pretty as her face. When her mother heard what good results we were getting, she started inviting me, along with Ralph, to her super-parties, and we became an ace in the hole for her, singing and playing for her famous guests. We all transferred to the West Coast about the same time in 1942, and her parties in Bel Air were even more spectacular than the Manhattan versions. I remember meeting Marion Davies there, among other legendary characters.

To me, Cobina was a legendary character. She was warm, spontaneous, enthusiastic, and encouraging. If people who need people are the luckiest people in the world, Cobina was lucky indeed.

The good-natured anonymous General kept his promise and I was inducted into the U.S. Army June 30, 1944. Fifty years later, I learned that on the same date and at approximately the same hour, Lena Horne entered Studio One at MGM and recorded my song "Love" for Arthur Freed's big extravaganza, *The Ziegfeld Follies*.

Looking back, I still wouldn't have swapped locations for any amount of money. I felt I was getting by far the better of the bargain as I exchanged the Dream Factory for real life! Real life, that day, consisted of a huge military shed that looked like a warehouse, sheltering a Second Lieutenant and a mishmash of sad sacks about to play soldier, eleven children (so they seemed to this old man trembling on the brink of thirty) and me—as motley a crew as I ever hope to see. We stood in a scraggly line looking very small and insignificant in the center of the building. But as we pledged allegiance to the United States of America and were given the official pronouncement, my heart swelled with pride and I blinked back tears. I had worked so diligently for this moment, and I memorized it. It is still one of my favorite "floats" in the harum-scarum Rose Parade of my life.

Immediately after the ceremony, one of the "children" timidly asked me if I would please show him how to shave. He had bought a Gillette safety razor, but he wasn't quite sure how to go about it. He was right off the farm, I learned, and no one there had noticed the fuzz on his face. But we had had an indoctrination class in which we had been told how many inches our hair length was not to exceed, and being clean shaven was stressed, so together we removed his fuzz and then headed for the barber shop. His crew cut looked better than mine, but that's not saying much.

Meet Me in Glendale

I felt better, however, when I got into uniform. Through some felicitous happenstance, I managed to get one that fit. This was an even better break than I realized at the time because my very first weekend pass coincided with the first preview of *Meet Me in St. Louis.* I have forgotten in which adjacent-to-Hollywood town it took place, possibly Glendale. I can remember very little about the film itself because the circumstances were so surrealistic they overpowered what was being flashed onto the screen. Most of it, to be sure, I had already seen in various projection rooms, but at that particular moment I had a feeling that something special was in the air.

Everyone showed up, even my mother and sister, much to my astonishment, because I thought they had gone back to Alabama. Dotted around the lobby or in the auditorium were Freed, Minnelli with Garland on his arm, Tom Drake, Mary Astor, Margaret O'Brien and mother, Roger Edens, Ralph Blane, Lucille Bremer, Leon Ames, Joan Carroll, June Lockwood, Marjorie Main, Chill Wills, Harry Davenport, and Henry McDaniel, plus the entire music and technical staff, the usual press people, and a few spies from other studios. Oh, yes, and there was Private Hugh Martin, looking, perhaps for the first time in his life, confident, secure, and possessing a smidgen of self-esteem.

Even Judy herself, the queen of the evening, graciously trained the spotlight on me for a few seconds, and I hope, and secretly believe, that in my summer khaki uniform I didn't look too shabby.

Afterward, there was the usual preview commotion, more than the usual this time since what Garbo once called "word from mouth" had been so positive. I was bidden goodbye by all my friends, some of whom no doubt wondered if they would ever see me again. That sort of uncertainty was in the air in July of 1944. A lot of them, I suspect, envied me deep inside though they verbally commiserated with me at the prospect of my returning, like Cinderella after her triumph at the ball, to sweeping floors and peeling potatoes. I was gladdened by knowing that there was one among the noisy crowd who was aware that I couldn't wait to get back to the brooms and the potatoes. My mother always knew me better than I knew myself.

I Don't Think I'm in Culver City Anymore

On my return to Fort MacArthur, I was given my first detail. That's "DE-tail" in Army jargon. Come to think of it, I wasn't given it, I volunteered for it. Every G.I. learns quickly that one thing you avoid is volunteering, but not this eager beaver. I was ready for anything and everything. Shoot the works, Army! For a few weeks I felt invincible. The "DE-tail" turned out to be, in the company of one lone young African-American, cleaning a many-stalled latrine. He didn't mind and I didn't mind, so it was an enjoyable, if unfamiliar, assignment. He had a good singing voice and we harmonized "Blues in the Night" as we scrubbed acres of urinals.

Chapter 29

I'm Tired of Texas

$\mathcal{I}$ HAD SEEN A LOT OF WAR MOVIES so I knew that soldiers, at least Warner Bros. soldiers, like to drink beer in PXes and shoot the breeze. Now that I was officially in, I felt it was time for life to imitate art, so on my last night at Fort MacArthur I was sitting at a table with some other new recruits. One of them was reading Walter Winchell, and there was an item in his column that day that listed the alleged three most rugged Army bases. The soldier read it aloud to us, then remarked, "With luck like mine, they'll send me to one of those."

Sure enough they did, the very next day, and we all went with him. Destination: Camp Hood, Texas, notorious not only for being rough on guys going through the seventeen weeks of Basic Training, but also for the most formidable weather this side of Hell at that time of the year. Camp Hood is between Austin and Waco and our seventeen weeks would coincide with blast furnace heat. The outlook was decidedly dim. I bitched at the turn of the dice along with the others, but secretly I still felt like a winner. I had set my sights on getting into the war, and I had achieved my goal. There are not many levels more humble than being a private in the Infantry, a dogface, but I didn't care. I knew that with the fate of the Allies still very much in jeopardy, I should not have expected anything more impressive, and I cheerfully accepted my classification as a rifleman. It seemed like monumental miscasting, but I was determined to give it everything I had. I got a good dose of invasion of privacy when we had to double up on the crowded train. I shared an upper berth with another G.I. We both figured we were lucky to get a berth and neither of us snored or fell out of bed. So far, so good.

However, when we scrambled off the train at a little whistle stop, it was not so good. The heat was withering and we had sweated through our uniforms, right down to our khaki shorts. A helpful supply sergeant issued new everything, and once more I lucked out, because everything fit. After a nice hot and cold shower we looked like the enlistment posters.

We reached Camp Hood the following day, a green and confused bunch of rookies. I was so gung ho to play my new role that I again ignored the old warning, "Don't volunteer" and recklessly held up my hand anytime there was something disagreeable to be done. So it was not surprising that I found myself digging ditches within a few hours of my arrival. It was an exhausting job more suited to the abilities of the five young huskies alongside of whom I was hacking away. They quickly caught on that I was a hundred-and-ten-pound weakling pretending I was John Wayne. Without humiliating me, they angled me into the least demanding position and made the old man take frequent breaks.

Immediately following that positive experience, I received a very negative one, so negative I had to consider seriously the possibility that I might not make it and would be sent home in disgrace. My familiar syndrome of ceasing to eat under duress came back to haunt me on day two at Camp Hood. I filed into the mess hall at lunchtime with a horde of hungry guys who started wolfing down huge portions of beef stew. I took one bite and realized I had made a mistake. I beat it to the exit door just in time to offer my mouthful of beef to a clump of bushes.

I returned that night for supper and asked if I might have some milk. There was none. I exited, feeling a slight sense of panic. I walked over to the PX and tried to buy some milk, the only food I felt I could swallow. There was none. My life had been salted with tiny miracles, and one of them occurred at that moment. The saleslady at the PX must have had a son of her own. Perhaps seeing my woebegone face she thought of him and said to herself, "If my son were in some fix, like this pitiful soldier, I would hope somebody would throw him a crumb."

I didn't want a crumb; I just wanted a glass of milk to keep from coming apart like wet cardboard. I explained my weird craving. Incredibly, she said, "I know just how you feel. I get that way sometimes, too, especially in a heat wave like this. Would you like me to bring in a quart of milk when I come to work?"

I was too dazed from low blood sugar to be very eloquent. I held up two fingers and said, "Two." Then I pulled myself together and added, "I'm so very, very grateful. I have money. I want to pay. I'll pay you double—triple—"

She interrupted me. "Nonsense," she said, "it will be my pleasure. I can do it every day except on my day off."

I don't know what would have happened if it had not been for that guardian angel. I insisted on paying, but her offer was a lifesaver. Twice a day I would lean against the outside of an empty barracks in the shade and guzzle a quart of milk. It must be a super food because it kept me vertical until my appetite returned about a week later. I was even able to dig a few more ditches.

Is There Life After Basic Training?

During the remaining sixteen weeks of this challenge I did things I never dreamed I could do. The calisthenics alone would have seemed beyond the realm of possibility, but I did them, not as well as some folks, but I did them. I roared through a little one-room house filled with poison gas. In my trembling fingers I held a gas mask, which I was supposed to plop onto my face at the very last minute before entering. I expected this caper to be my final one on earth, because in civilian life I had been totally unable to open a can or change a light bulb. Providence came through for me yet again because Button A actually fitted into Latch B and Cord C held it all together. I emerged sweating and panting, but the important thing is, I emerged.

I didn't like the mornings when we had to sit on the ground with legs spread-eagled and touch our foreheads to the ground. I, of course, couldn't manage this, and when a tough sergeant forced it to happen, I could almost hear crunching bones, and I shed a few tears.

"Don't do that, soldier," said the nice G.I. squatting next to me. "Don't give him the satisfaction."

The one exercise I was never able to bring off was pulling myself over a ten-foot wall with a rope. Those skinny old piano-playing arms of mine shrank at the very thought of that little maneuver.

One of my favorite memories is of a morning when the thermometer went up to three digits. We were drilling out in the sun and I turned my head and discovered, to my surprise, that several soldiers in the first row of my squad had fainted. I was practically the only one still standing, the skinny, over-aged Hugh Martin looking down at a bunch of muscular young bucks face on the ground! It was a delightful experience!

One memorable afternoon after we had marched nine miles, a refrigerator truck suddenly pulled up with a surprise ice cream treat for us. I got the last scoop of ice cream, just before it ran out, and promptly dropped it on the ground.

My nickname during Basic Training was "Windy." No, I wasn't garrulous; on the contrary, I kept a very low profile. I never talked about Hollywood or Broadway because I was enjoying the company of real people and thought I'd try being one myself. No, I acquired my new name this way: I was chronically late each morning when we lined up right after reveille. One fine Texas morning I straggled in two minutes late, as usual, and was yelled at by my Sergeant. "I'm sorry, sir," I said, "I really don't understand it. I went like the wind." I didn't expect this to break everybody up but it did, and from then on I was "Windy."

One day we were told that we were going to have a marksmanship contest at the rifle range and that whichever platoon got the best score would be given weekend passes to Austin or Waco. Disaster, thought my colleagues. Surprise! Private Martin shot a sensational string of bull's-eyes that Friday and several subsequent Fridays. We won the prize more than once, thanks to Private Martin, and I was suddenly the sweetheart of the regiment.

They even forgave me for not being able to assemble my rifle. The pivot on which everything turned for a rifleman was his M-one rifle. It had to be cleaned daily, and there's no way one can do that without taking it apart, a very complicated procedure. With great effort I did master taking it apart. The problem was that never once in seventeen weeks was I able to get it back together again. God bless these noble, wonderful friends. Someone always did it for me. They took turns, and they never poked fun at me. Oh, they made little jokes, but they were not nasty or humiliating jokes.

Eventually I allowed myself to sit on a piano bench in one of the recreation halls. But I had waited until I was absolutely certain that these buddies of mine liked me for myself; I didn't show them my signed photos from June Allyson and Judy Garland, not until I felt the warmth of these real life people. Real life! Yes, that's how they seemed to me. Not that show people aren't as wonderful as Irving Berlin wrote them to be, and I dearly love them. But what a revelation meeting young adults and kids from Ohio and Kansas and Kalamazoo and Kankakee and Keokuk and other points North,

South, East, and West. There wasn't a phony in a carload, not even among the brass.

Speaking of the brass, my Captain, a very Clark Gable-ish gentleman, tried to convince me that I should apply for Officers Candidate School. I tried to persuade him that I would be a flop as an officer. "I'm barely making it as a private," I pleaded.

"Don't sell yourself short," he barked. "You look like an officer. You talk like an officer. You talk a heck of a lot better than I do."

I finally caved and sent in a form requesting a hearing. The hearing turned out to be one of the worst disgraces of my life. It not only disgraced me, which I didn't really worry too much about, but it disgraced Captain Beauford, and I felt awful about that. My replies to the test questions brought looks of disbelief to the inquisitors, and I could see my poor faithful sponsor, the Captain, in the back of the room with his face buried in his hands.

"Some are born great, some achieve greatness, and some have greatness thrust upon them." People very flatteringly kept trying to thrust greatness upon me in the Army, and I kept letting them down with a crash. The Sergeant of my squad made me squad leader, probably because I looked a little more Warner Bros. than the others, but every time I gave an order, my men would assemble on time and I would show up ten minutes late. The Sergeant finally gave up and wrested greatness from my hands.

Somehow, Heaven only knows how, I performed all the strange things people do in Basic Training. I drove bayonets into straw men that looked like Ray Bolger in *The Wizard of Oz*. I walked open-ended miles and ate K-rations. I lived intimately with cockroaches; every time I opened my footlocker, legions of them streamed out. I shot at people and people shot at me, not with actual bullets, but it got my attention.

During the last week, we performed a little maneuver with live ammunition. We were, fortunately, told in advance that we would spend an hour on such-and-such a date crawling on our

bellies through exploding hand grenades to a make-believe forti-
fication. I bought a bunch of ear plugs, gave some to my best buddies, and came through the war game relatively sane, saner than
the poor lads who had been nearly deafened by the sham battle.

During none of these shenanigans did I ever regret having
fixated on entering the service. But there was one night, I recall,
when something inside of me snapped. We had walked miles to a
God-forsaken spot in the middle of nowhere and had eaten a horrible supper sitting on the ground in heat that was indescribable.
I looked across the expanse of sand and saw something that puz-
zled me—large wheels rolling around kicking up dust like crazy.

"What on earth is that?" I asked my comrades. One of them, a
native Texan, said, "You mean you ain't never seen a hoop snake?
Them is a bunch of hoop snakes, hoopin' it up."

"Are they poisonous?" I inquired.

"Oh, yes," he said with a certain amount of pride.

I was beginning to suspect I was not in Hollywood anymore. It
was not, however, the hoop snakes that cracked my morale. Two soldiers and I pitched a tent and just as we were about to hit the road to
dreamland, the heavens opened and rain of Noah-like proportions
descended on our pup tent. It leaked. It got pretty soggy in there and
there wasn't a thing we could do about it 'til the blazing Texas sun
came out the next morning. Sleep was impossible and our clothes
squished. It was at that point I yelled, "What am I doing here?"

By the time the seventeen-week test had resolved itself, we were
shivering in our barracks and wondering, "Where do we go from
here?" Many felt we'd be sent to the South Pacific. I prayed they
were wrong. I dearly love the European culture, and I speak French,
albeit haltingly.

I was standing in line with my platoon one morning about 4: 30
a.m., when a little messenger came rushing up with a telegram for
Private Martin. I was not allowed to read it until later, but it turned
out to be from Arthur Freed.

"Tune in *Hit Parade* tonight," it read. "'Trolley Song' number three." My buddies and I huddled over a beat-up little radio in the PX and waited breathlessly for Frank Sinatra to sing my song. He got about halfway through it, lost his place in the cue card, stopped singing altogether, and said in a rather hostile voice, "This song has too many words in it." My moment of glory was short-lived.

But I was having the time of my life. I would never be the same. I was a different person from the rebellious musician who didn't want to be fenced in, not even by the most glamorous movie studio in the world. Then, too, there was a very carnal side to my feelings upon completion of Basic Training. The very last day before leaving Texas I happened to spy a scale in a drugstore. I stepped on and wasn't quite sure I could believe the numeral I saw. "One hundred forty," it read. My cup ranneth over. I had been scrawny and flat chested all my life; now I sought out a mirror and confronted it. "Not bad," I said.

Chapter 30

We Who Are About to Die
Go to Musicals

AFTER BASIC TRAINING I was given a couple of weeks leave. The Army had ordered me to report to Camp Miles Standish, near Boston, the last week in December. This was 1944 and the Battle of the Bulge was raging in Europe. Nevertheless, I was relieved that I was being sent east to Europe rather than west to the Pacific. I high-tailed it to New York for the shows.

The Astor Theater held memories for me. My first film, *Best Foot Forward*, had successfully opened there. Now it was the words *Meet Me in St. Louis* that blazed across the billboard above the theater, and under the title was a picture of a singing Judy Garland and the first four bars of "The Trolley Song." My first weekend pass in July had allowed me to see *Meet Me . . .* at its first sneak preview. Now its official debut was about to occur at the Astor Theater, and I was on hand once more to enjoy the hoopla.

The night before the opening of *Meet Me in St. Louis* in New York, Sally Benson threw a dinner party for her family, Ralph, and me. Their names were not "Smith," as Sally called them in her New Yorker pieces, but there they all were except for the older members, the mother and father and "Grandpa Prophater," who had all three passed on. But "Rose" was there, and "Esther" and "Lon" and "Agnes" and of course "Tootie," because Sally herself was "Tootie." It was a memorable evening, one touching two centuries, and the historic old Astor Hotel seemed just the right place for it.

Perhaps this is an appropriate place to say a passing word about Sally Benson. So many bouquets have been tossed to Garland and Minnelli and Freed and Margaret O'Brien and the songs, and I am certainly not one to say them nay. But Sally was the author of the original stories from which *Meet Me in St. Louis* was derived. She was doubly involved because in addition to writing the stories so eloquently, all of the material was truly autobiographical. The unsung hero of *Meet Me in St. Louis* is Sally Benson. The basic story is both funny and true, and as we all know, the funniest lines are always the ones that ring true. Irving Brecker knew that, too, and fashioned a screenplay that was faithful to Sally's voice.

Another seemingly minor player who was actually very major was Ralph Blane. I have mentioned that after *Best Foot Forward* Ralph mysteriously stopped writing and seemed content with his role as demonstrator de luxe and front man. This is the truth, but it's not the whole truth. Ralph was a very important part of the equation. His affability, not only with the big wheels but with me in the critical moments of creativity, was essential. His responses to my work, that is, insisting I resurrect "Have Yourself a Merry Little Christmas" after I impatiently discarded it, his changing "clang, clang, clang *said* the trolley" to "clang, clang, clang *went* the trolley," his suggestion that I incorporate the addresses of the young lovers into "The Boy Next Door," these were not insignificant.

Chapter 31

The S.S. Sea Tiger

*I*to go on forever, but the day of reckoning arrived. The Camp Hood contingent reported to Camp Miles Standish a couple of days before being shipped out. I was a tiny speck among thousands of servicemen now equipped physically and psychologically for combat. I was not ready either to kill or be killed, but I had knocked myself out to get into the fray, and I was almost ready for whatever lay ahead.

The fifteen-day voyage across the Atlantic was suspenseful enough for a war movie. *The Sea Tiger* was the vessel that carried me "Over There." It was a victory ship that pathetically failed to live up to its triumphant name. There were tiers of bunks; each tier comprised eight bunks ranging from floor to ceiling. They were actually hammocks and as we fell out of line into them, mine turned out to be directly in front of a huge ventilation blower that belched freezing winter outside air directly onto me for the next two weeks.

The Sea Tiger zigzagged between German submarines as part of a huge convoy of similar crafts. Destroyer escorts and large Coast Guard ships darted in, out, and around like water bugs on a lake.

Providentially, our whole convoy of perhaps twenty-five ships made it to port. Depth charges going off all around us caused a certain amount of panic at first, but we grew accustomed to the sound and managed to tune it out. I was so ignorant I thought the muffled booms were German subs trying to sink us, but I eventually learned that it was the other way around, we trying to knock out the subs.

I did more music-making than eating during the voyage. I was so violently seasick I didn't even attempt to make it to the mess hall. Friends brought me scraps of food, and oranges, and Hershey bars were available. There was a piano on board. The sea was rough, so my little upright piano was lashed to a hatch cover. I tried to play every homesick soldier's favorite song.

Peter Dattilo

I received a letter in 1985 that describes that unforgettable journey better than I could.

Dear Mr. Martin,

Every year, at this time, for decades, I reflect on an occasion in my life that began on Jan. 2nd, 1945. I was standing on a pier in Boston harbor with hundreds of other G.I.s, preparing to board the S. S. Sea Tiger, a very small victory ship.

As we stood around, smoking cigarettes, eating Red Cross doughnuts and drinking coffee, listening to an Army band entertaining us, and doing what we did most and best, stand and wait, a buddy of mine said, "See that guy over there, he wrote Meet Me in St. Louis. My being in love with our "then" music and knowing of its composers, I knew he meant Hugh Martin. Memory relates that you were then a Frank Sinatra stature guy. But then at 5'11" and 140 lbs., I was, too. We were called to attention, told to shoulder barracks bags "A" and "B" and march on board (struggle is more like it) to the strains of brass band stimulus. Now what I remember to me was pure irony, and for 40 years I have wondered if you remember it. You were three or four soldiers ahead of me in line, when suddenly after finishing one song, the band on the dock broke into "The Trolley Song."

I was fairly depressed at our circumstances and future, and I am not going to say your song revived my spirits. Hell no, but what I often thought about was... what were your feelings just then? Do you remember the incident?

Our crossing to Le Havre took 15 days. Your bunk was about three away from mine. We had casual conversation from time to time, nothing for you to remember. I was a skinny 19-year old from Brooklyn and I don't remember being the least bit clever or profound at that time. However, you helped to settle a dispute by agreeing with me. The argument, my argument that Frank Sinatra was a better singer than Bing Crosby, so I guess we were both prophetic.

If there was any sensitivity on that voyage of destiny it was listening to you playing a beat-up old upright piano positioned on a below-deck hatch cover. You did it for hours, and I thank you now for that.

Near the end of the voyage you were taken to the dispensary and treated for pneumonia. I remember the day of the night we disembarked, several of us looked in on bedridden you and said goodbye and we hoped better health. You were ill—mighty ill. And this is what I wanted to relate to you forty years later.

My memory now is sort of like the surface of a nickel; you know it's Jefferson but some of the features have been worn away. However, this chapter in my life is crystal clear. Mr. Martin, Hugh, I thank you for a cherished memory in what I reflect upon as being better times, maybe naïve, certainly romantic, and of course beautiful music played. "Have yourself a merry little Christmas!"

Good health and happy 1986,
Peter

Today, over twenty years since he wrote that letter, I consider Peter Dattilo a valued friend. We still have never met, not since the *Sea Tiger*, but one can bond very deeply by mail, telephone, and e-mail.

One part of Peter's story needs a little amplifying. When the brass band on the dock struck up "The Trolley Song," it was, to my impressionable mind, a moment to remember. I have never been one to nudge a stranger and say, "Hey, I wrote that song," but on this occasion the sequence of events was so bizarre my normal behavior seemed expendable. I turned around to the soldier immediately behind me in the line that was waiting to walk up the gangplank.

"That song," I said, "the song the band is playing. I wrote it!"

The G.I. yawned deeply. "I know, buddy. And I'm Rita Hayworth."

Peter and I still exchange memories of that January voyage through submarine-infested waters. Another shipmate was Duffy Brown. Duffy phoned me recently and casually told me something that made my hair stand on end. He said that our fragile little ship tilted one stormy night.

"Two more degrees," he said cheerfully, "and we would have capsized."

I was just about to ask him how much two degrees was, but I suddenly decided I didn't really want to know.

Chapter 32

The Forty and Eights

AFTER FIFTEEN DAYS ON THE *SEA TIGER*, we all hoped that whatever came next would be an improvement. It wasn't. We scarcely had touched foot to soil or our port of debarkation, Le Havre, France, when we were lined up and marched off to a railroad yard. Masses of boxcars stood waiting for us on the tracks ready to whisk us off, each to our respective replacement depot. My particular consignment was a five-day journey away, so the word "whisk" is inappropriate.

Most of the infamous boxcars were inscribed with the words *"Quarante hommes ou huit chevaux,"* that is, "Forty men or eight horses," the recommended cargo for the size of the car. The officer in charge of loading us failed to observe that the cars were not all the same size; some were smaller: "Thirty-six men or six horses," these were marked. The same infallible bad luck that positioned me in front of a cold air blower on the Victory ship propelled me and thirty-nine other soldiers into one of these smaller rolling prisons. We were pushed in and mashed together like baby squid in a jar. When the doors clanged shut we discovered that there was almost no ventilation and only one lamp, a small battery affair given us along with water and K-rations, enough for two days.

I recall trying to figure out, along with the soldiers closest to me, which arms and legs belonged to which of us. It seemed funny at first, but the humor soon dried up. There were no accommodations for sanitation; we had to take care of that in the fields during our stops—frequent and interminable ones. During these stops, the doors were opened for us so we could relieve ourselves, but the January cold was so biting that I, for one, chose to remain constipated the entire trip. Even inside the carriage, it got so cold that we tore off some of the extraneous wood and kindled a small fire with it in the center of the floor. We soon observed that the smoke had no way to escape, and we were beginning to asphyxiate. We doused the fire and resigned ourselves to life in a freezer. Then the food and water gave out and most of the laughter with it.

About the third day, the train ground to a halt and we asked a passing Second Looie, who was counting bodies, how long he thought it would be before the long caravan would start up again. He said he had no idea, and I believe he was telling the truth. There was an air of mystery about the whole operation; no one seemed to know where we were headed or how long it would take to get there. We mentioned to the Lieutenant that we were ravenous for food and he said the officers on board were just as hungry as we were. There was always an element of cynicism toward the brass among us foot soldiers, but in this instance we believed him. He looked as cold and hungry as we. There was no sound in the Arctic-cold wasteland except for distant guns, so we knew we were not far from the front.

My High School French Comes in Handy

One of the more adventurous in our elegant club car pointed off in the distance to what seemed like a little town.

"Are we in France?" he asked the Looie.

"Haven't a clue," was the reply.

After the officer left, the same G.I. said, "Does anybody here speak French?" There seemed to be an idea germinating in his mind.

"I do," I said. As the words were coming out of my mouth, I had a strong feeling I should have kept it shut.

"Listen, buddy," said the troubleshooter, "what would you say to taking off up that hill to that little town up there?"

"I can barely see it," I said doubtfully. "It would take maybe a good hour."

"How long do we usually sit here on these God-forsaken tracks?" persisted the private.

"Hours and hours," I admitted.

"That's right!" he shouted. "Hours and hours. You could make it there and back."

"To do what?" I asked.

"To get food, man!" he said with emotion. "It's a town! Towns have shops and it's the middle of the day."

"What if the train moves on with me still in the town?"

"Oh, man!" he cried. "You'll get back in plenty of time. And this miserable train moves so slowly you could probably chase it down and hop on board."

My blood ran cold at the thought of missing it and getting left out in the middle of nowhere and then being court-martialed for going AWOL. But the die had been cast. I couldn't face the thought of rolling on through the ice and snow with all those pairs of accusing eyes silently saying, "You! You're so chicken you're willing to take the food out of our hungry mouths just so you can come out smellin' like a rose." I put on my helmet, wrapped what few clothes I possessed tightly around me, said, "So long, fellas" and climbed out of the boxcar. A cheer went up and that helped because I have always been dependent, not on the kindness of strangers, but simply on being loved, or rather, on feeling loved, which is not quite the same thing, is it? Anyway, I have always been willing to try almost anything for that warm, fuzzy feeling. That's the only possible explanation of my derring-do, since the little skirmish I was starting out on was a reckless and irresponsible mission.

My heart beat faster when I reached the town on the hill, and sank when I perceived how tiny it was, not a town at all, a village perhaps, maybe a hamlet. I made a few encompassing turns around the handful of winding, cobblestone streets and alleys. Suddenly I saw a sign that brought my heart back to its proper place in my breast; *"Boulangerie"* it read, and no word ever looked so beautiful to me. A bakery was just what I had been hoping for. We had no cooking facilities, obviously, but *bread* could stave off hunger pangs indefinitely if I played my cards right.

I entered the modest little shop. A white-aproned man was selling his freshly baked bread to three or four elderly ladies dressed rather seedily. The smell was overpoweringly delicious to this hungry G.I. I waited for the right moment, then softly tried out my high school French on the baker.

"Est-ce possible," I began tentatively, *"Est-ce possible á acheter un peu de pain?"* (Would it be possible to buy a little bread?) I explained that it would be for my fellow soldiers and I pointed to the train lying in the valley like a huge caterpillar.

He began to speak very rapidly and I hadn't the foggiest idea of what he was saying.

"J'ai d'argent," I declared, showing him some American dollar bills.

He didn't seem impressed, and I had the feeling the conversation was closed. Suddenly the ladies in the shop swooped down on the poor man. He was like a rat being pecked to death by chickens. The women were all talking at once. My French is far from fluent, but I got the gist, there was no mistaking it. What they were screaming, in essence, was "You wretched, miserable serpent! How dare you refuse to give this American soldier whatever he desires? He and his friends have come thousands of miles to save our country, and you . . . ! I will never buy a scrap of anything from you ever again!"

I felt terrible. I was sorry for the poor fellow, especially when we all finally understood the problem. It was not the money; he was willing to give me bread. I almost thought he was going to shout, "Let them eat cake!"

No, the problem turned out to be a matter of ration coupons. If the baker couldn't show a sufficient number of coupons, the government could make it really hot for the fellow. He could even lose his license. The furious mother hens stopped clucking long enough to let him explain, and they finally forgave him, not without a few Gallic gestures and dirty looks. Then the women had a little conference and presented me with a handful of ration coupons. I demurred with all the fervor I could muster, but they persisted with equal fervor.

Finally, I broke the tug of war by pointing to a long loaf of crusty French bread hot out of the oven, and I communicated to them, half in fractured French and half in pantomime, that two such incomparable items would meet our needs.

The eldest of the ladies adjudicated, "For that, Monsieur, only two coupons will be required."

She pressed the magic vouchers into my hand and we all cried, even the baker.

I went down the hill with a light heart. Thank God the train was still motionless on the tracks! When I got near enough to the train to be visible, I waved my two four-foot-long *pièces de resistance* over my head. Cheers! Whistles! Cowboy whoops from hungry comrades! All was well at least for the next few hours. Looking into their grateful eyes, I felt—the only time during the entire span of my service—like a hero. And I felt loved!

Chapter 33

Saved by the "Clang"

AFTER FIVE DAYS, we finally pulled into our destination in Givet, France. We were dirty, smelly, constipated, and extremely hungry. The Army chow never tasted so wonderful, partly because we were famished, but also because America was sending its choice foods to the battleground areas. The Army did its best to feed its servicemen well everywhere, but the cream of the crop was going to the Pacific and to the forces in Europe.

The pneumonia had turned into a painful sore throat by then, so I was disappointed that our quarters were in a bombed-out warehouse. There were huge windows all around with the glass blown away. Still, the floor was reasonably clean and there were plenty of blankets. They felt good enough for all normal purposes; when the winter winds blew through, none of us felt like bitching because we knew the extent of the suffering being endured at the front. The Battle of the Bulge had been going on for weeks and we learned from our marvelous newspaper, *The Stars and Stripes,* how woeful our losses had been in that area. It was touch and go for Allied victory in Europe, so missing glass windows and sleeping on the floor seemed like minor matters.

Recently I read the book *Witness to America* by the late historian Stephen Ambrose. He noted that, if asked, his nomination for "Man of the Century" would be G.I. Joe.

"In my opinion," said Ambrose, "he, more than anyone else, saved the world from the forces of evil and put it in the domain of the forces of good. Especially," he added, "the G.I. Joes who fought the Battle of the Bulge in northern Europe in December 1944 and January and February 1945."

As I read that, I enjoyed a moment of self-glorification as I rolled around in my mind the fact that I, Private not-so-first-class Hugh Martin, Serial Number 39592238, had joined the ranks who offered themselves up as fodder in the infamous Battle of the Bulge. But my moment of glory was short-lived as I reflected on, and thanked God for, the hedge Heaven placed around me during that terrifying moment of World War II.

Yes, I had voluntarily, even obsessively, put myself into those ranks. But once I reached foreign shores, there was nothing heroic about my performance in the European Theater of Operations. It was spent mostly at a piano in a morale-boosting variety show with an all-soldier cast. I lost my voice after my umpteenth rendition of "The Trolley Song," but that was insignificant compared to the arms and legs and lives being sacrificed wholesale all around me: 80,000 Allied casualties, 100,000 German ones. That winter of 1944-45 was the coldest in northern Europe in fifty years. The suffering was indescribable, but it turned the tide.

I am proud, not of myself, but of my buddies. Not just the ones I traded Cokes and jokes with, but the whole kit and caboodle of G.I. Joes, those wonderful, self-deprecating heroes "of whom the world was not worthy."

When I shipped out New Year's Day plus one from Boston Harbor, "The Trolley Song" had finally been replaced in the Number One spot on the *Hit Parade* by Cole Porter's "Don't Fence

Me In." "Trolley" had a long and honorable seven-week run in the top position, so I didn't feel any resentment in having to yield to Mr. Porter. Imagine my delight, however, when we tuned in the *Hit Parade* on Armed Forces Radio Network after we landed in the Repple Depple, as we called the Replacement Depot. My songwriter's heart leaped up when I discovered that the *Hit Parade* programs being sent to entertain the American forces in Europe were on a seven-week time delay. What an ego trip! On the first program I heard in Givet, Andre Baruch, the *Hit Parade* announcer, welcomed "Trolley" as Number One for the first time. It seemed I was to have my day in the sun for seven extra weeks and just when I could really use it.

I wasted no time using those extra weeks as an excuse to visit the Special Services Office, where I let them know that one of their riflemen was moderately newsworthy at the moment. I had an ulterior motive, of course. I was scared out of my wits at the realization that I was probably a few days away from facing the kind of horror I had heard about but couldn't conceive of. Already men were being hastened to the front to fill the gaps in our decimated ranks. I had bidden farewell to a few guys I had gotten to know on the *Sea Tiger*, and some of them had come back all too soon, either shot up or, worse still, in canvas bags.

It was not noble of me to attempt to stave off the call of duty. I had known when I enlisted that it might come down to the crunch, and I prayed making myself available for musical duty was not an act of cowardice. I still don't know whether it was or not. I only know my terror made me do it and I didn't feel guilty about it. I still don't.

The Worst Case of Stage Fright I Ever Had

Guilty or not, my timing was good. Just at the time I offered my services, a new edition of an all-soldier variety show was being assembled and was due to open in a local movie house two days hence. They were at a loss for a next-to-closing act. Here was that old bugaboo, the eleven o'clock number, and it looked as if it were going to be me.

Now I had a different kind of fright—stage fright—but that was less formidable than fear of being blown to bits on the field of battle. I had confidence in my ten fingers and their ability to please, but my throat was in bad shape, so I wasn't sure what would come out when I started to sing.

Opening night for me was fearsome, but for the rest of the troupe it was business as usual. They had been playing the show for weeks. I stood in the wings shaking in my boots. A couple of comics were on stage getting good laughs. Thank God, I thought, a warm audience. That turned out to be an understatement. When I stepped out after being introduced, I was stunned by the sheer size of the audience. The interior of the theater was very European with balconies up to the ceiling and tiers above tiers of boxes bulging out from them. Every seat was filled and the boxes were so crammed they made me think of the boxcars we had been traveling in.

My knees threatened to buckle as I made my way to the little spinet positioned in front of the footlights. A soundman mercifully hung a microphone around my neck; without amplification I would have been a dead duck. My voice at its healthiest is small, and it was a long way from being at its healthiest. I spoke a few words about Judy Garland and about *Meet Me in St. Louis.* They had, of course, not seen it, but there must have been quite a number present who had heard the most recent *Hit Parade* because when I sang, "Clang, clang, clang, went the trolley," there was a buzz of recognition. I followed "Trolley" with two or three other songs I had written, and each one was received with generous enthusiasm.

The blockbuster was my closing number. Just before I went on, I remembered a little song I had written for Meredith

Willson before I was inducted into the Army. He was doing a series of forty-eight state songs, one each week, to be sent to servicemen overseas on the Armed Forces Radio Network. He needed a song for Connecticut; he said that nobody wanted to tackle it because the name was so awkward and unwieldy. I submitted one to him, and he was delighted with it. But I was to find an even better use for it as a closing number to my act that dark night in Givet, France. It had occurred to me that America has the same number of syllables as Connecticut and that the accents fell in the same places. So instead of singing "Connecticut is the place for me," I sang "America is the place for me!" A theater full of homesick soldiers resonated to *that* thought like gangbusters! They rewarded me with a roar that still thrills my soul when I replay it in my mind. And I have to confess, I replay it rather often.

Strangers in the Dark

What followed was even more gratifying. The show had been normally lit, but every chink of every wall had been plugged and every opening concealed so that the military blackout could be observed to the letter. In the modicum of moonlight we all wended our way back to our quarters as best we could. After the show, I walked alone back to the barracks in total darkness. I was one of the new boys in town, so I became lost almost immediately. In addition to being unfamiliar with Givet, my sense of direction is zilch. I stumbled into someone whom I couldn't see, but he had a friendly voice.

"Are you as confused as I am?" I said.

"More so, I suspect," he said, and I laughed.

"How can you sound so happy?" I asked him. "I mean when everything is so lousy."

"Everything *is* lousy," he admitted. "I'm so homesick I'm about to explode. But a crazy thing just happened to me tonight. I was lower than a snake's belly when I walked into the theater tonight. Did you see the show?"

I realized that it was so dark neither of us had any idea what the other looked like. It seemed a good chance to get an honest reaction. I told him yes, I had seen the show.

Soldier: Wasn't that guy great, the one who played the piano and sang his own songs?

Hugh: Oh, that guy.

Soldier: Yeah, *that* guy. Those songs! He writes really terrific songs. I've heard one of them on the *Hit Parade.*

Hugh: "The Trolley Song."

Soldier: Yeah, that was it. But it was the last song he sang that knocked me out, the one about America.

Hugh: You liked that song?

Soldier: What do you mean, did I like that song? Didn't you?

He sounded almost angry.

Hugh: Yeah, I liked it, but I'm biased. I wrote it.

My silhouetted friend was flabbergasted. I wasn't sure whether identifying myself was the proper thing to do, but I think it was. There is a lot of monotony in the Army, even during wartime. I thought, "Give him something to put in his letters home, for goodness sake."

What he had done for me was immeasurably greater than anything I had done for him. When he became convinced I was not putting him on and that the onstage entertainer and the bumbling person in the dark were one and the same, he confided even more to me.

Soldier: Listen, fella. I'll probably never see you again.

He laughed.

Soldier: Can't see you now for that matter. But I want you to know what you did for me. I was so blue two hours ago I felt I couldn't take it anymore. Now, after hearing your songs, I, well, I know I can take, whatever I have to take.

We parted. He was in a different billet from mine. But every time things got rougher than usual, he popped into my subconscious and gave me a shot of courage. Maybe I did the same thing for him. I hope so.

In Belgium. Winter, 1945.

(photo by an Army buddy)

Chapter 34

Ciney, Belgium

*T*HREE MONTHS LATER, I would pick up the *Stars and Stripes* and read that "The Trolley Song" had not won the Academy Award for Best Song of 1944. It had been expected to win, but it lost to a song from *Going My Way* ("Swingin' on a Star"), a song I have detested ever since. But in March, 1945, when the Oscar winners were announced, my friends were surprised I didn't seem more disappointed. One reason was because "The Trolley Song" had literally saved my life. That was enough to expect of any song.

The other reason is that I've always wished Hollywood hadn't chosen to glorify itself in just this way. I was pleased when Janet Gaynor was voted "Best Actress" at the first Academy Awards ceremony, held on May 16, 1929. It was a quiet affair compared to the glamour and glitz that accompany the ceremonies of today. Two hundred and fifty people attended the black-tie banquet that evening in the Blossom Room of the Hollywood Roosevelt Hotel.

I'm sorry I never won an Oscar so that I could join George C. Scott in refusing it. When I try to explain why I'm against awards and award shows, the usual response is raised eyebrows and an accusatory, "Sour grapes."

No, fellas, it's not sour grapes. I love to see good work recognized, especially if we're in a loftier zone such as the Nobel Peace Prize. But I call the contemporary Oscars ceremonies the Golden Calf Awards because they're not about honoring good work as much as they are a political process to make more bucks. In so doing, they divide actors and technicians alike in a frenzied race for popularity, and actors and artists need to be unified, not divided. Has the Academy of Motion Picture Arts and Sciences ever heard the phrase "ensemble playing?"

Getting back to Belgium and the Army, I sang "Trolley" night after night in January and February of 1945, postponing my annihilation as long as I possibly could. However, singing on vocal cords inflamed by pneumonia had finally taken its toll on my throat. My "clangs" got weaker each night, and, finally, when I opened my mouth to sing one night, nothing at all came out and I was given my walking papers from the show. Instead of shipping me off to the front, however, they stashed me into an Army Hospital in Belgium, near a little town named Ciney.

I had mixed emotions on having to withdraw from the production. There is enough ham in me that it went against the grain to leave a show when I was stopping it every night. But it was lovely the first night in the hospital, actually being warm enough to be able to sleep for the first time since leaving America. When I awoke the next morning, I found myself under several thick blankets. Delicious! The room was pleasantly warm, too—a huge ward containing perhaps fifty tiny cot-like beds. What actually woke me up that first morning was a radio in the medication area. Coming from the speaker was the gorgeous voice of Eileen Farrell singing "The Boy Next Door." When that ended, she spoke a few words about the *Meet Me in St. Louis* movie and then sang "Have Yourself a Merry Little Christmas." It seemed like a good omen.

Eventually I was sent to Captain Sachs-Wilner, head of the Eye, Ear, Nose and Throat Department. He examined my throat with a laryngoscope and told me that by persisting in singing on my inflamed throat I had gradually developed two thick nodules, one on each vocal cord. He was delighted with them and brought in several of his colleagues to look at his new guinea pig—me. Then he casually pronounced my sentence: six months of total silence.

"Use a pad and pencil, my boy, you'll get used to it after a while. Oh, and by the way, this condition will probably plague you the rest of your life."

He seemed pleased as punch by this prospect and continued smilingly, "The nodules will heal up all right, but after that, when you're talking or singing, your voice, with no warning, will *crack*!"

He pronounced the word "crack" with relish, like someone in a scary movie. In my opinion it was a sadistic thing for a doctor to tell his patient, especially considering that his prognosis proved to be untrue.

No, what cracked was not my throat, it was me. For the next few months I had a colossal pity party. It was the first of several crack-ups I was to experience in my life, a neurotic pattern I repeated over and over. Here is a brief quote from one of my songs that shows I was not unaware of this syndrome:

> *The same mistakes,*
> *I make them still,*
> *And I guess I always will.*[1]

They gave me enough penicillin, the new miracle drug, to float a battleship. Unfortunately, penicillin was not a cure for what ailed me. The primary cause of my profound melancholy went beyond frustration at not being able to be a good soldier, at least in the area of entertainment for which I was well suited. Over and beyond that fact was the demon of being thought a slacker, a man so cowardly he would go to the length of pretending to have a disability in order to get a medical discharge from the Army. There was a cruel irony in this since I had knocked myself out to be accepted and passionately wished to stay in and acquit myself well.

---

1 *The Story of My Life,* music and lyrics by Hugh Martin. Unpublished.

With "Louie," an army buddy in Belgium, winter, 1945.
(photo by an Army buddy)

After a week in the warm, sheltered Ward Room of the hospital, I was transferred to a cold drafty barracks with my fellow G.I.s, waiting to be shipped out to the Battle of the Bulge. I could hear them whispering about me. I wondered that they even bothered to lower their voices since, with no walls between us, everything said was an open secret.

The gist of what was being said about me was more or less like this:

> *You know that guy who goes around with a pad and pencil, pretendin' he can't talk? He can talk! I was in the doctor's*

office yesterday and he was talkin' up a storm. Shoot, he's just buckin' for a dis-charge, that's what he's doin'.

It's true I had been talking to Captain Sachs-Wilner. He had me come in once a week to check my progress, and my suspicious barracks mate happened to hear me testing my vocal strength for the doctor. It wouldn't have done any good to explain. It was far too complicated, especially since I had been ordered not to use my voice.

I was an obedient patient; I used my pad and pencil at all times, even though I was given a job in the Post Office. People reacted in various ways to my muteness; almost none of those ways was kind.

During the period before my throat healed, two requisitions for a transfer reached my C.O. The first was from Captain Joshua Logan in Paris, wanting me to join Mickey Rooney, Bobby Breen, Paddy Chayevsky, Red Buttons, and himself in the top entertainment center for Army morale. His request was refused because of my hospitalization.

The second was from Major Glenn Miller, wanting me to join Miller's legendary Army orchestra. This was refused for the same reason, and the next time I heard the name Glenn Miller I was to learn, to my horror, that he had died when his plane crashed in the English Channel.

A Friend in Need Is a Friend Indeed

A memorable kindness was extended to me at this critical time by one Paul Abramson, a Captain in the Medical Corps attached to the military hospital where I was working in the Post Office. He observed me doling out stamps and weighing letters and was sensitive enough to perceive that the smile on my face was not a real smile. He picked up on the fact that my fixed, joyless expression was a not too successful attempt to conceal a lot of pain.

He tried, most tactfully, to draw me out and discover the cause of my melancholy. I resisted at first because I couldn't face the possibility of being condemned one more time as a specialist in self-pity. He took me to his office where he asked me questions that I answered on my pad. My emotions were pounding, and finally the floodgates burst with a lot of frustration, anger, and grief. Captain Abramson sensed a crisis and instantly went into action. His specialty was surgery but no psychiatrist could have done a better job on me. Without his intervention, I don't like to think how total would have been the breakdown I was heading for.

"We can't remove your nodules surgically, Hugh, we don't have the instruments," Captain Abramson told me.

This seemed like bad news at the time; actually, it was the best possible news. The operation is usually successful, but it's not 100 percent foolproof. Many years later, when surgery cost Julie Andrews her glorious soprano voice, I wished she had been required, like me, simply to cease using her voice for an extended time.

During this uncomfortable period, life went on, sometimes in a monotonous daily grind, other times most dramatically. One fine day Captain Sachs-Wilner said, "Hugh, you have been so faithful about using your pad and pencil that the nodules are gone, and you have my blessing to start speaking again."

This after only three months instead of the six he had originally recommended. Three guesses, dear reader, as to which brought me more joy, V-E Day or the mandate to start talking again. You got it. Me an idealist? Maybe, but only to a point.

After the restoration of my voice I began to receive weekend passes to the nearest metropolis, Brussels. During one of these trips I had a brush with a streetcar. (The Brussels trams are almost as hair-raising as Paris taxicabs.) After I'd caught my breath, I ran to the front of the streetcar to find out exactly what was written on that little placard on the front of the car. It read: *Chanson du Tram. Grand Succès Decca!* Freely translated it proclaimed, "The Trolley Song, Big Hit on Decca!"

Chapter 35

I Love Paris in the Summer
When It Sizzles

WHEN I WROTE TO JOSH LOGAN from the Ciney hospital to tell him my throat was healed, he sent a jeep to pick me up and drive me to his headquarters near Paris. The date was the fourth of July, 1945.

Paris was sensational. What made Paris sizzle that memorable summer was, quite simply, love. I don't think many of us, visiting Paris in the years following that dramatic one, have felt especially loved. We did then. If you were an American soldier, you couldn't walk very far without being kissed by a Parisienne. Even when we were not actually kissed, we felt kissed by their very eyes, and by the charm and graciousness of their expressions, their smiles, their body talk, sometimes their touch. It was a wonderful time to be alive, especially in the queen of European cities, Paris, France.

I was not stationed in Paris. I was billeted in the attic of a half-demolished chateau, eight and a half miles northwest of Paris in the town of Chatou. There were perhaps fifty of us crawling in and out of every nook and cranny of the beautiful old edifice. My attic cubicle was tiny, but my summer there was one of the happiest times of my life. I lucked out with roommates, sharing my few square feet of flooring with Billy Halop, once the ringleader of the Dead End Kids, and Joe Pevney, then married to Mitzi Green, with whom I had had so much fun singing and dancing in the Hoagy Carmichael–Johnny Mercer musical *Three After Three*.

There was only one bathroom for the fifty of us, but it boasted a good old iron bathtub that occasionally gushed warm water for a few minutes. Still, the old chateau seemed luxurious after boxcars and bombed-out warehouses and hospitals and icy barracks. And the war was over, at least in Europe. Glory, hallelujah!

I was alive, I could talk, and the most beautiful city in the world was laid out at my feet like a magic carpet. We were not in Paris, but weekend passes were not hard to get.

Later in the summer, we all moved to Le Vésinet, a few miles further from Paris; fascinating to me because an illustrious French Impressionist, Maurice Utrillo, had lived and painted there. I recognized several of the town's landmarks from Utrillo paintings I had seen at the Louvre and the Orangerie.

For me, the center of all this magnificence was the Louvre. I love the visual arts as much as the aural ones, so the Louvre became my pleasure dome and I was Kubla Khan. There was fine live entertainment to be had, as well. The opera was off and running again (for the French, not the German invaders). There were ballets, and exhibitions of contemporary art, and walks along the Seine and in the Bois de Boulogne.

There was a new star in the entertainment scene, Édith Piaf. One of my buddies told me I should try to get a ticket to see her at the huge Théâtre Olympia. He was someone I trusted, so I scooted across town to the box office. Piaf had been sold out for days, but two cancellations were phoned in just as I arrived at the window, two seats in the front row. I don't know why—I took them both; I knew no one in Paris, but I was lonely—and hopeful. Within minutes, I ran into an old friend, Ella Logan. She was wearing a uniform, and looked cute as a button. After a hug, I said, "How would you like to take in the show at the Olympia tonight?"

"Who's there?" she said.

"Édith Piaf."

"Who's Édith Piaf?"

"I really don't know," I said, "but somebody tipped me off that she's a new sensation."

"Let's go," said Ella, "what can we lose?"

Sitting in our front row seats, we were deafened by the pit orchestra and wondered what was in store. What we were not expecting was a petite, 4-foot-11-inch gamine, not endowed with beauty or glamour, wearing her famous plain black dress. The moment she began to sing, goose bumps took possession of Ella and me. During the next forty-five minutes, we were riveted; I involuntarily squeezed Ella's hand from time to time, and she occasionally clutched my arm. I can't tell you what Piaf sang that night; I only remember the galvanizing effect she had on the two of us. And I recall Ella grabbing me at one point and whispering, "Look! Look! Look at the way she touches her hair when she's singing. I do that! I've never seen another singer touch her hair that way!"

There were many such serendipities as seeing Piaf with Ella, too many to enumerate. But one of them was too unusual to omit. It was an evening spent with Gertrude Stein and Alice B. Toklas. The ladies felt an urge to do their patriotic bit for us friendly troops, so they opened their famous residence at 27 Rue de Fleurs one night a week. Two lucky soldiers would show up at 8:00 P.M., and Gertie and Alice would entertain them with hors d'oeuvres and wine and some really classic conversation. No one in my memory generated such extraordinarily fascinating talk in French or English or both. In my case, my companion and I felt we would be on safer ground in English so they graciously steered the dialogue to our native tongue. (Theirs, too, since Miss Stein sprang originally from Allegheny, Pennsylvania, and Miss Toklas from San Francisco, California.)

We sat directly beneath Picasso's famous portrait of Miss Stein, which made us feel somehow part of history. While she was fixing some tidbits for us in the kitchen, Alice leaned forward surreptitiously and whispered, "Gertrude is in one of her anti-capitalist cycles at the moment. Oh, I do hope she lets me have one more afternoon in Macy's basement!"

Potsdam and Berlin

But my main thing was to keep the main thing the main thing. That was the little band of troupers Josh Logan had plucked out of Army units all over the E.T.O. Now that victory had finally been won in Europe, Josh had a free hand. His biggest catch was Mickey Rooney. The most reliable polls had named him Number One at the box office for four years just before he entered the Army. My friendship with this unique genius began at the Capitol Theater when he and Judy, plus Ray Bolger, Bert Lahr, and The Martins, had combined to launch *The Wizard of Oz* with a personal appearance stage show. No one had time to catch his breath doing five shows a day, but Mickey and I hit it off from the start. He had married a beauty, Betty Jane Rose, from my home town. In fact she was Miss Birmingham of 1944. This was just a few months before he was shipped overseas.

Josh sent Mickey and Red Buttons and me, along with Eugene List and a concert violinist, to the Potsdam Conference to entertain Churchill, Stalin, and Truman. Mickey and Red were not invited to the state dinner, nor was I, although the five of us lived together in a tent on the premises. The organizers of the affair decided to play it safe with classical music instead of comedy. I think they made a mistake. Rooney and Buttons would, I think, have cracked up even the impassive Josef Stalin, that's how funny they were together. I had seen them entertain troops, and the laughter they generated was dynamite. Their double act was funnier than anything I had ever seen them do separately or with other partners. They were a dream team, and it hurts me that they never got together after the war for a movie or a Broadway show.

What fascinated me was their material, by which I mean their lack of it. The absence of writers, I suppose, was what baffled me. When I was a regular on Fred Allen's *Texaco Hour,* I was impressed that Fred was the sole creator of comedy material for the show. But what I was seeing Mickey and Red do was even more amazing. It was obvious they didn't know what the heck they were going to do when they walked out on stage in front of hundreds of servicemen. They sparked each other in an almost supernatural fashion. Mickey would suddenly become an old man, or a baby, or a stuffy general, or a tramp, or a woman. This would activate all sorts of responses from Red. Sometimes the process would be reversed. I watched them dozens of times, and I never saw the act go flat. The results were invariably hilarious.

While on the fringes of the Potsdam Conference, we were bussed into the heart of Berlin. There we witnessed first hand what our planes and bombs had done three months earlier to this once gorgeous metropolis with its tree-lined boulevards and magnificent buildings.

My heart went out to the Berliners, especially the women, who had suddenly lost everything. I wanted to give them . . . I don't know what. All I could give them was my quota from the P.X. of candy bars and canned soft drinks that even the humblest G.I. was entitled to.

I was surprised, when facing a ring of tattered housewives with outstretched hands, to learn what they craved most passionately. It wasn't Hershey's chocolate, or Cokes that these wives and mothers were desperate for. It was *soap*! Any kind of soap or detergent was the coin of the realm. These women felt filthy. Some of them may have felt morally filthy. But all of them longed for the soap that would allow them to feel clean again.

Joshua Logan

Josh commissioned his writing stable to create two original musical shows, each about two hours long and each geared to circulate to all the posts where American troops in Europe were stationed. One was a revue, *O.K. U.S.A.,* and I wrote a few songs for that one. The more interesting one was a "book" show called *No T.O. For Love;* "T.O." is an Army acronym meaning "Table of Organization." The reason it was interesting was the quality of the writing. I went to see it expecting a mediocre soldier show that would get by because there was almost no live entertainment at Army camps overseas. Halfway through the first act, it began to dawn on me that the dialogue and lyrics were exceptionally good. I took a peek at my program, and learned the name of the soldier who had provided them was Paddy Chayefsky. This was, of course, many years before he wrote *Marty* or *The Americanization of Emily* or *Network.* In fact, he had no credits at all at that point.

There was a lot of exciting talent lighting up the sky in the Paris of 1945. But for me, the one that overshadowed all the others was our Captain himself, Joshua Lockwood Logan, Jr. of Mansfield, Louisiana. By the time you reach the end of this book, you will know that I have met a legion of wonderful and gifted folks from the world of entertainment and worked with quite a few. And it will be clear that, to my mind, the king of them all was my commanding officer in 1945, Josh Logan. Forty years later I would have the unsurpassable privilege of writing a musical with Josh. Without a doubt, if I had to choose the show biz person who looms largest in my life, it would be dear, warm, brilliant, loving Josh.

Chapter 36

Back Where I Started

I WAS IN PARIS WITH MICKEY ROONEY, one of the funniest people in the world, when the United States dropped the bomb on Hiroshima—though there was nothing funny about that catastrophe. We reflected whether there would soon be any world to be funny in. And we were horrified by the accounts of the magnitude of the destruction. At the same time, being human and being soldiers, we couldn't help wondering what effect this event would have on our travel orders. We had both fully expected to be sent next to the South Pacific. Was there, we wondered, a ray of hope for us concealed in this ghastliness?

As it turned out, there was. Neither of us had to travel six thousand miles to a zone that held no charms for us.

When it came time to "separate" me, the Army in its inscrutable wisdom, sent me by troop ship to New York, which is exactly where I wanted to be, and thence by train to Los Angeles, which is exactly where I wanted not to be.

March was its beautiful California self in 1946, and I decided to put thoughts of New York aside and just enjoy the gorgeous early spring in Hollywood. It was exciting seeing Ralph again, and Jerry Lawrence and Bob Lee and Marsha Hunt and Marilyn Maxwell and the Kellys and Ted Reid and my skimpy collection of sheet music.

My friends treated me as if I were war hero Audie Murphy. They knew full well I had probably been a sad, sad sack, but the fact that I was still alive filled them, and me, with amazement.

Before kissing sunny California goodbye and going back to my beloved New York, something happened that I find difficult to talk about because I behaved so badly. However I've been the Truth Squad so far—no use backsliding now.

There was a large and affable lady in Hollywood named Louise Long; Louise was a superb masseuse and she had had the good fortune to find a perfect niche for her talents. The movie industry is perhaps the most stressful milieu in the world, for performers and executives alike. Imagine being scrutinized eight hours plus, five days a week, sometimes more:

"Is she putting on a little weight?"
"Is he developing a few age lines around his mouth?"
"Has she become a liability to the studio?
Look around for someone younger."

As for the wheeler-dealers and their side-kicks, the climate was not much more relaxed. So in desperation for many, it was back to the massage table. And it did help to take the edge off the nervous strain of movie-making.

Louise gave a big party once a year for her high-powered clients, one of whom was Arthur Freed and another, Ralph Blane. Ralph's mission at this moment was to get me into Arthur's office with the hope of business-as-usual after a two-year interruption of the greatest war in history. I had opted just not to show up—surely one of the most foolish and ungracious decisions of my life. Freed had given me the finest opportunity, so

With Elllen and my father, Big Hugh
in 1946.

far, of my life. The least I could have done was to go to him and
thank him profoundly for *Meet Me in St. Louis*.

The reason that I didn't is not quite clear to me even now.
If I had been a career-driven person, there was no other road in
show business more promising than the one back to the Freed
Unit at MGM. Unfortunately (or perhaps fortunately), the two
things I wanted most were, not a flashy career, but a right relationship with God and an ideal mate. Mind you, this was years
before my conversion, but the Hound of Heaven had picked up
my scent and I was a marked man. So it was *Home Sweet Heaven*
more than *Hooray for Hollywood*.

With my brother, Gordon, in 1946.

Another very big factor in this equation was that I didn't quite trust Arthur. I had tried so hard to be, not just a dutiful employee, but more, a loving friend. I sincerely admired him but he had on more than one occasion betrayed my trust. The first shock was the gratuitous tongue-lashing he gave me out of the blue—about nothing really of any importance.

The second shock was more serious. I had sought his help in trying to get a 1-A classification so I could serve in the Army or Navy. He did a really treacherous thing; he took me to one of Metro's top lawyers and told him to pull a few strings to get me into uniform. Privately, as I discovered through a sympathetic friend, he had instructed the lawyer to keep me *out* of the Army at all cost. It was flattering that MGM wanted me enough to resort to a double-cross like that, but it also made me very, very wary of Arthur Freed.

I don't like working with people I don't respect and it was hard to respect Arthur after the lawyer episode, especially after my exemplary association with Messrs. Rodgers and Abbott, two gentlemen almost as honorable as my saintly father.

But back to the party: Ralph, in a single-minded drive to get me back into the fold, had invited me to Louise's shindig, knowing Freed would be there.

"I know you hate parties, Hugh, but every big wheel in Hollywood will be there and you might enjoy a bit of star-gazing."

Poor Ralph—his little plan backfired. When Arthur spotted me across a crowded room, his face lit up. It fell just as suddenly when he observed that I was not in uniform.

"How long have you been out?" he said crossly. "Why didn't you come to see me?"

"Why, I . . . I . . . was just about to call you, Arthur. Tomorrow in fact." Very lame. It was a lie and it sounded like one.

"I'm sorry you didn't let me know," Arthur said. "I wanted you to write the songs for *The Pirate* for Judy and Gene." He walked away abruptly.

I watched him across a crowded room. He looked as if he were about to say, "We are not pleased," like Queen Victoria. He simply closed the door on me with finality, and things were never the same between us again.

It was a stupid and foolhardy thing I had done. Worst of all, I suddenly realized how boorishly I had behaved to a man who had given me the greatest career opportunity of my life. The really terrible part of it all is that, in retrospect, I think Arthur really loved me, he just didn't know how to show it. There was a lot of the child in Arthur, and I had deeply hurt that part of him. I felt even worse years later in New York with a couple of fresh flops to my discredit and no offers in sight. How earnestly I wished I had not burned the bridges between me and this powerful but vulnerable guy with an extraordinary gift for making film musicals.

As Leo Hubbard in The Little Foxes,
Ogunquit, Maine.

Chapter 37

Hits and Misses

R. Rick Simas, Musical Theater Specialist at San Diego State University, wrote an interesting reference book[1] about flop shows. When he gave me a copy, I was not surprised to see the name Hugh Martin crop up more than once! The first reference was *Look, Ma, I'm Dancin'!* It had sounded sure-fire. Nancy Walker was our star and was never funnier. Lawrence and Lee contributed an engaging "book," George Abbott produced and directed it, Oliver Smith designed the sets, Harold Lang, already a great ballet dancer, proved he could sing and act. Most importantly, Jerome Robbins conceived the show, based on his own life, and choreographed it brilliantly.

Shanghaiing Harold Lang into the project was a delicate matter inasmuch as Eddie Winkler is a character based on Robbins himself. It's understandable Jerry should have found me offensively aggressive in pushing Harold into the role of Jerome Robbins, slightly disguised. In retrospect I probably owe Robbins an apology for my tenacity, but Harold triumphed in *Look, Ma . . .* and on the

---

1 Simas, Dr. Rick. *Musicals No One Came to See*, New York and London: Garland Publishing, Inc. , 1987.

strength of our show became an important Broadway star, eventually recreating *Pal Joey* in a production that ran longer than the original Gene Kelly version.

Just to show my faithful readers how clever I am, let me confess that while auditioning actors for *Look, Ma . . .* I turned down two men who became huge stars in the world of entertainment. The first was Gordon MacRae; years later he would portray Curly in *Oklahoma* and Billy Bigelow in *Carousel,* Rodgers and Hammerstein's two biggest movie blockbusters.

The second reject was Tony Bennett—can you believe it? It was not lack of enthusiasm on my part where Tony was concerned. When he auditioned for me in my apartment he totally blew me away. I thought he was marvelous and I told him so. The roadblock was that my boss, George Abbott, had a block about amplification. Microphones are omnipresent today; there is no theater in New York today where you can find refuge from the latest variations of Stereophonic Sound. You are sure to be blasted out of your seat with ear-shattering decibels.

But Mr. Abbott, God bless him, liked the sound of the natural human voice and he put a ban on mikes. I adored the sound of Tony Bennett's voice, but I feared (I think correctly) that it might not "carry" over a large Broadway orchestra without a technological boost. So I sadly passed up the singer whom Frank Sinatra called, "The best singer in the business."

I was, however, able to help Tony get one of his first big breaks. He had a coterie of supporters who were fighting to get him a record deal. They finally found some people willing to finance one if they could get him an endorsement from a celebrity. Evidently they thought I was qualified because they phoned me to ask me what I thought of Tony's possibilities. I told them that I thought he was absolutely tops. "This kid is another Martha Raye," is the way I put it. I've been kidded about this comparison ever since, but it's not as dumb as it sounds. Martha was more famous as a comedienne than as a troubadour, but in truth her singing was out of this world. She is, even today, my favorite female vocalist, above, even, such superb artists as Judy Garland and Ethel Waters. I realize that Judy and Ethel were greater singers overall—but Martha Raye had a special timbre in her jazzy soprano that reached my heart. More than any other songbird, her passionate love of music trembled and vibrated on every note, like a sweet clear bell.

Another subtle connection between Tony and Martha is this: they both approached a popular song with deeply felt emotion. Tony and Martha subconsciously choose a key that is, perhaps, a half tone higher than the one in their comfort zone. This higher key requires an extra vocal effort, and that little extra effort gives us a little extra thrill.

We had a dazzling opening night at the Adelphi Theater with celebrities galore, including Greta Garbo and Truman Capote, cheering us on. But in spite of all we had going for us, we closed after six months. Our investors got their money back because Paramount bought the screen rights for Fred Astaire and Betty Hutton, but the film was never made.

What went wrong? I wrote four top-notch songs, "Gotta Dance," "I'm the First Girl in the Second Row of the Third Scene of the Fourth Number," "Tiny Room," and "I'm Tired of Texas." Then I got lazy and failed to meet the high standard of the first four. It was the first time I had had control over the selection of songs, and I was much too uncritical of my own work. In the past, I had Dick Rodgers or Arthur Freed to throw out songs when they were below par; even Ralph Blane had been helpful with an occasional, "Hugh, you can do better." In short, I believe if I had rolled up my sleeves and sweated a little to achieve excellence, *Look, Ma* . . . might have been a hit. But who knows? What I've always needed, but didn't realize at the time, was a sounding-board, a Big Daddy, someone with the authority to throw out my inferior songs and say "No!" loudly and clearly.

It is so easy to Monday-morning-quarterback a show and say, "If only they had listened to me." But in the case of this troubled musical, I'm convinced if I could have gotten through to Jerry and Mr. Abbott with some ideas I had, I could have made a difference.

Here's a "for instance": one of the characters was a female rehearsal pianist. "Build that part up," I pleaded, "and let Kay Thompson play it. Not only is she a dynamite singer, but she also plays piano like a whirlwind and moves like a ballet dancer. Put the four Williams Brothers in the ensemble and give the five of them two spots, one in each act."

Jerry said, "Who is Kay Thompson?" and Mr. Abbott added, "Who the devil are the Williams Brothers?" I told them that Walter Winchell had told his millions of readers the five of them were "the greatest act that ever hit humanity," but the Messrs. Abbott and Robbins were not impressed.

I was startled to read in Amanda Vaill's superb biography of Robbins[2] that Billy Rose offered Jerry the Ziegfeld Theater for *Look, Ma . . .*—plus the entire financial backing required to get it on if Robbins would fire me and get someone else to write the songs, and yet Jerry refused to unload me. I was grateful for the information, otherwise I would never have known about this somewhat out-of-character gesture of loyalty on Jerry's part. I was amazed and touched, especially since he was more associated with betrayal than with loyalty.

The Queen Mary—First Class!

Even though *Look, Ma . . .* had not been the blockbuster we all had hoped for, I decided to reward myself by going to Europe. Not only did I go to Europe, I went first class on the Queen Mary.

---

2 Vaill, Amanda. *Somewhere: The Life of Jerome Robbins.* New York: Broadway Books, 2006.

It was the only time I ever splurged on total luxury, but working with Jerry Robbins had been such an ordeal I felt nothing short of the biggest ship in the world could ease my pain.

The pastime I have enjoyed most in my lifetime has been my trans-Atlantic crossings on the ocean liners, and I was fortunate enough to do it many times. The Cunard Line was my favorite, namely the Queen Mary I and the Queen Elizabeths I and II. The time span on these huge ships was usually five days. If I traveled Holland-American or Italian, it took seven or eight, but they were great fun, too.

These voyages had a supernatural aura for me; I always felt I had left Planet Earth and was cruising somewhere in outer space. The food was impossibly good, the passengers colorful, and the goings-on exciting to the point of making me feel happily guilty.

My most unforgettable crossing began on a fine spring day in 1948 when I walked across the gangplank onto the Queen Mary, docked at 50th St. and the Hudson River on New York's waterfront.

I was glad I had opted for first class, because if I hadn't, I probably never would have met Martha Raye. Martha was big in the forties, both in Hollywood and on Broadway, and she was even bigger on my personal hit parade. I think, finally, I love her singing above all the others, because she had an unsurpassable passion for music, and it shone out in every note she sang.

I introduced myself, half expecting to be brushed off. Instead, she lit up like a Christmas tree and exclaimed, "You wrote 'The Boy Next Door'! Truthfully, it's my very favorite song!"

I was "in," and the next four days were giddy and grand. She learned a few of my other songs, and we gave a concert in the ship's deluxe restaurant on the top deck of the ship. Martha was delighted with my accompaniments because I knew all her arrangements by heart and could anticipate all of her complicated changes of key and tempo.

She drank a lot, clowned a lot, and danced a lot with her new husband, Nick Condos. Her first husband and most fruitful collaborator had been David Rose. Her recordings with the David Rose Orchestra were responsible for some of the greatest "singles" in the annals of popular American song.

"Life's Full of Consequence," Yip Harburg wrote, and as a consequence of all the fun we had, she broke her leg! This was a complication because she was scheduled to open almost immediately at the Palladium in London. To her everlovin' credit, I can tell you she did open, on time, broken leg and all, and was just as big a hit with the loyal British, as she sat on a grand piano, as she could possibly have been dancing around on her two beautiful legs.

Grandma Moses

Another big failure was on the horizon, but sandwiched in between the disasters, fortunately, was a most felicitous and prestigious success, a lovely documentary about the phenomenal American painter Grandma Moses, Anna Mary Robertson Moses.

When I took on the assignment of writing the underscoring for it, I didn't realize I would have the pleasure of being a guest in her upstate New York farmhouse, and have her brew tea for me—even play the piano for me!

The producer of the film was Jerome Hill; I met him in Paris in the summer of 1945 when we were both in the Army. Three years later he had become a filmmaker, and he invited me to compose the music for a one-reeler concerning the life and the paintings of Grandma Moses.

"It calls for classical music, Jerry," I wailed. "I am strictly Tin Pan Alley."

He wore me down by sheer persistence, but it took two years to get a commitment out of me. I had never done underscoring and

Jerome Hill, whom I met in the Army in Paris,
1945

wasn't sure I could. I worked furiously for three months, and then, with fear and trembling, demonstrated the results for him.

He said almost the same words that Dick Rodgers had spoken in 1938 when he heard my arrangement of "Sing for Your Supper": "It's exactly what I wanted. I think it will work."

It must have worked; "The Grandma Moses Suite," perfectly orchestrated by Alec Wilder, was recorded the same year. The film itself is an absolute gem. The paintings, of course, are masterpieces, and the unusual approach to displaying them as conceived by Jerry was exciting. Jerry paid me the ultimate compliment a film composer can receive—he cut the picture to accommodate the music. Ordinarily the music gets cut to accommodate the picture.

Back to the house in upstate New York, Jerry Hill had arranged an evening with Mrs. Moses, and we drove up from Manhattan, Jerry, Alec Wilder, my sister Ellen, and I. The elements conspired to turn the scene into a Grandma Moses painting as we drove into her front yard. We wished we had been in a sleigh, but with snowflakes falling thick and fast, we still felt like figures in one of her winterscapes.

She was graciousness personified. We marveled at the spic and span condition of her house, a large farmhouse that she swept and cleaned herself.

There was something other-worldly about that evening. It seemed another culture, another century. Everything seemed to be suffused with a kind of purity that was startling after the sophistication and superficiality of Manhattan. The snow-washed air reminded me of childhood trips to the country. But there was a spiritual purity, too; a purity that came from Mrs. Moses herself. You felt it looking at her paintings, and the feeling was multiplied when meeting the lady herself—seeing her smile, hearing her talk, and watching her move with a grace and sprightliness that belied her eighty-nine years.

Preston Sturges and Make a Wish

My life has been liberally salted with geniuses. Just lucky, I guess. Perhaps I shouldn't declare they were geniuses, for who knows what a genius is? I don't pretend to. But for all of us who care about the arts, there are certain icons who strike us as being geniuses.

When my fantasies run a montage of those who seemed to me to be geniuses, the faces who most often pop up are Kay Thompson, Ed Wynn, Dick Rodgers, Judy Garland, Mickey Rooney, Grandma Moses, Preston Sturges, Noël Coward, and Beatrice Lillie.

But my list is strictly my list. I make no claims for my five men and four women. It just happened that when I was around them they seemed to have emanations of genius shooting out from them like light around characters in a science fiction movie.

The one with the strongest emanations was Preston Sturges. After tangling with the complex problems of *Look, Ma, I'm Dancin'!*, I began to be restless, anxious to "Pick myself up,/Dust myself off,/Start all over again."[3]

With Jerry Lawrence and Bob Lee, my colleagues of *Look, Ma . . .*, I hatched a little plot about a young girl in Paris. She was an orphan; I seem to be attracted to orphans. Three of my heroines have been "motherless chiles." This one was the first of the three.

When Jerry and Bob and I hit some snags in putting together an original story, they dropped out, but my musical comedy urge continued to dart about, looking for, what else, an orphan . . . just the right orphan, a kind of Hugh Martin orphan.

I remembered a film called *The Good Fairy* that had delighted me when it was released in 1935. *The Good Fairy* was originally produced on a European stage. Ferenc Molnar wrote it, and it came to

---

3 Kern, Jerome, and Dorothy Fields, *Pick Yourself Up*. T.B. Harms Co., 1936.

277

Broadway with a very young Helen Hayes as the hapless but enterprising orphan.

I read Molnar's play and it let me down a bit. But then the movie played a couple of days in one of the art houses, and I watched it again with excitement. Margaret Sullavan was the orphan, one who bore almost no resemblance to Mr. Molnar's orphan. Preston Sturges, Paramount's master of screwball comedy, created a new orphan, Luisa Gingelbusher, a new story, and new dialogue, dialogue that I still regard as the most beguiling ever heard in anything. Preston Sturges was to become a top movie director in a year or two, but he was merely the writer of *The Good Fairy*. William Wyler, a fine *réalisateur*, as the French say, directed it.

I couldn't contain myself. I've never been noted for going slow, thinking things through, then acting with confidence and steadiness. I am precipitous! I booked myself onto *The Twentieth Century* and *The Sunset Limited* and checked in at the Chateau Marmont in Hollywood.

The quiet, dignified old Chateau Marmont was a good, though accidental, choice for a strategic attack on Preston Sturges because he owned The Players restaurant, a stone's throw from the Marmont.

I had brought Jack Gray with me to demonstrate the handful of songs I had already written, the same Jack Gray who soon after changed his name to Timothy Gray and co-wrote *Love from Judy* and *High Spirits* with me.

Jack and I went straight to The Players, and had dinner there the first night. We asked for Mr. Sturges, and Preston came to our table, bought us champagne, and totally overwhelmed us with his social graces. His toasts, stories, limericks, and songs had us falling off our chairs with laughter.

And we seemed to entertain him as well. There was an upright piano in a corner, so Jack and I performed a couple of songs I had written for *The Good Fairy* as I remembered it from seeing the film several times.

With one of my greatest show biz heroes, Preston Sturges.
My other great hero is Joshua Logan.
The year is 1950, at Preston's home in Hollywood.

Just before we had our final glass of champagne, Jack sang, and I played, "How Are Things in Gloccamorra?," which, of course, was written by Yip Harburg and Burton Lane. It is a gorgeous song, and Jack, who is full Scottish, had the brogue and the sweet tenor voice in control. Everyone cried, Preston hardest of all, and as we left, he shook our hands warmly and said, "I'll do the show." We returned to the hotel in a euphoric haze.

Preston Sturges is the most charming human being I've ever met, and the wittiest. I couldn't have enjoyed the evening more if Mark Twain himself had risen and spent it with us. Some charming people can captivate you in a social situation, but are unable to translate it to their creative output. No wonder I loved a line in *Top Banana* delivered by Phil Silvers, who, as a burlesque comic badly in need of good jokes, looks contemptuously at one of his writers and grumbles, "Oh, you're funny, aren't you? You're oh, so funny! Put a pencil in your hand—nothin'!"

Not so with Preston. His work is superb. His *The Lady Eve, Sullivan's Travels, The Miracle of Morgan's Creek, Hail the Conquering Hero*—all are true comic masterpieces both in the writing and direction.

So why did *The Good Fairy* flop? I'm not sure. Producing a Broadway musical is the iffiest business known to man. My personal theory is that Preston so hypnotized me I was a guy who couldn't say no. He insisted on scuttling the magnificent screenplay he had written for adorable Maggie Sullavan. He wanted to throw it out and start from scratch, write a brand new story line and dialogue. My big mistake, one that probably killed the show, was letting him do it. I couldn't resist him and so my original dream fell by the wayside. I simply was not the immovable object that should have held firm against Preston's irresistible force. I blew the whole show in a moment of weakness and one lamentable decision.

At this point, I phoned George Abbott and tried to convince him he should produce and direct it. I struck out with Mr. Abbott but he caught me off guard with a counter offer.

"Why don't you put your show on hold until you do one for me, one I'm very excited about?"

He explained he was planning a musical based on Betty Smith's exquisite novel, *A Tree Grows in Brooklyn.*

It takes courage for me to confess that I turned him down. My fixation with Sturges had, I think, rendered me temporarily insane. Even if Mr. Abbott had asked me to write a piece of garbage, the right thing to do would have been to say, "Yes, a thousand times yes!" But to have said no to his offer to let me do music and lyrics for *A Tree Grows in Brooklyn*! Thinking about it always brings on a migraine.

The mission was accomplished with Preston Sturges, so I returned to New York and pressed on with making selections

With Kaye Ballard and Nanette Fabray, backstage No, No, Nanette,
at a theater in Long Beach, California, 1994.

for the show that was now called *Make a Wish*. I chose Gower
Champion to be our choreographer. He had never done a book
show, but I had seen his work in several revues, notably *Lend an
Ear*. He and his talented wife, Marge, who served as his assistant
on *Make a Wish*, did a superb job and made a great hit with both
audiences and critics. Gower received much praise, especially for
a brilliant ballet called "The Sale," and he deserved every bit of it.

I had gone about this whole endeavor backwards. Finding a
responsible producer should come very early in the game. I had
painted myself into a corner by rounding up an unpredictable genius
to write the script, a scintillating star, Nanette Fabray, a choreographer who was on the verge of becoming one of the most important
figures on Broadway, and a charming pair of dancers, Harold Lang
and Helen Gallagher.

Raoul Pène du Bois did extraordinary work with costumes
and sets of great quality, including a show curtain that opened
and closed like a Venetian blind—ingenious and lovely.

*Harry Rigby and Jule Styne, two of the young neophyte
producers of* Make a Wish. *The third one was Alexander Cohen:
it was a first effort as producer for all three, 1950.*

But my deepest pride is reserved for our star, Nanette Fabray. Nan epitomizes one of my favorite Noël Coward stories. A nondescript young teenage girl pounced on him at the airport and gushed, "Oh, Mr. Coward, would you tell me how to become a star?"

"Twinkle," said Mr. Coward.

And my darling Nan, even today, twinkles more brightly than most of Hollywood's stars, past and present. Even more than I admired her performance, I admired her behavior. There was an enormous amount of infighting during our turbulent rehearsals, factions within cliques within caucuses, everyone blaming everyone else. Nan stayed serenely above all the malice; she hardly seemed even to see it, and she certainly never allowed herself to become

A conference regarding Make a Wish.
Left to right, Preston Sturges, Nanette Fabray, me, Jule Styne, 1950.

involved with it. She is a great lady and there aren't a whole lot of those around.

Make a Wish was produced by three neophytes who shared my enthusiasm: Jule Styne, Harry Rigby, and Alexander Cohen. Jule and Harry and Alex made every mistake imaginable, but, happily, they all three went on to become top Broadway producers.

The tryout on the road was agony. When we premièred in Philadelphia at the Shubert Theater, most of us thought we had a hit in spite of all the feudin' and fussin' and fightin'. But by the time the curtain fell on opening night in Philly, we knew we were in big trouble. We all kept struggling to keep the ship afloat, but we knew in our sinking hearts that we had struck too many icebergs and the leaks were too massive to repair. I remember Jule Styne literally locking me in my Ritz-Carlton apartment until I wrote a new title song, a duet for Nan and Stephen Douglass. I remember the horrible newspaper reviews and the equally bad one in

Variety. I remember vast rows of empty seats, the deserted matinees, the endless rehearsals.

Against my will, a decision was made by the three producers to replace Sturges. I remember a string of good writers who brought in trial scenes; one was Anita Loos, who, I believe, would have been a better choice than Abe Burrows, who was finally given double duty as director and play doctor. Abe was a fine craftsman, especially when he was in his natural habitat, like *Guys and Dolls*. But the innocently risqué subtleties of Messrs. Molnar and Sturges escaped him completely. We opened at New York's Winter Garden Theater on April 18, 1951, to bad notices, and we collapsed and closed three months later.

Chapter 38

Dr. Feelgood

IN THE 1950S, I fell into the clutches of a very dangerous doctor named Max Jacobson. I was not the only sucker by any means. During his marathon working hours, his 73rd Street office, between Third and Lexington Avenues, was crammed with the royalty of New York show biz. One would see Tennessee Williams, Leonard Bernstein, Alan Jay Lerner, Van Cliburn, and many others. Max was gregarious, so sometimes it seemed as if Truman Capote were giving one of his galas in the doctor's office. We were all getting powerful intravenous injections; my punctured arm made me look like a war casualty, and all of us were told the same thing, "They're liquid vitamins."

Pretty potent vitamins, Max. They did everything but make the blind see and the deaf hear. The congregation in the waiting room often included crippled patients limping into Max's office and emerging shortly after with their crutches gaily tucked under their arms.

Several years later, the scandal broke on page one of *The New York Times*. The exposé revealed how Dr. Max Jacobson, also known as "Miracle" and "Dr. Feelgood," had been injecting his patients with amphetamines—"speed," as it is commonly called. The article described the case histories of some of his patients, especially some of the more shocking cases that had resulted in nervous breakdowns, severe psychiatric problems, and, in a few cases, death. The article ended by stating that his license had been permanently revoked.

Eddie Fisher likes to comment casually, during his interviews, "Yes, it's true I was a junkie for many years. My accompanist, Hugh Martin, got me started." True, Eddie, old boy, but I'd appreciate it if you would add a clarifying phrase to the effect that Hugh Martin was a fellow victim, not a pusher.

When Eddie and I flew to London to appear at the Palladium, he took Dr. Jacobson with him. I remember how surprised I was when I stepped onto the plane and there was Max in the aisle giving shots. I blush today at the realization that I could have been so stupid as not to have known that something very weird was going on, but I didn't. Maybe I didn't want to.

In the 1960s he practiced his skullduggery at the White House, as well. We now know JFK suffered from severe and almost constant back pain. Jackie Kennedy had been led to Dr. Jacobson by her friend, Leonard Bernstein. She, like all of us, was taken in by Max's magnetic persona and his spectacular healings. She loved her husband and longed to see his suffering diminished, so she arranged for Dr. Jacobson to make frequent visits to the White House. *The New York Times* had a field day with that one.

Chapter 39

Look for the Silver Linings

THERE WERE A FEW SILVER LININGS in the 1950s. It was not my favorite decade by any means, but it was not all gloom and doom—after all, there was the Palace. Even in 1951, when Judy Garland asked me to play for her there, I was convinced she led the field, not only as a singer, but as a comedienne, an actress, and a dancer. There seemed to be nothing in the world of entertainment she couldn't do better than anyone else. So for me, sharing that dressing room with her twice a day, six days a week, for over four months was a fascinating experience. Yes, there was a sheet between us, but only for the relatively short time when we were *déshabille*. I was so awed by her talent I suppose I expected her to be a kind of creature from outer space, which she was anything but. As most of her fans know by now, she was fun-loving and down to earth, at least when she wasn't falling apart. Happily, those moments of despair and self-destructiveness were very much in the minority.

It was an especially happy time for Judy. Scads of visitors floated in and out of our room, including every celebrity in New York—Marlene Dietrich, Noël Coward, the Duke and Duchess of

The second Martins Quartet: Timothy Gray, Gwen Harmon,
Preshy Marker, and Don McKay, 1957.

Windsor, the full roster of the Jet Set, the Beautiful People, and
Show Biz Icons.

She seemed happiest, though, when the celebs left and she could
let her hair down with Sid Luft, or one of the seven dancing gentlemen in her act, or Ernest Adler, her campy and comforting hair-
dresser. Her compulsion to entertain was so strong she was almost
always "on," telling inimitable stories, doing burlesque bits, or imi-
tating the MGM's highfalutin' sopranos, notably Kathryn Grayson
and Jeanette MacDonald. She had a strong "head" voice that served
her in good stead when she sang wicked impressions of "Indian Love
Call" and "Make Believe."

At the time, Judy Garland fanatics were not the most sophisticated people in the world, and Judy was very canny. She wanted

to grow and broaden her horizons, but the fans wanted her the way she was—sweet, wholesome, a girl-next-door type, not too far from Dorothy Gale and Betsy Booth. When she strayed and stretched her image, the box office was quick to respond and to chastise. *The Pirate* was one of the few Garland movies that lost money, and the mail from *Ziegfeld Follies* was downright hostile. Her fans didn't care for the sexy, satirical "Madame Crematon," and they let her and the studio know it, P.D.Q.

The banter occasionally turned bitter. One week, on our day off, she arranged a little party for "the act," the seven dancers, Sid, Ernie, and me. We were treated to a showing of a couple of Judy's films, two of her favorites, *Babes on Broadway* and *Meet Me in St. Louis*. We all sat together in the balcony of Loew's State. It was double fun. The movies themselves were enjoyable, and her loud ad-libs during them (most at her own expense) were even more so.

She had forgotten how young and beautiful she looked in those earlier films. Back in the dressing-room that evening as she was making up, a horrible thing happened. She stared at her incomparable face in the mirror, weighed it on the scales of beauty, and found it wanting. A little cry of distress alerted Ernie, resting on the sofa at the time. Quick as a flash, he wrested a curling iron from her trembling fingers. He is a sensitive man, and his intuition told him that Judy was a second or two from pressing the searingly hot metal curler into the flesh of her face. She had desperately and neurotically wanted to call back her youthful freshness, and when she couldn't, all she could think of to do was to mutilate herself. Thank God for Ernie and the speed of his response.

Judy wept for a few minutes. Youth is not an easy thing to lose, especially for someone who had become a metaphor for springtime. But she had also become a metaphor for "the show must go on," and go on it did.

The rest of the engagement was remarkably glitch-free, considering the load Judy was carrying. Many happy moments from those nineteen weeks float back to me still, like an MGM montage, complete with sounding brass, tinkling cymbals, and angel voices on the soundtrack. For instance, the night I modulated into a wrong key for an encore. It was totally my fault, but my error made Judy look stupid, so I thought the show would never ever end that night, I was impatient to apologize to her, which I was finally able to do, tearfully.

"Oh, Hughie," she said with sweet surprise, "it wasn't your fault, I just couldn't get with it tonight."

Memorable, too, was the night Alec Wilder watched us from the wings. It was the only time I ever presumed to ask Judy's permission for anyone to do that. I dared to do it because I knew her reverence for Alec matched mine. He stared for a solid hour without moving a muscle at the hijinks happening simultaneously on and off stage. He looked like a child watching Santa Claus in the very act of emerging from the chimney.

There was a spot in the show when Judy and I were alone in the wings for a minute or two before making an entrance together. If she was feeling good, we often chatted about this and that, and one night she startled me by saying, "Would you like to know how I make people cry?"

"Judy," I replied, "I've often wondered."

"I smile!" she said as she grabbed my hand and pulled me onto the stage.

There was something miraculous about Judy's smile. No wonder she could manipulate us with it. The same was true of her laughter and her tears. Music is hard to define; even punk, rap, and rock 'n' roll are called music, but calling it that doesn't mean it is. The sweetest sound I've ever heard is Judy's laugh. Listen to her breaking up at Mickey Rooney's antics in an early reel of *Girl Crazy*. That, fellas, is music—a waterfall, a cascade, an avalanche of the most beautiful music imaginable.

Even a crying jag, if it comes from Judy, somehow manages to be music. No scene in any film tears my heart out like the cafeteria scene in *The Clock*. The music she makes in that scene, without singing a note, is as moving as anything one might hear in the opera house or at Carnegie Hall.

There was a phenomenon that seemed to me to set Judy Garland apart from all other singers. When others sang, there was always an unspoken assumption that there had been a writer, or writers, who had created the song now being sung. When Judy sang a song, that assumption seemed to vanish. Something else was happening. The song seemed to be emerging for the first time, not by way of anyone's pen or piano but straight from the heart of the girl, herself, whether the emotion was sorrow or joy. That little miracle, I believe was, more than any of her other gifts, a major source of her power.

Some rare recordings of Judy's voice when she was still a child were given to me recently by my good friend, Jeff Freeman. Listening to them, I discovered that this miraculous power Judy had been given was even stronger and purer during her adolescent years. She gained much as she grew into womanhood, qualities that would inspire critics to call her "the greatest entertainer of the century," and I agree with the critics about that. But to those of us who are deeply touched by innocence and purity, there will never again be a phenomenon like Judy Garland between the ages of thirteen and seventeen.

When the Palace engagement finally ended, someone threw a little party for all of us in the lobby of the theater. All the popular newspaper columnists were there, plus a battery of photographers, publicity people, television personnel, etc. Judy saw I was ill at ease, and thoughtfully latched on to my arm protectively and marched me over to where Sid was standing.

"Sid," she said in a mock-earnest voice, "I can't stand to say goodbye to my roommate. Can't we adopt Hughie?" Then with a sly look she added, "Oh, no, I guess not. He's a little too young for Liza."

*Timothy Gray (right) and I did vocal arrangements
for the Patrice Munsel TV show on ABC, 1957.*

Liza with a "Z"

When Judy made me smile with that remark about Liza and
me, Liza was five and I was thirty-seven. The next time I saw her
she was seventeen and I was forty-eight. A young man named
Arthur Whitelaw had asked Ralph and me if we would work
with him on an off-Broadway revival of *Best Foot Forward*. We
happily agreed, and one morning in January 1963, I found myself

*This photograph was taken in the 1920s when
Adelaide Hall was Duke Ellington's girl singer at the Cotton Club.
In 1952, for Timothy Gray and me, she played an important
role in* Love from Judy.

waiting to audition Liza Minnelli. She was two hours late, and I recalled the reputation of her famous mother for keeping people waiting. But her excuse was legitimate; she had missed her commuter train. She took off her heavy coat, and we saw that she was wearing a modest little dress of utmost simplicity. Simplicity was the hallmark of her audition for us. She placed a copy of "They Can't Take that Away from Me" on the music stand for our pianist, then sang it with sweetness and great musicality, making every nuance of the Gershwin song felt and revealed. George, I believe, would have loved it. I certainly did. And Ira would have been thrilled by the way her movement so faithfully expressed the intent of his beautiful lyric. Most surprising of all, instead of going into her dance at the end of the chorus, she danced as she sang it—subtly, expressively, and gracefully. I fell in love with the daughter of a lady I had always loved. She was, of course, accepted by all of us.

Liza caught the fancy of the hard-boiled Manhattan critics, which put us in the hot ticket category. We probably could have run a couple of years at Stage 73 Theater, but Liza suddenly gave her notice. "Mama wants me to come home," she explained. The show closed abruptly.

I Delete You

In 1952, Timothy Gray and I did a show in London's West End that turned out to be the longest running show either of us ever had. It was *Love from Judy*, and it was adapted from a novel and play by Jean Webster, *Daddy Long Legs*. The role of Judy had been already immortalized by Mary Pickford and Shirley Temple among others. These ladies notwithstanding, the girl Emile Littler, our very British producer, found topped them all. Her name was Jean Carson, a winsome, green-eyed, young Scottish

Jean Carson in Love From Judy *by Hugh Martin and Timothy Gray.*
Opening on September 9, 1952, it ran for almost two years
at the Saville Theater in London's West End

charmer who swept London off its feet in our show. It ran a year and a half at the Saville Theatre and everything about it was felicitous. Everything that is, except its composer, Hugh Martin, who was very sick during the entire period. The experience was so painful I choose not to write about it. It is sufficient to say it was a huge hit, everybody loved it, and it nearly killed me.

Chapter 40

A Mixed Bag of Musicals

DALE CARNEGIE, ONE OF MY HEROES, wrote, "Don't make a case against yourself." Good advice, and perhaps I'm contradicting it by saying my glory days were somewhat over by the fifties. If I'm honest, I have to admit that after the *Meet Me in St. Louis* movie, everything I did was slightly anticlimactic. I actually didn't enjoy doing *Meet Me . . .* as much as I did less prestigious projects. All the same, I knew I was monumentally fortunate to fall into something as perfect as the Garland-Minnelli musical. Everything about it was winsome; you'd have to be a sourpuss of the first order to fault it in any way.

But my later shows, flawed though they all were, were more fun! The clout of the Mayer-Freed-Edens Empire was extremely effective, but also a little oppressive. These craftsmen were all so good at what that they did there was not a whole lot more for me to do, and that frustrated me after the artistic freedom I had had on Broadway.

The shows and movies that followed didn't, for the most part, light up the sky, but they lit up my *life,* and I personally find life more important than success. Here are a few knee jerk reactions to the jobs that kept me busy after I was discharged from the Army.

Ziegfeld Follies and Good News

The single songs for these extravaganzas were written before my Army tenure, but the films were released afterwards. Lena Horne sang "Love" in the *Follies* and most seductively.

Gene Kelly heard "Pass that Peace Pipe" by Roger Edens, Ralph, and me. He liked it so much he suggested it for the Astaire-Kelly get-together in *Ziegfeld Follies*. However, Fred had expressed a desire for them to sing and dance "The Babbitt and the Bromide" by the Gershwin brothers, and Gene deferred to his senior partner.

Eventually, "Pass that Peace Pipe" was sung and danced by Joan McCracken in *Good News* and boasted a good Kay Thompson vocal arrangement. It gave me my second Academy Award nomination.

Top Banana

This is one of two pseudo-burlesque Broadway musicals I did vocal arrangements for, the other one being *Sugar Babies*. I remember it with affection because of Phil Silvers, who was delightful onstage and off. I remember it even more because it gave me an opportunity to renew my friendship with Johnny Mercer. He was easily one of a handful of the finest lyricists America has ever produced, and this was the first time he wrote his own music instead of collaborating. I felt enormously honored that he chose me to do his vocal arrangements because it was obviously a milestone in his illustrious career.

Athena

This was a very ditzy Pasternak Technicolor splash featuring Jane Powell and Debbie Reynolds among other capable performers.

Debbie Reynolds, me, Jane Powell, and
Ralph Blane in the MGM commissary, 1954.
(photo by MGM)

I have to confess loving the songs, especially "Love Can Change the Stars." MGM released it in 1954. It was Joe Pasternak who reunited Martin and Blane for this movie.

The Girl Rush

This was an out-and-out disaster, the worst I've ever been sucked into. Shooting was prolonged for months during which Edwin Lester invited Ralph and me to write songs for the Mary Martin-Jerome Robbins *Peter Pan,* which was a smash and became a television classic. Rosalind Russell held a contract with us and wouldn't allow us to do *Peter Pan,* even though *The Girl Rush* was in the middle of a layoff of almost a year. Oh well, if you can't take heartbreak, show biz is not for you. We finally got over it, but losing *Peter Pan* was a terrible disappointment to Ralph and me. All we got out of *The Girl Rush* was embarrassment and one modest hit, "An Occasional Man," which Gloria de Haven sang fetchingly.

The title, "An Occasional Man," came to me courtesy of a very dear lady named Clifford Edison, who worked for the Martin family. Clifford was an Afro-American widow who started cooking for us when I was born. During a brief crime wave in Birmingham, my mother became concerned for Clifford's safety.

"Clifford," said my mother, "I'm worried about you. What about that stretch of woods you come through every morning to get to work?"

"Oh, Miz Martin," Clifford laughed, "there ain't nothin' in those woods, [pause] 'cep' an occasional man."

The year after *The Girl Rush*, Rosalind Russell had her greatest triumph when she opened at the Broadhurst Theater in New York in *Auntie Mame*. If anyone ever wants to know what Roz was really like, they have only to watch the equally successful movie of that hilarious comedy, because Roz *was* Auntie Mame. She plays her with bull's-eye accuracy because she had been a reasonable facsimile of Mame for the last forty years.

Miss Russell took Ralph and me to Las Vegas to do research on the movie and it was one of the weirdest weeks of my life. Roz drank too much but never got drunk. She ate too much but never seemed gluttonous. She gambled too much but never lost a penny.

During the run of *Auntie Mame*, I took my mother to meet Roz in her posh apartment at the Hotel Pierre in New York. Roz came on like Queen Marie of Rumania, and in her most upper-clahss voice said, "Mrs. Martin, I was just about to have a glass of sherry. Would you care to join me?"

Ellie Gordon, in her bird-like little Southern voice, replied, "Do you think I could have a double whiskey?" Roz's double take was something to remember.

Thereafter, when I encountered Roz across a crowded room, she would cup her hands around her mouth for greater projection and shout, "Hey, Hugh, how's your whiskey-drinking mother?"

The Girl Most Likely

Though not a pretentious film, it was one of my favorites. Cute story about Jane Powell trying to chose one of three boy friends. I liked working with Stanley Rubin, who produced it with style and taste, and Gower Champion's choreography was stunning, especially "Balboa," in which he dunked a handful of brilliant dancers in the RKO studio's re-creation of Newport Bay. Knockout! Nelson Riddle orchestrated our songs to perfection, and Kaye Ballard was at her comic and vocal best.

Hans Brinker or The Silver Skates

This was the only time I ever wrote an original score for a live TV special—a hair-raising experience, by the way. We couldn't have had better people for it.

Sponsor: Hallmark Hall of Fame

Producer: The talented and gracious Mildred Freed Alberg

Network: NBC

Source: The children's classic by Mary Mapes Dodge. Very outdoorsy and cinematic, with ice skating races and lots of action.

Star: Teen-age idol, Tab Hunter. He looked every inch the heroic young Dutchman, and did his own singing and his own ice-skating. His acting, also, was all we could have hoped for.

Director: Sidney Lumet. Getting him was a coup; he was fresh from the success of his film *Twelve Angry Men*. His ideas were fresh, too; he had never done a musical, and brought some new concepts.

"Rikki," Hans's girlfriend: Peggy King. The high spot of the show was Peggy singing "I Happen to Love You," one of my best ballads. She sang it to Tab in that unique, heartstoppingly beautiful Peggy King voice that "sends the shivers up and down your spinal column."[1] (Thank you, Ira!)

Hans's chum: Dick Button, Olympic ice skating champ, doing his thing on NBC ice.

Book: The redoubtable Sally Benson, no less

Hans's father: Basil Rathbone

Hans's mother: Famed operatic soprano and wonderful actress, Jarmila Novotna

Music director: Franz Allers, who had just completed the same service for *My Fair Lady*.

Orchestrations: Irwin Kostal, soon to become tops in that field. I discovered him on the *Patrice Munsel* TV series, and offered him this assignment, his first crack at a "book" musical. His work in *Hans Brinker* struck me as being absolutely gorgeous.

Tab Hunter wrote a book of memoirs.[2] In it he states, "*Hans Brinker* not only came off without a hitch but also scored a ratings bonanza, becoming the most-watched show in the history of that Sunday-night staple, the *Hallmark Hall of Fame*, a distinction it would hold for the next fourteen years."

---

1 Gershwin, George and Ira, "My Cousin in Milwaukee," from *Pardon My English*, New World Music Co. Ltd.

2 Hunter, Tab, with Eddie Muller. *Tab Hunter Confidential*, New York: Algonquin Books, 2005.

Chapter 41

A Star Is Born

ECENT BOOKS HAVE DESCRIBED MY FALLING OUT with Judy Garland during the making of *A Star Is Born*. Most of them are inaccurate, but one or two authors have recounted the incident truthfully, notably John Fricke in *Judy Garland, World's Greatest Entertainer*[1] and Edward Jablonski in *Harold Arlen: Rhythm, Rainbows and Blues*,[2] both superior biographies.

As early as 1951, while we were still performing at the Palace, Judy and Sid Luft spoke to me about their dream of doing a musical film based on the 1937 Janet Gaynor film, *A Star Is Born*. They told me they were thinking of asking me to provide the songs for it. This did not materialize. Three years later, after signing Harold Arlen and Ira Gershwin for the score, they brought up the subject again.

"Would you consider doing the vocal arrangements and being my vocal coach?" Judy asked me. I told her I thought Roger Edens

---

1 Fricke, John. *Judy Garland: World's Greatest Entertainer*. New York: Henry Holt & Co., 1992.

2 Jablonski, Edward. *Harold Arlen: Rhythm, Rainbows and Blues*. Boston: Northeastern University Press, 1996.

would resent my doing what he had always done for her so brilliantly.

"Oh, no," she assured me. "Roger wants you to do it, hopes you will do it."

I briefly considered saying, "What about Kay Thompson?" Instead, I said, "You bet your life I'll do it. When do we start?"

I flew out to the coast in the spring of 1953, took a room at the Chateau Marmont and, with the hotel's permission, rented a piano for my room. I reported to the Luft residence on Sunset Boulevard, as huge and depressing a home as the mausoleum on the same street where Gloria Swanson told Mr. DeMille she was ready for her close-up.

I showed up there on two consecutive days only to be told by the maid that Mrs. Luft was too ill to rehearse. The third time Judy herself greeted me warmly and led me to a small music room with a piano.

I have berated myself repeatedly through the years for not having been sensitive enough to pick up on her real problem. She was well dressed, her face was the charming oval we all loved, she was appropriately sociable, but there was a kind of suppressed unease behind it all; a demon of fear seemed to possess her. Consequently, we were like strangers, incongruous after the intimacy we had shared in our dressing room with a sheet between us at the Palace. I thought this awkwardness would disappear when we started making music, but it increased. She was in marvelous form vocally; the energy was there, and the intelligence. *What is missing?* I asked myself. The smile, I suddenly realized, that's what was missing. Judy's singing had always sparkled and bubbled and jumped for joy.

She was cranky, too, in a way totally unlike her. She had always latched on immediately to little musical ideas I tried on her. Today, our first crack at the lovely Arlen-Gershwin songs, there was an unspoken resistance to whatever I suggested, especially when we arrived at "The Man that Got Away." I had dreamed of how she would sing it ever since Harold Arlen had sung it for me. He had come to my apartment, performed the entire score for me, and I had been hypnotized. When he sang for me "The Man that Got Away," he dropped his volume to a smoky whisper that evoked the little after-hours joint where Esther Blodgett and her orchestra buddies congregated after their gig, to play and sing just for themselves. I remembered the way Arlen had sung it, and I could already hear, in my imagination, Judy singing it with moody, understated emotion. I felt she and I would be in perfect accord about how it should be done. I was even convinced she would want to sing it in B flat.

"Put it in C," Judy said, imperiously.

"C?" I asked, with genuine surprise.

"Yes, C," she said irritably. "Any objections?"

"Well, yes," I replied, trying not to sound rude. "If you sing it in C, you're going to have to yell by the time you get to the end of the bridge."

"Yell!?" she said so loudly I cringed. "I never yell." She was angry. What had I done, I wondered. I'd been looking forward to this moment for months, and now I'd blown it.

"Well, try it," she demanded. We tried it. She liked it. I hated it.

"Don't you see?" she said, "There has to be a flash of something extraordinary at this moment. If I croon the damn thing, why would Norman Maine see the possibility that I might be a star?"

I didn't argue. We ran it twice, and she did have to yell when she sang, "Fools can be fools, and where's he gone to?" She broke off the rehearsal abruptly and sent me home. I felt like a schoolboy being sent to the principal's office.

In retrospect, I believe Judy's problem was she felt she had to reinvent herself in order to stay on top. In actuality, she was never anywhere except on top. You can't improve on something that's perfect. Have you any suggestions for a rose? Or an orange?

George Cukor tells a story about Judy that is both amusing and revealing. During the making of *A Star Is Born*, he said to her, "Judy, why do you agonize over every scene you do? You know better than anyone what a good actress you are."

"George," she said, "I know that. But every time the camera rolls I think to myself, 'maybe this is the time they're gonna catch me.'"

I love the story because it tells me so much about why Judy does everything a little bit better than anyone else.

"You Gotta Have Me Go with You"

If demons were still hassling Judy when she arrived to make her first sound track, they were certainly nowhere in sight. She was lively, full of jokes, fashionably dressed, and apparently feeling wonderful, which shows what a good performance a star can give when her back is to the wall. The truth was, she felt ghastly; between takes of the number, she had to disappear discreetly into a tiny dressing-room-type cubicle to throw up. I knew so well what she was going through, wanting to be a powerhouse when the red light went on, and fearing she would not live up to expectations.

She needn't have feared. Ray Heindorf stood on the podium in front of one of those incredible Hollywood orchestras, about forty-five top musicians poised to play. One would expect such a large group to be unwieldy and too heavy to swing. *Au contraire!* The minute Ray's baton came down, feet were tapping, fingers were snapping, and the large recording studio was crackling with rich, titillating rhythms from the pen and heart of Harold Arlen.

Then the red light went on, and someone in the control room said, "'You Gotta Have Me Go With You', take one," and

Judy began to sing. It was the first time she had worked since the Palace, and she went at it like a starving man who has been given food. Her voice was rested and clear, her face was animated, and her rhythm was in perfect sync with the orchestra. Indeed, she seemed to be in perfect sync with life. Gone was the nausea, gone were the hostilities, gone were the demons—at least they seemed to be for the few precious moments she was singing.

Two lads from the famous vocal group, The Hi-Lo's, stepped up to a microphone a few feet removed from Judy, and the three of them began to sing my vocal arrangement. Take one was a success with all the staff and tech people on the set, and the engineer in the control room pantomimed "okay" from behind the glass pane.

"We have to do it again," Judy said. "I forgot to laugh."

"Laugh?" came a surprised voice on a loudspeaker.

"Yes, laugh," she repeated. "In the movie, I'm supposed to be leading James Mason through a dance routine. He's all left feet and stepping on me and that breaks me up and I laugh. I forgot to do it."

She turned around and looked at me. "Hugh, Hugh, if I show you which bar that bit comes in, could you do something to make me laugh? I'm so sick it's hard to laugh."

I immediately said, "Of course," then panicked. What in the world could I do to make her laugh when she was feeling so terrible?

"Take two" came the funereal voice. I had about sixty-four bars to get an inspiration. I got it! When I was in grammar school, a little girl had taught me how to make a fish face. Could I still do it? I practiced. I could still do it! I did it, right in the proper two-bar pause. She laughed. We all laughed! I mopped my brow.

"The Man that Got Away"

The next important recording date was "The Man that Got Away," and this one didn't generate laughter except for some at my expense. But I'm getting ahead of myself. "The Man that Got Away" was to be a critical moment in the film. Everyone loved the song, but no one agreed as to how it should be presented. Judy, of course, won the day and her version prevailed. But I was not the only one opposed to her belting, arm-waving, flamboyant concept. Her director, George Cukor, was distraught about it. "If she does a *tour de force* in the first thirty minutes, I have no picture! There's no place to go from there. She's demonstrated that she's a star too soon. Too soon!"

I hugged him. I knew it was presumptuous; I hardly knew the man, but I was so relieved to have an ally.

George looked bamboozled. "I thought *you* put her up to all that carrying on."

"No way," I protested. "I've been imploring her to sing it simply. I told her that she is singing this song as if she were Vicki Lester, and she's still Esther Blodgett. Please," I urged him, "come in right now and tell her that you agree with me. She reveres you. She will listen to you!"

"She will listen to no one," said Mr. Cukor, and he vanished.

I walked onto the recording stage with strong feelings of apprehension. The musicians were tuning up, tootling and scratching and blowing—always such a happy sound. The stage was full of people, not kibitzers, but go-fers, secretaries, technical people, staff, and lackeys.

Enter the star. She looked every bit the star but, unlike the earlier recording date, she was not smiling. The Garland mouth, usually so soft and sweet, had a determined set to it.

"Hi, Ray! How's the orchestration?"

"It's great!"

"Where do you want me?"

The sound engineer approached Judy respectfully. "Miss Garland?"

"Call me Judy."

"Judy, we all know how you hate earphones."

"Oh, golly!" she groaned, "You're not going to . . . ?"

"Not if it really bugs you. But if we could isolate your voice on a separate track, we could do tremendous orchestral things, and I think the final result would really please you."

She consented and was shown into a tiny glass booth, just big enough for two people. The two people were Judy and me. We entered the booth and sat down, each on a little stool. She warmed up on takes one and two. Then, on take three she let us have it—all the stops pulled out.

Cheers, applause, embraces.

"Now," said Judy, "Let's do it in Hugh's key."

I looked as bamboozled as George Cukor had looked. "Judy," I said, "you can't expect forty-five musicians to transpose a complicated orchestration at sight. Especially in five sharps!"

"Of course not. I had Ray order the whole thing copied in 'B'."

Mixed groans and snickers from the band. "B" is an s.o.b. key for instrumentalists.

"Now, now, men and women," said Ray, "it's not that difficult. You've done it before."

I had really wanted it down a full tone but beggars can't be choosers. I was elated that she would throw me a crumb and try it even a half tone lower. Judy sipped coffee while the players ran through the transposition. Then we stepped back into the glass booth and restored our earphones.

About sixteen bars into the number, it was obvious to me that the jig was up. She was very subtly going to humiliate me, going through the motions of singing it with passion but actually walking through it. Her body was there in the booth, two or three feet away from me, but her emotions were miles away in limbo. My heart sank.

When she finished the take, she went back to the vast recording stage and settled back with a couple of friends. She was happier now because she had won the first round; especially happy because she knew she had turned in a strong performance on take three in the key *she* had chosen.

She requested playbacks on the gangbusters take three, followed by the lukewarm rendition in the lower key I had begged for. After the second playback, no one spoke because no one wanted to risk disagreement with Judy. Then a voice rang out, not loud but sharp as a stiletto. "Hugh, you're so f-----g wrong."

Embarrassed giggles came from the entire assemblage, including the large orchestra. The voice could only have come out of one person. Judy's voice has a unique timbre. I froze like a hunting dog in mid-point.

"Come on, Hugh," Judy continued, "Don't you honestly think the higher key is better?"

I tried not to sound angry, but I sounded angry. All eyes were on me.

"I don't know why you ask me, Judy," I said with not much conviction, "I'm always so f-----g wrong."

"You're so f-----g right," she said.

I picked up my briefcase with shaky fingers and headed for the huge iron door. As I fought my way through it, a roar of laughter from the sound stage rang in my ears as I made a clumsy exit.

I was a hazard on the road as I drove back to the Chateau Marmont. Fortunately I got there without killing anybody. I went to the desk and mentioned that I would like to keep my room two more nights. I spent the next day packing, and drove out the day after that. My piano was rented, but the car was my own, so I simply pointed it toward the rising sun and kept driving.

Roaring through the Rockies, I was listening to a CBS newscast. There was an entertainment report with an interesting item about my ex-boss. "We asked Judy Garland to comment on the defection from *A Star Is Born* of Hugh Martin, her vocal coach. She replied, 'I have no time for prima donnas in my life.'"

This quote boomeranged slightly since the media by this time perceived Garland as the mother of all prima donnas.

There are few things more contemptible than running out on friends when they are in trouble. If I had had any idea of what Judy was going through at the time she was beginning to film *A Star Is Born,* I would have swallowed my pride and stayed on to help her. What I thought at the time was hostility, I now realize in hindsight was fear at the thought that she might fail in this project. I was offended, of course, at being the object of her profanity. No one relishes being the butt of a joke, especially if the jokester is getting solid laughs. Not snickers, mind you, laughs—big fat bellylaughs. It's an acknowledged fact that Judy Garland, not primarily a comedienne, was almost the funniest lady in a town that likes to laugh, especially at the expense of others.

I was watching *A Star Is Born* lately and the realization that I had done the wrong thing when Judy attacked me in front of a sound stage full of people suddenly hit me. What I did was quit, the exact opposite of what I should have done, which was to laugh and forgive her.

I learned early in our partnership that she loved to belt. She loved to belt because it was the fuse that sparked the explosion, the kind of audience reaction that sets a performer's heart on fire and starts the adrenalin flowing. It's hard to resist but it can be self-destructive, artistically and physically. Take belting a step too far and it becomes yelling.

"I never yell," she had said to me. But Judy, dear, you did yell. Not only did you occasionally yell, you started the whole cycle of yelling. Pop singers never did that before you; now it's standard procedure.

It was mainly her fault, but her audiences, intoxicated by her persona, must share some of the blame. The louder she sang, the more they applauded; the more they applauded, the louder she sang. It became a neurotic game, the crowd lusting for what she gave them, and she, drinking it all in and saturating her spirit with denials of the fears and phobias and paranoia. Eventually, of course, the Garland voice itself, that Stradivarius of human instruments, fell by the wayside. I listened in sorrow to the wreckage of her voice, and grieved that she had not allowed me to protect it.

Sid and Judy must have been angrier at me than I was at them because they decided to deny me screen credit for my work on *A Star Is Born*. Just for the record, I did the vocal arrangements for the following numbers: "You Gotta Have Me Go with You," "Here's What I'm Here For," and "Lose that Long Face." In addition to the vocal arrangements, I wrote an introduction and coda for "The Man that Got Away."

Judy and I were never romantically involved. My love for her was strictly based on a kind of soulmate relationship, a strong, compelling trust we thought could never be broken. It was I who broke it, unfortunately, when I compulsively walked off *A Star Is Born*.

I was present at her historic Carnegie Hall appearance in April, 1961. There is no denying that it was a *tour de force* of almost unparalleled power. As I sat in the top balcony, after she had sung about a half-dozen songs, I found myself acting out the lyrics of one of Jimmy Durante's trademark comedy songs:

Did you ever have the feeling that you wanted to go
And still have the feeling that you wanted to stay?
You knew it was right, wasn't wrong.
Still you knew it wouldn't take very long.
It's tough to have the feeling that you wanted to go

And still have the feeling that you wanted to stay.
Start to go. Change your mind.
Start to go again and change your mind again.[3]

I finally had to leave the auditorium because almost every song began with the orchestra driving, driving, driving. Soon her little foot began stamping, stamping, stamping, and the audience was screaming, screaming, screaming. I couldn't take it. Out on 57th Street, I could still hear the cheering, cheering, cheering from inside.

I am probably the one person in the world who didn't like Judy at Carnegie Hall. I know I sound like a kook; I would have had to be insane not to know that I was in the presence of genius. But Miss Genius and I had been through a long-standing tug-of-war about her singing style. Vincente Minnelli and I envisioned Judy as a musical Sarah Bernhardt, a consummate singing, dancing actress of enormous sensitivity and subtlety. Frances Gumm (Judy) had the blood of vaudeville in her veins and eventually succumbed to the razzmatazz of the two-a-day. I was able to sit through only about fifteen minutes at Carnegie Hall. I knew I had lost and I'm a bum loser, so I picked up my marbles and left.

Reconciliation

I'm often asked whether Judy and I ever reconciled, and the happy answer is "yes." Two or three years after our donnybrook, I got a great idea for a musical I wanted to write as a starring vehicle for mother and daughter, Judy and Liza. What to do? Do I dare present it to her? Will she shove it in my face and slam the door after me?

---

3 Music and lyrics by Jimmy Durante. Published by Jimmy Durante.

Faint heart never won fair lady, I decided, and I made my offer in a letter. It reached her at her New York hotel just as she was checking out. She wired me her response. The telegram was about four feet long, almost as tall as she was, and it was as loving and dear as anything I've ever read. I framed it and hung it where all could see because I was so proud of it. When I transferred to the West Coast, one of the movers ripped it off, but the sweetness of it will always remain in my heart. They can't take that away from me.

Chapter 42

The Crash

I HAVE GONE THROUGH MORE IMMOLATIONS AND RESTORATIONS than a phoenix. I had a propensity for making bad choices that kept me in some kind of trouble most of the time. I played fast and loose with morality, and deep in my guts, I knew I'd eventually get my comeuppance. I did, big time, in 1960.

I was forty-six years old, happy and healthy, and I had tasted success and failure in large draughts. In 1960 I was on the upswing because Noël Coward had given Tim Gray and me the rights to musicalize his comedy, *Blithe Spirit*. I had loved the play ever since I saw it on Broadway at the Morosco Theater in November of 1941. Many consider this to be Noël's finest comedy. Amazingly, when we asked him how much he wanted for the rights, he had said, "Nothing, boys. Just do a good job."

We were doubly amazed because a month earlier, we had inquired of Garson Kanin the possibility of our acquiring the rights from him to musicalize *Born Yesterday*. His reply had been, "You can have it, fellas, for a million dollars."

I love Noël Coward for many reasons, certainly not the least of them being this extraordinary act of generosity. Tim and I were very much johnny-come-latelies in the London scene. Noël was king of the roost. But he had been a fan of our *Love from Judy* and had let it be known to all and sundry that he thought it was the best musical originating on British soil in many years. His praise for our efforts was a factor in the show's success and probably helped it achieve its gratifying year-and-a-half run at the Saville Theater.

Timothy and I were back in America when we learned of Noël's gift, but we felt that, ideally, the show should play London before Broadway, so we went back to England to write it. Tim flew over a month before me to look for suitable and reasonable living quarters. I followed by ship in the company of a good friend, Vernon Lusby. We crossed the Atlantic eastward in the summer of 1960 on the Dutch ship *Noordam* and I had hardly had time to sharpen my pencils when I had a full-blown nervous breakdown. The ability to sleep, or read, or concentrate vanished almost overnight. Worst of all, I was unable to eat. I mean at all! I could force myself to swallow food, but instead of strengthening me, as food is supposed to do, it weakened me and made me ill. My world collapsed in less than a week.

When I reached London, Tim was naturally very upset. Noël was notified and he was more than upset; he was disgusted with me. Not a whit more, you may be sure, than I was with myself.

I managed to suppress the news back home in the States, but London's theatrical community is small and tightly knit and the news spread quickly; "Have you heard? That American songwriter, the one who wrote *Love from Judy,* has cracked up rather seriously."

Tim Gray hung in with me for a reasonable length of time, but when I got worse and worse, he split. I do not say this in anger. It was the normal thing to do under the circumstances. I had led him to Fort Knox and slammed the door in his face. I might easily have done the same thing to him if the situation had been reversed. But he was very supportive the first few weeks. He fed me, medicated me, even gave me enemas when my body totally shut down. He took me to a psychiatrist named Malcolm Pines. Even today, fifty years later, the mere mention of his name starts me quivering. Our first conversation ended like this:

Hugh: Dr. Pines, is it possible that I may be losing my mind?

Dr. Pines: We'll have to see about that.

He stashed me into a commune for loonies. I only stayed about ten minutes. I happened to spy a typed menu on one of the walls and it announced that supper would consist of Toad-in-the-Hole and Cornish Pasties. I didn't know what they were and was not eager to find out.

I stayed longer at the second facility, three weeks. It was the Atkinson-Morley Hospital in Wimbledon for mentally disturbed patients and it was grim but endurable. It looked like Manderley in *Rebecca*, and I recall hoping that Judith Anderson would appear some night and set fire to it.

I still couldn't sleep or eat; they fed me eggs to keep me alive, but most of my hours were spent simply weeping. Nothing histrionic, mind you, I just sat in a chair and wept quietly, going through cartons of tissues.

It was probably the single most horrible event of my life, and one of the daily traumas of it was shaving. When they admitted me to the hospital they took from me anything sharp that might be a suicide aid, including, of course, my razor. They replaced it with an electric one, but the real suicide aid was not the shaver, it was the mirror. Every morning when I got out of bed after an interminable night of sleeping pills, but no sleep, I had to face that mirror as I passed the Norelco over my haggard face.

"You're crazy," I would say to that face in the mirror. "You're stark staring insane, and you'll never be anything else."

I had absolutely nothing to do so I walked incessantly. I couldn't eat or sleep but I could walk; I didn't want to sit in a crowded ward all day with a lot of people even more disturbed than I. So I walked and walked and walked—around the quaint old English streets when I could occasionally get permission to go outside, but usually just all over the hospital, down every corridor searching for I didn't know what.

Having thoroughly done all three floors, I went down to the basement one day and came upon a little chapel. I walked in tentatively, found I was alone, and sat down and looked about. It was a neat place to worship. It had the usual accouterments—an altar covered by a white and gold cloth, a large Bible on a stand, a stained-glass window, and little soft kneelers such as are found in Catholic churches, although this chapel had a sign posted to the effect that it was non-denominational.

Suddenly I became a child, a small and terrified child, one who has just had a hideous nightmare, or one who has had a fight and lost, or one who has, without explanation, been rejected by a parent.

"God!" I sobbed, "What is happening? I don't understand. Don't you love me? I've tried everything and nothing works. Am I going crazy? Should I kill myself? Help me! Help me!"

I threw myself on the floor, face down in front of the altar and wept for a few minutes. Then I cried out, "I don't even know that there *is* a God. But if there is, if you can hear me, please, please, pull me out of this miry pit."

"Miry pit" was a strange thing for me to say, and I don't know what put it into my unstable mind at that moment. It's a phrase from the Old Testament, but I had hardly ever read the Bible.

Weakly, I got to my feet and went back to the ward. I thought it was the end, but it was the beginning. Sometimes there is only one place to start from—the bottom.

After three weeks of that scene, I found a public telephone and dropped a coin into it. "Timmy!" I cried, "I've got to get out of this nuthouse. If I'm not bonkers already, I soon will be!"

God bless my partner! He jumped in a cab, was in my room an hour and a half after my phone call, and started throwing my meager possessions into a suitcase he had brought with him.

"Don't we have to tell the doctor?" I asked.

"No," Tim said firmly. "I can't stand to see you like this."

We stopped by the cashier's desk to get the bad news. I was braced for a sum that would wipe out my life savings.

"How much does Mr. Martin owe you, please?" inquired Tim.

"Nothing, sir," was the astonishing reply. Hooray for the British National Health Service!

It was the first good news I had received in weeks and I cried again, tears of relief this time. What was happening to me was a horror story, but if it had to happen, I'm glad it happened in the U.K.

About a month later, I was walking along a street near Buckingham Palace. I passed a small health food store and stopped to look into its large display window. A tiny jar of cashew butter caught my eye and for a split second I thought, "Mmm, I bet that would taste good."

When I realized the import of my fleeting thought, I blinked. Had I actually thought what I thought I had thought? Pretty insignificant to a normal guy, but to someone who had had no desire for food of any kind for months, it was a memorable moment. I went into the store, bought the cashew butter, along with a round tin of what we call crackers and the British call biscuits. That evening at suppertime, instead of the baby food I had been forcing down in order to stay alive, I had biscuits and nut butter and two glasses of cold milk. It was the most enjoyable meal I had eaten in months.

My appetite slowly returned and by Christmas I was eating normally. *What on earth had happened to me?* I wondered. The only person who came up with the correct answer was Vernon Lusby. Vernon was a living saint, probably the most unselfish friend I ever had. After our ship had reached Southampton, Vernon had gone on to the continent for several months. When he returned to London, he was the first person to come up with the explanation.

He gave it to me straight. "For ten years you ran to that devil, Max Jacobson, every time you got depressed. He pumped you full of amphetamines and you're surprised to have a nervous breakdown? You're lucky he didn't kill you."

Vernon was smart. How had I missed anything so obvious? But I had. It never occurred to me I was just another victim of Jacobson's hold on some of the theater's brightest and best. What fools we were to be taken in by this Rasputin.

"Of course," I said to Vernon instantly. "What an idiot I am not to have figured it out myself."

Vernon Lusby was one of four people who stuck by me all the way, no matter how many chips went down. So did Del Hanley, my talented demo singer, Anne Cox, my sweet, wonderfully British secretary, and my psychiatrist, Dr. Peter Hays. None of them ever gave up on me. They supported me physically and emotionally, and I gratefully place them in my little choir of guardian angels.

When I returned from England, I was feeling, understandably, not a little insecure. I had reached a fork in the road; I knew the wrong choices would take me once and for all out of the theater and I wasn't ready to give it up. I don't love the theater the way I used to; indeed, when I watch the "Tony's" each year. I am increasingly appalled at what Broadway has become. Broadway! The apex of all my fantasies! The erstwhile heaven on earth that had made me tingle with delight when I fled Birmingham, Alabama, for the domain of my dreams. Is this what you've come to?

But I digress. In 1961, after spending time in the cracker factory in Wimbledon, my self esteem was at a new low. Some beautiful melodies were coming out of my fingers, thank you Lord, but lyrics had sometimes been a stumbling block and I decided for once in my life to play it safe. In my little black book, two names were etched as being potentially top of the heap lyricists: Sheldon Harnick and Marshall Barer. Whom to pop the question to? I agonized over it for some time and chose Marshall. I was dazzled by Sheldon's brilliance and I still am, but Marshall's poetic soul had a great appeal for me.

Marshall came across a three-page outline by George Bradshaw and Bob Thomsen called "Music in the Night." It was a dead steal from a famous short story by John Collier, but it intrigued Marshall and he asked me to write it with him.

"Someone to Talk to," "You're About to Be Beautiful," "The Up Number" "The Face On the Cutting-Room Floor"—these are memorable songs and I will always bless Marshall for jump-starting them. Yes, each lyric came from his magical pen before I ever had at them, much as Rodgers and Hammerstein used to do. Our *pièce de resistance* was a lyric Marshall wrote called "Wasn't It Romantic?" He assigned me the task of setting it to music that would harmonize with the Rodgers and Hart masterpiece, "Isn't It Romantic?" The plan was to have Jeanette MacDonald sing it in counterpoint against her own image in a clip from the 1932 film *Love Me Tonight*. Years later, Marshall and I had a date to play our double whammy for Dick Rodgers but our golden chance passed us by.

We fashioned the show for Jeanette and Liza Minnelli. Liza adored it and was gung ho to do it. Jeanette was impressed, too, and I think she would have done it, but Ol' Devil Cancer got there first. Another burst bubble; they go with the territory so if you can't survive them, just don't fall in love and get your heart broken.

The day Marshall Barer visited me in Encinitas, he was wearing a yellow shirt with a magenta neck scarf and orange socks. I attributed this combination of colors to a lapse in his color sense, but I couldn't have been more wrong; if ever a man was a total artist, it was Marshall. When we took long walks together, he spoke in rhymes the entire time; some of it beautiful poetry that he had already written, some of it verse that he composed as we walked along. All of it was first-class.

When we got back to my house he pointed to his car, which was parked in front of it. It was a Mercedes that had been transformed into a decoupage; he had covered the whole chassis with denim from vintage blue jeans. While we had been walking, it had attracted a small crowd and a lot of snapshots were being taken. This was classic Marshall Barer.

With Joni Eareckson Tada.

Chapter 43

Three Overwhelming Experiences

WHY FOURTEEN YEARS WENT BY after the Wimbledon experience before I had a real conversion is something I can't explain. I was trying during those years. I radically changed my lifestyle and terminated some addictions I thought I could never kick.

Finally it happened in 1974. I was in Birmingham with my family, almost completely recovered from the 1960 breakdown but still far from having robust health. My doctor did a checkup on me and recommended I enter St. Vincent's Hospital as an in-patient for some tests.

My brother Gordon accompanied me the December afternoon I was admitted. Halfway to the reception desk, I heard, over the murmur of a crowded foyer, a Voice. The Voice said quite clearly (but not audibly), "Hugh, share your room!" I sloughed it off and thought I was having a kind of delusive daydream. But the command in my head was repeated. "Hugh, share your room!"

It was even more compelling the second time, so much so I said to my brother, "Gordon, you're going to hate me. Do you suppose I could get a semi-private room? Or even a ward?"

My long-suffering brother shot me a dirty look. "After I knocked myself out to get you a private room? You said you couldn't face people."

"I know I did. Please be patient."

I didn't have the guts to tell him about the Voice. I wanted him on my side. He marched me to the receptionist and made the request for me. The young lady at the desk shot *him* a dirty look.

"You said on the phone—"

"I know what I said," Gordon replied politely. "The plans have been changed."

"Well, your plans may have changed, but ours haven't. We're booked up solid. Sorry."

The phone on her desk rang and she picked it up. After a few seconds, a surprised look came onto her face and she said, "Really? I thought you were going to check out after the weekend. Well, thank you."

She gave us a sweet Alabama smile. "You must have a little pull with the Almighty. I can put you in a room for two in about an hour. Go up to the second floor and wait there while the bed is made up."

My roommate turned out to be William Lester, an assistant pastor in a local black Seventh-day Adventist church. He was a personable, middle-aged gentleman who had just undergone surgery. I could see in his face that he was dealing with a lot of pain. The doctor, with the help of the nurse, eased Mr. Lester into bed, and gave him medication for the pain. He also instructed him to call for assistance if he needed to get out of bed.

After supper, I saw Mr. Lester painfully crawling out of bed. I was uncomfortable at the thought of him doing it against orders, but I didn't feel I knew him well enough to protest. He dropped to his knees, holding onto the bed and appeared to be praying silently. Afterward, he began to inch himself back into bed.

I couldn't keep silent this time. "I heard what the doctor told you. Why don't you—I mean it's none of my business, but why did you just do what he told you not to do?"

"Oh," he said, "I'm a Seventh-day Adventist. We like to kneel at sunset and thank and praise the Lord. Friday night, you know, beginning of the Sabbath."

I was surprised. More than that, impressed. I felt I had been led to that room for a specific reason. The next day I asked him a lot of soul-searching questions and I liked his answers. But it wasn't his answers that triggered my conversion. It seemed orchestrated from above: the mysterious Voice in the foyer, the sudden availability of a room for two patients, the unusual coincidence of my roommate being a devout Christian, most of all, his genuine reverence. Put them all together and it seemed undeniable that it was the most important day of my life.

I am a simple man who has never seen the inside of a seminary. My theological education is zilch. I can try to tell you how I felt after my Brother Lester experience but I can't explain it. I can only tell you the phenomenon occurred to me not gradually, but suddenly, like a black-and-white movie that suddenly bursts into Technicolor. I had never had any aptitude for prayer. It had always been something I felt I was supposed to do, so I went through the motions. Ditto going to church. Now I wanted to go and go and go, even when there was no worship service or any people there except me. Now it was God's House, not just a building with stained-glass windows and religious symbols.

I had the same feelings about the Bible. I had tried to read the Bible off and on my whole life, and there were certain passages that made sense to me, but 95 percent of it was gobbledygook. Oh, but now, what a difference! When I read it, the truth of it leapt off the page at me. I understood it! I couldn't believe what was happening.

Of course, it must be understood that in defining the moment when I was "born again," I was not saved by doctrine, or dogma, or creed, or legalism of any kind. I was saved by Jesus Christ, who gave His life to save sinners, of whom, I can truthfully say along with the Apostle Paul, I was chief.

More than thirty years have passed since that life-changing experience. The ups and downs of daily life have continued, but the joy and the "blessed assurance" have never left me.

Del Delker

My next overwhelming experience was serving as accompanist for a marvelous gospel singer named Del Delker. I used to hear her on a Christian radio ministry called "The Voice of Prophecy." I had been captivated by her rich, velvety contralto. She seemed to me the gospel singer deluxe—a spiritual "other side of the coin" to Judy Garland.

As I listened to Del on the radio, she gradually became a kind of "magnificent obsession" to me. I was convinced that I was the only person in the world who was qualified to be her pianist. My friends all laughed at my megalomania. They said I was reaching for the moon, but I had the last laugh—able to say (as Audrey Hepburn murmured happily in Billy Wilder's *Sabrina*), "I think the moon is reaching for me."

I got the job by sheer audacity, but the important thing is I got it. Del and I criss-crossed the whole U.S.A. for four glorious summers (1994–1998) doing concerts in churches and at camp meetings. I begged her to take me along on her overseas assignments but she never relented.

"It would kill you, Hugh," she said." I'm a tough broad but even I come home totally zonked out. You wouldn't come home at all except possibly in a pine box."

I accepted her verdict. But those four glorious summers were the high spot of my life, not just spiritually, but in every way. Sometimes, even now, when I'm waiting to fall asleep, I see the faces of the good folks we sang for: sweet, godly faces, like no other faces I've ever seen. We loved them a lot and they loved us a lot. There were standing ovations at some of the meetings; those thrilled us, of course, but there was little ego in our appreciation. We knew it was for Someone greater than we. Regardless of whom it was for, we ate it up!

Del Delker, my remarkable gospel singer,
with Elaine Harrison and me on a camp meeting tour in1987.

Sharing the Palace stage with Garland, Arthur Freed musicals at MGM, hit shows on Broadway with long lines at the box office and rave reviews from the newspapers—none of these could ever hold a candle to a good old-fashioned camp meeting with all the stops pulled out. *"Give Me that Old Time Religion!"*

Joni

Another overwhelming experience was meeting a lady named Joni Eareckson Tada. Joni is one of the most selfless and dedicated Christians I have ever been inspired by—in a class with Corrie ten Boom, and Dr. Martin Luther King, Jr.

If anyone was handed a lemon it was Joni (pronounced Johnny); as a beautiful young girl of seventeen in 1967, she dove into Chesapeake Bay (not realizing that the tide had gone out) and broke her neck. The doctor's verdict was shattering; Joni would never walk again, nor would she be able to use her arms. At such a vulnerable age, Joni was a quadriplegic.

It would have crushed almost anybody else in the world, but it was especially hard for Joni because she was a superb athlete: she excelled at horseback riding and used her perfect body to swim, run track, and dance ballet.

It is difficult for me to conceive of triumphing when life hands you a lemon like that. She took it and made the most gigantic, Technicolor, ginger-peachy, God-kissed lemonade ever concocted. She created a ministry for the disabled called *Joni and Friends,* which has brought hope and help to thousands of disabled persons. There is a branch of *JAF* called *Wheels for the World,* which distributes wheelchairs to thousands of crippled men, women, and children in third-world countries.

A word about Joni's face. Yet even as I write this, I know that there are no words to describe it. My little friend, Reyna Delgado, just brought me a photograph of Joni smiling, and she said, "I can't tell you what her face does for me. It is something I don't understand myself." And she left the room.

Five minutes later, she returned and said excitedly, "I have figured out what it is. It is God's love. I've heard about God's love all my life and never could quite imagine it. But there it is—when I look at Joni's face."

A face that could have been twisted with bitterness because of her immense suffering, instead is radiant with God's love.

Chapter 44

High Spirits

$\mathcal{I}$ HAVE POIGNANT MEMORIES of Dr. Peter Hays, my seeing-eye dog during the psychological blindness I experienced in 1960 when I became unglued in London. The memory I treasure most is a conversation in his office fronting Hyde Park Corner. I was huddled miserably in a chair opposite the desk where he was seated. He said, "Hugh, you know psychiatrists are warned not to become too involved with the suffering of their patients. But I have to tell you, I've never treated anyone whom I wanted so passionately to get well."

Let me fast-forward to December 1963. Dr. Hays has traveled 3,000 miles to Boston, Massachusetts, for a medical conference. In a taxi, on the way from the airport to his hotel, he catches a glimpse of the marquee of the Colonial Theater. The name "Hugh Martin" is emblazoned there in bright lights. After checking in at his hotel, he gets my address from the stage doorman and finds we're both staying at the Touraine Hotel. When he finally reaches me, he learns that *High Spirits* is none other than *Blithe Spirit*. "Is that the show you swore you couldn't write? In fact, didn't you swear you would never write again?"

Marquee of Alvin Theater, N.Y., for High Spirits, *1964.*

There are times when it's a pleasure to be wrong. I got seats for my beloved psychiatrist for an evening performance. I was still a baby Christian, but even then I recognized that a coincidence is often "a little miracle in which God chooses to be anonymous."

Re-winding to December 1960, I gradually regained my health and was even able to have myself a merry little Christmas in London. In January 1961, I flew back to New York, having given up all hope of our *Blithe Spirit* project ever materializing.

Two years went by and then, on an impulse, I called Tim in London. We had not spoken to each other since we parted company at the low spot of my breakdown.

Hugh: Timothy, I have a hunch the voice you're hearing is one you never want to hear again.

Tim: Who is this?

Hugh: It's Hugh, Tim. Hugh Martin.

Tim: Hugh! How are you? Where are you?

I filled him in concerning the three years that had elapsed since our dream project had broken up and washed away like a sand castle under the ocean's waves. As I told him what a rough time I had endured, I could hear him softening.

Tim: That Max Jacobson! I knew he was killing you. I tried to tell you and you wouldn't listen.

Hugh: I should have. Have you heard about his losing his license? Big front page story in *The New York Times*.

Tim: Oh, good night! Poor Max. The terrible thing is I couldn't help liking Max in spite of himself.

Hugh: I know, I feel the same way. But you're right. He did come close to killing me. Listen, about *Blithe Spirit*, would you, I mean, could you—that is—

Tim: Would I what? What are you driving at?

Hugh: It's too good to scrap. Why don't we finish the job on spec, I mean, we won't even tell Noël we're doing it. And then . . . and then . . . we'll sing the whole score to him. He won't be able to resist it. We'll bowl him over.

Tim: Hugh!

I could hear him choking up.

Tim: I want to. I really do. But I'm working in a show.

Hugh: Listen, friend, when your show closes, you can stay with me till you find work here.

Tim: Hugh!

He was choking again.

Hugh: You don't have to talk. Thank God for your enthusiasm. I can't stand apathetic people. Let me know when you can come.

He flew to New York after his show closed and this time we went to work in earnest. We agreed on a schedule and adhered to it faithfully. It included times when we worked separately and times when we came together to blend, throw out, agree on, wrangle over, whatever it took to whip the thing into shape for Noël. Unlike my collaboration with Ralph, which had been essentially the pooling of songs

Timothy Gray and me, 1964.

written by one or the other of us, this partnership was very vital and synergistic. We fed on each other's creative talents like parasites, so our writing sessions were stormy, frustrating, and often thrilling.

One of Timothy's working habits that delighted me most would occur when I presented him with an idea that set him off. He would smile a beatific smile, grab my hand, and place it over his heart. He wanted to show me that my idea had pleased him so much that it physically caused his heart to beat faster!

I remember the night we wrote "You'd Better Love Me," which has had a decent exposure through the years.

Hugh: Tim, I've written a little tune I hope you'll like. It sounds very Vernon Duke-ish, but I didn't steal it; it's original.

I played the first few bars for him. Tim looked thoughtful.

Hugh: You don't like it.

Tim: Don't be so hasty. I do like it.

Hugh: But?

Tim: But that low note at the end of the first phrase. Does it have to dip so low?

Hugh: Of course it does. If it doesn't, there's no point to all those thirds.

Tim: Now, Hughie, wait a minute. You know a hell of a lot more about music than I do, but sometimes you get a little highfalutin'. Bear with me. What if that line went like this?

He sang it, slipping in a higher note to replace the offending low note. It was my turn to look thoughtful.

Tim: You hate it.

Hugh: I want to hate it because I didn't think of it.

Tim: And, Hugh, I think it cuts off a minor third of the singing range. That's a plus.

It was and I was sold. We started fishing about for ideas for a lyric.

Tim: It sounds like Elvira.

Hugh: When I was a teenager, a hundred years ago, I liked a

song called "Gather Lip Rouge While You May." I just wondered if we could do anything with the phrase 'while you may.' It has a nice sound, I think.

Tim looked blank, then suddenly his eyes and nose and mouth all went in different directions.

Tim: *"You'd better love me while you may."*

Hugh: I love it!

Tim: Wait a minute.

Hugh: We sound like Ann Sothern and Robert Young writing *Lady Be Good.*

Tim: Shut up.

I shut up. He sang a couplet to the new tune we had just operated on.

Tim: (singing) *You'd better love me while you may. Tomorrow I may fly away.*

We gave each other one of those "aren't we wonderful?" looks.

Hugh: In the second half, what about *You'd better love me while I'm here?*

Tim didn't miss a beat. *"I have been known to disappear,"* he said smugly.

Hugh: We *are* Ann Sothern and Robert Young.

Tim: Which one are you?

Looking back over my life and good times, it's apparent to me that Timothy Gray was the best writing partner I ever had. We were yin and yang, harmoniously congenial in many ways but just opposite enough to create a nice stimulation for our lyrics. A good example of this is "I Know Your Heart by Heart" from *High Spirits*. I wrote it one day in London and presented it to him expecting kudos and pats on the head. Instead, I got knit brows and a faraway look. He could see I was disappointed so he hastened to say, "This is really good, Hugh, we can use this. But I have a crazy idea of how to make it better. It's true Charles is infatuated with Elvira, so it's logical he should sing a paean of praise. But he also was well aware of her infidelities and loose ways. Better we write a lyric bringing out both her virtues *and* her vices."

Writing a vocal arrangement of High Spirits, *1963.*

I immediately wrote the line "I'm drawn to you, but I'm on to you."

"That's it," shouted Timothy, "You've got it!" Tim rewrote the lyric as a mixture of sweet and sour, and the results were twice as exciting as mine, and infinitely better for the story. The ending, which used to be,

> *I know your heart by,*
> *Your loving heart by,*
> *I know your heart by heart*

now became

> *I know your heart by,*
> *Your cheating heart by,*
> *I know your heart by heart.*

Tim wrote the "book" adaptation of Noël's play, *Blithe Spirit*, entirely by himself. He offered me the opportunity to collaborate with him on the script, but I declined. Not that I wouldn't have thoroughly enjoyed doing it, but I felt if I didn't give my full attention to the score, it would suffer. So I concentrated on the music. We wrote the lyrics together, approximately fifty-fifty. The responsibility for being faithful to Noël's play, while at the same time opening it up inventively to accommodate the songs, fell totally on Tim's shoulders. Every time I see that show, I marvel at how expertly he did it. It never sounds as if anyone other than Noël had written it, yet there are long stretches of material added by Tim that blend with the original play seamlessly.

We kept chipping away for several months, never talking about it to anyone except our closest friends, because we were so afraid Noël would hear about it and put the kibosh on us. We must have succeeded in our secrecy because when the awful moment arrived and we phoned to ask Noël if he would listen to our efforts, our request obviously took him off guard. He had flown in from London just about the time we finished the first draft, so we pounced on him. Usually so poised and suave, he sounded flustered when we told him we had bitten the bullet and written the whole kit and caboodle without rights or permission of any kind, strictly on spec. We said, "All we want is to perform it for you; if you don't like it, we'll just ditch the whole thing and never mention it again."

What happened next is told so well in Cole Leslie's *Remembered Laughter*[1] that a brief quote from Coward's diary tells the story better than I ever could.

> *A great surprise happened. Hugh Martin and Timothy Gray came to play the score of their musical version of* Blithe. *I was all set to turn it down because it really has been going on far too long and I was sick of all the frigging about. Coley and I sat with our mouths open. The music is melodic and delightful,*

1 Cole, Leslie, *Remembered Laughter*. New York: Alfred A. Knopf, 1977.

the lyrics witty, and they have done a book outline keeping to my original play and yet making it effective as a musical. I am not only relieved but delighted. I have told them to go ahead.

I shall never forget that afternoon in the living room of Noël's New York apartment. There were five people present: Noël, Leslie Cole, Del Hanley, Tim, and myself. Tim and Del sang the score with great energy and humor, and I was in good form at Noël's piano. There was a moment I especially treasure: Del, during the final song, hit a high note with such power and precision that the dozen roses in a vase on the piano simultaneously dropped all their petals. While everyone was laughing about it, Noël said he couldn't resist an audition with a finish that slick! He added, "Yes, of course you can have the rights. Would you like me to direct it?"

"Would we like you to direct it? Did we hear you all right? Ask us some more funny questions, Master!"

After a few sketchy plans, we departed, walking several feet above the ground. We spied a Catholic Church, crept in and pushed some bills down a slot, lit a big beautiful candle, and gave thanks.

With Noël now sponsoring us and even offering to be our director, finding a producer was suddenly not a problem. Tim had a friend named Robert Fletcher, an excellent designer of sets and costumes for the theater. Bob suggested we contact Lester Osterman, which we did. After hearing the score, he offered to produce it in association with Fletcher and Richard Horner. Noël approved the setup and we were off and running. After several conferences, we chose Fletcher for décor, Danny Daniels for choreography, Fred Werner for musical direction, and Harry Zimmerman for orchestrations.

Now the fun part began—choosing our cast. Dozens of names were tossed into the ring and most were unceremoniously tossed out again. We had gone through a scroll of possible "Madame Arcati's" when Lester casually said, "What about Beatrice Lillie?" The response was so loud I think it scared him. Noël berated himself for not having thought of his oldest and one of his dearest friends in show business; but he won some brownie points by suggesting Tammy Grimes for "Elvira," a role as tricky to cast as "Arcati." It turned out to be an inspired suggestion. Tammy's performance was not as spectacular as Miss Lillie's, but it was equally effective. She looked enchanting in her gray ghost costume, especially designed by Valentina. When she sang our songs, their mocking innuendoes and seductive nuances were vastly enhanced by her unique vocal style.

Timothy Gray, Beatrice Lillie, and me, 1963.

We wanted Laurence Olivier to play "Charles Condamine," and since he was in New York briefly at the time we were casting, we closed in on him in his tiny room at the Algonquin Hotel. We expected a polite refusal, but to our amazement, he said, "Yes, I'll do it."

We were thrilled, naturally, but our elation diminished a bit when he added, "If you'll wait a year for me. I have some commitments I can't extricate myself from."

Lester and Noël had to make the painful decision not to wait for Sir Laurence. We were all bitterly disappointed; it's not easy to turn down the greatest actor in the world! Instead, we engaged Edward Woodward, a fine actor who did a first-rate job. In hindsight, Lester and Noël made the right choice. They had the theater, they had the backing, and if we were to get Lady Peel (Bea Lillie), we all knew it was now or never. We had heard disturbing rumors that her memory was on the verge of vanishing. We didn't have the luxury of waiting another year for her.

Tim and I, blindly optimistic, pooh-poohed the rumors about Miss Lillie, but when we went into rehearsal, we discovered they were not rumors, they were facts, and very distressing facts at that. Bea was dynamic with the script in her hand; the minute it was taken away, she couldn't remember a single line.

Osterman and Coward called a secret emergency meeting. A vote was called for in regard to releasing Beatrice Lillie and engaging another actress. The vote was unanimous in favor of replacing her, except for one vote. Mine. I stood firm to hang in with her. "This is insanity," I pleaded. "She is the funniest woman in the world. Lots of actors can't remember their lines after only three days, especially those first three stress-filled days of being eye-balled by hordes of strangers. Keep her at least a week," I begged. "If it's hopeless after a week, I'll give you my consent."

Legally, according to Equity rules, they couldn't fire her without my vote, and they could see by my clenched teeth and steely eyes that I was not about to give in.

I got my reward. After a week, Bea's memory slowly began to function, and I had the intense joy of being able to say, "I told you so!" to all and sundry. The performance that ultimately resulted is the most wildly funny one I've ever witnessed, and many theater buffs agree with me. It's not often, during out-of-town tryouts, for the staff and authors of a play to be observed nightly falling into each other's arms, tears of laughter happily raining down on each other's blue serge suits. The public, even the critics, concurred. Watching Bea Lillie play Madame Arcati was pure unadulterated delight, a comic joy seldom surpassed.

A stupid decision I made was to make the overture of *High Spirits* mild and polite in the style of English drawing-room comedy. As a matter of fact it was so mild and polite that it put people to sleep before the show even began. Noël came to me and most courteously asked, "Do you suppose we could goose up the overture a bit?" I hesitated because I didn't want to admit I was wrong, but the evidence was against me as was everyone on the production staff. Timothy suggested Luther Henderson to redo it, and it turned out to be one of Tim's more brilliant inspirations. Luther was a skillful black gentleman whose specialty was "le jazz hot." Luther—and I do not exaggerate—orchestrated an overture that has passed into musical comedy history, along with *Gypsy* and *Candide*, as one of the greatest beginnings to a show ever written. Some of the show's devotees would drop by the Alvin Theater just to hear the overture and then leave. I must say I can't blame them because it took the top of our heads off in a most marvelous way.

High Spirits was a happy experience—blue skies all the way. There were two tiny black clouds, however. One was Bea Lillie's agent, John Phillips. He was a troublemaker of the first order. An ex-chorus boy from Bea's revue, *Inside U.S.A.*, he had caught her eye and found himself, probably to his own surprise, certainly everyone else's, her lover. He used this new-found clout to alienate himself from everyone, even going to the absurd extreme of knocking Noël down backstage after a performance. It was Timothy who wrestled him and prevented him from further mayhem.

Beatrice Lillie as Madame Arcati in High Spirits,
1964.

Later, after the show was a hot ticket, we received a movie offer from Ross Hunter, who had been greatly impressed with Bea. He wanted to give her and the show the full Technicolor big-budget glitzy treatment. John Phillips, drunk with power, demanded such a ridiculously high salary for Bea that Ross Hunter, in frustration, dropped the project. It was a loss for everyone, but mainly for the movie-going public who would have seen Beatrice Lillie's finest hour, just a few months before she became too ill to work.

*With Elaine Harrison in front of
the Encinitas Seventh-day Adventist Church
where we met in 1975.*

Chapter 45

Explain Elaine

$\mathcal{A}$N OLD SCHOOL CHUM OF MINE, LESTER FOSSICK, whom I recently rediscovered, phoned me after receiving a letter from me. I had evidently carried on rather effusively about my adored manager and best friend, Elaine. His last remark to me on the telephone was, "Oh, by the way, explain Elaine."

I realized at that moment that I can't, but I keep trying.

My passion to "explain Elaine" was fruitless until one day I persuaded her to tell me something about her parents. It was the "open sesame" to help me understand why she has such a compulsion to save people from disaster.

Elaine was born of two of the most saintly people I've ever known. Actually I didn't know Victor Lindsay, her father, only Mary Lindsay, her mother, but they were legendary people in Encinitas, California, where Elaine has lived her entire life. Dr. Victor was a general practitioner, and he was the only doctor in the area. He literally worked 24/7 and made house calls and delivered babies. Those were the days before health insurance, so the sick babies went to the Lindsay home where Nurse Mary frequently stayed up all night keeping them alive. Medicine in those days was not so much a calling as a ministry.

Another specialty of Mary's was caring for drunks; she immersed them in tubs of hot water and plied them with lemonade until all the alcohol was out of their systems. During the great depression many of their patients were farmers, so impoverished that they had to pay their fees in produce: corn, lima beans, seafood, and the like.

There you have Dr. and Mrs. Victor Lindsay, of whom the world was not worthy. No wonder Elaine is an angel from Heaven—one who rescued so many people including this grateful songwriter.

Fortunately for her legion of admirers, of whom I am the most fervent, she is sweet about 99 percent of the time, but watch out for that 1 percent. She always tells me it's to save me from myself, and I believe that. She is convinced I was born yesterday, and I am the most naïve, vulnerable, and gullible of mortals. She could be right.

I was asked for a mini-bio for the program of a National Company of *Meet Me in St. Louis*, and at the end of it I wrote:

> *Mr. Martin wants to thank Elaine Harrison for putting his music and his life back on track when both were in serious jeopardy, and for saving his life over and over and over again.*

This is an understatement. If Elaine hadn't arrived on the scene (about 1975), I would possibly be in an assisted-living facility, but more probably I would be dead.

Elaine is tall and blonde. When we visited New York in our younger days, she was often mistaken for Constance Towers.

She is paradox unlimited; she insists she is a peasant, but no aristocrat has a more gracious manner. She claims to be a small-town girl, unimpressed with social position and superficiality in general, yet I would trust her much more than the fashion magazines when assessing *haute couture*. She claims to know nothing at all about music, yet many is the time, when I've hit a snag during the writing of a new song, that she has led me out of the wilderness and onto the right track. She once made Josh Logan roar with laughter when he asked her opinion of a theatrical nuance. Her reply was, "Oh, I don't know anything about the theater, Mr. Logan. I'm a registered nurse." But I have learned through the years that she has a crystal ball tucked away in her nurse's kit. She has an infallible theatrical instinct.

She does not have a big ego. Nor is she proud or boastful or aggressive. She just knows what she knows and she knows that she knows it. I made one of my typically asinine remarks to her one day for which she soundly squashed me, as I deserved.

"Ellie," I said, "I gladly admit I am less intelligent than you, but aren't you kind of glad I am? Would you be happy over the long haul with someone who's smarter than you?"

She thought for a moment, then said, quite seriously, "I don't know. I've never been in that situation."

The way we met was like this: my born-again conversion experience in Birmingham had made me much happier spiritually and psychologically, but my physical condition was still wretched; I had not been able to shake off the ill effects of the ten years on "speed" and the nervous collapse that resulted from it. Shortly after a visit to see my folks in Alabama, I fled the bitter winter of the East to Encinitas, California. I was excited about my recent conversion, so the first Sabbath after my return, I showed up at a Seventh-day Adventist Church in my area.

Let Elaine Tell the Story

One day a frail little old man appeared at the doorway of my church just before our worship service began. He was wearing a black gaucho hat, a full-length Army overcoat, and black gloves. He had fleece-lined moccasins on his feet, he carried a cane, and he had two-day's growth of beard. Unselfconsciously, he marched down to the front row and took a seat.

Two happy people by dawn's early light.

After the service, everyone gathered around the entrance to chat and exchange greetings. I felt it was my Christian duty to be kind to this old bum, so I went over and introduced myself and extended an invitation to come again.

I was surprised when a taxicab arrived just then to pick him up. No one in our congregation had ever had any need for a taxi. I asked him where he lived and when he said, "Third Street," I said, "I live on Fifth Street. Don't hire a cab. I'll pick you up for services."

He took me up on my invitation and during the next few weeks we began to get to know each other. The trip was about eight blocks, giving us time to become better acquainted. As he became more comfortable with me, he began to expand on his obvious physical problems.

"But," he said defensively, "at least I can still work."

It sort of stopped me when he mentioned that he could work. "What kind of work do you do?" I asked, trying not to look dubious.

"I'm a songwriter."

"Would I know any songs you've written?"

He rattled off three or four titles that were among my favorites during my high school years.

"Well," I said, "I know you."

I couldn't wait to get home to my family to say, "Do you know that that bizarre old man is a famous songwriter?"

This episode occurred during my Dark Ages. Between *High Spirits* and *Sugar Babies*, my telephone hardly ever rang, nor, with very few exceptions, did anyone write to me. It was very restful in a way, but it was only natural that I felt as forgotten as Norma Desmond in *Sunset Boulevard*.

Today, more than a quarter of a century later, I live with Elaine and her husband, Fred, in a spacious and beautiful house overlooking the Pacific Ocean. We're "The Folks Who Live on the Hill."

I've never gone in for an extensive wardrobe so I haven't requisitioned *all* their closet space. But, alas, the music—tons of music, Niagaras of music, avalanches of music! And tapes, and CDs, and videos by the carload!

And the "old bum" who got no letters for approximately fifteen years, now receives letters, gifts, flowers, e-mails, and phone calls from all over the world. Elaine and Fred and I watched the movie *The Man Who Came to Dinner* recently. The resemblance to Sheridan Whiteside's takeover from the Stanleys, the host couple in the play and film, to my insidious takeover of the Harrison hacienda gave the three of us a good laugh.

Little did I know how dramatically Elaine would change my life when I met her in that church parking lot. I'm convinced it was Providence that brought her into my life. I believe that God in His infinite wisdom knew that something was woefully lacking in Hugh Martin, and Elaine Harrison was the jigsaw piece who could fit the missing space. Thank you, Elaine. Thank you, Lord.

The greatest thing you'll ever learn
Is just to love and be loved in return.[1]

---

1 Abhez, Eden. *Nature Boy*. Creative Concepts.

Chapter 46

Sugar Babies

My NEXT JOB WAS BAGGY PANTS COMEDY with a touch of genius. Harry Rigby called me in 1979 to tell me about a Broadway musical that he and Terry Allen Kramer were producing.

Harry: It's called *Sugar Babies*, Hugh. The score is 100 percent Jimmy McHugh. No new songs, just a whole bunch of his biggest and best, most of 'em with lyrics by Dorothy Fields.

Hugh: I love them both.

Harry: Well, you've got to fly to Detroit and do a couple of vocal arrangements for us. We have two old friends of yours, Mickey Rooney and Ann Miller. The first act finale is more or less a long duet of great Jimmy McHugh standards by Mickey and Ann.

Hugh: Where are you calling from?

Harry: San Francisco. I think we have a great show, but there's something wrong with that first act finale spot. Will you come help us out?

I told him I'd love to, but I didn't tell him how much. No one had offered me a job since *High Spirits,* and that was over fifteen years before. My telephone had been so silent I used to wonder whether I had paid my bill.

Hugh: Harry, could we bring Timothy Gray into this deal?

Harry: Absolutely not.

Hugh (surprised): I thought you liked Timothy.

Harry: I don't. He's so bossy, Hugh. He comes in like King Farouk and tells us all what to do and how to do it. You don't *need* an assistant, do you?

Hugh: Not really. If I had a big strong voice like Kay Thompson or Ralph, I wouldn't need anybody. Hey, speaking of big strong voices, would you accept Ralph?

Harry: Yes, I would. At least, he's pleasant.

Hugh: Okay, let's compromise on Ralph.

Hugh: He doesn't give me ideas for the arrangements the way Timothy does but he does have the big voice. I need that to help me teach the harmony parts. I'll settle for Ralph.

Harry: I'll go ahead, then, and give him a contract. You're sure you won't be unhappy?

Hugh: I'm always happy working for you, Harry.

A deal was quickly worked out for us to fly to Detroit. I've always liked Harry and found him a sweetheart to work for. He had started at the bottom with my *Make a Wish*. It had failed, but it hadn't dampened his ardor for producing Broadway musicals. Now he had a tremendous hit to his credit, the revival in 1971 of *No, No, Nanette* with Ruby Keeler.

Ralph flew into Detroit from his home in Broken Arrow, Oklahoma, and I flew in from California. We booked a suite at the Phoenicia Hotel, rented a piano, and together reported to the theater to catch the evening performance. Harry squeezed us into two seats in the last row as the orchestra played an overture of Jimmy McHugh songs.

After the show:

Harry: Would you like a drink? I feel like celebrating.

Hugh: When?

Harry: Can you meet me in the bar at midnight?

I did, and he poured out his heart to me in regard to the little problems he was facing.

Harry: I think this could be a really big one, but I'm walking a tightrope. With no story line, just bits and sketches and beautiful girls and wonderful songs, we can't have any boring spots. And that medley that Mickey and Ann do at the end of the first act—if that doesn't top everything, I think we've had it.

After a reasonable time, I said I should probably try to sleep since I had an early call at the theater. As I was leaving the bar, I had a sudden idea and I went back to Harry's table.

Hugh: Harry, did you know that Mickey plays piano?
Harry: No, I didn't.

Hugh: And not just plinkety plunk piano. He's really good.

Harry: Interesting. You're driving at something. What is it?

Hugh: Oh, I don't know. I was just fishing for a gimmick of some kind for that medley that's so crucial.

I showed up at the theater the next morning on time and walked through the wings toward the auditorium. Out of the corner of my eye I could see, dead center on stage with a spotlight on it, a nine-foot grand piano. I felt a little light-headed. When I saw Harry, he had a quirky expression on his face. I hugged him and said, "When I saw that piano, I felt as if I'd given birth to it."

"You did," said Harry.

Ralph and I fiddled around musically with the medley, but it was really in pretty good shape. Starting Mickey out all alone made the difference. His tiny body seated at the huge piano, the dexterous, exploring fingers, and finally the unmistakable Rooney voice bringing with it memories of Judy Garland and the shows in a barn, as well as echoes of Busby Berkeley extravaganzas with Mickey leading the parade. He sang the first song, "I Can't Give You Anything But Love" in E major much to my surprise, a difficult key (four sharps yet) for people who play the piano, but I've learned not to be surprised by anything that Mickey does.

Myths about Mickey

I have never believed the stories about Mickey Rooney being temperamental and difficult to work with. Stories like that usually stem from people who have heard stories from people who have heard stories—seldom from folks who have actually observed Mickey behaving badly. Yes, he has a short fuse plus strong convictions about his work, so it's inevitable that he occasionally erupted like Mt. St. Helens. But he and I worked hard and intimately during the pre-Broadway tryout of *Sugar Babies*, and I have become a little cynical about his detractors. With me, he was the very soul of cooperation, and not only with me but with all of his colleagues. I saw not a trace of competitiveness or jealousy. I cannot, in fact, think of anyone I've ever worked with who threw himself into the fray with more willingness and joy than Mickey Rooney.

As for his standing in the Hollywood colony, I think perhaps his peers more fully realize his genius than even the public, although he was rated number one at the box office for four years. I know of at least four gentlemen of great taste who have stated publicly that Mickey Rooney is the finest actor that ever came out of Hollywood. They are: Cary Grant, Tennessee Williams, Anthony Quinn, and Sir Laurence Olivier. Nice going, Mickey!

Ann Miller

Ann Miller was a whole different ballgame. This gifted lady was a great asset to the show and a perfect foil for Mickey. However, I felt, whether wrongly or rightly, that Annie negated some of the charm of her singing by overbelting. She admired Ethel Merman, as do I, as do we all, but I felt strongly that the Merman approach to these songs didn't suit Annie, especially in the sentimental Jimmy McHugh—Dorothy Fields songs like "I'm in the Mood for Love" and "Don't Blame Me." I longed for her to caress the notes of those tender love songs rather than to sock them—to sing them (in her mind) to one lucky man, not to an auditorium full of theatergoers.

The closest I got to achieving my goal for Annie was one day during a break in rehearsal. She had been fighting me tooth and nail because she loved to use a voice that one newspaper critic described as "calling trains."

The dancing ensemble had just given its all for a couple of grueling hours, and Ernie Flatt (choreographer) had given the girls and boys permission to collapse for a much-needed fifteen minutes.

I had a sudden idea. "Annie," I said, "the mikes are on and the stage is clear for a while. Do you suppose you could take this microphone and sing "I'm in the Mood for Love" in that quiet, romantic style that I was begging you to use this morning? Just see how it feels to you."

I held my breath.

"Okay," she said. She must have been in a "why not?" mood, but I was grateful for whatever caused her to consent to the experiment.

I wanted to go out front to listen, but I felt it would be safer to accompany her myself since that's what she was used to. She walked down front and center. I played the intro and she began to sing. It was as sweet as Garland singing "Over the Rainbow" and it had a powerful effect on everyone present. The stagehands stopped hammering, the dancers put down their cokes, and everyone got very quiet. She sang only one chorus, but that's all it took. The mike level was fairly high, but she was singing quietly, tenderly, with a low-key kind of intensity.

When she finished singing, there was a burst of applause that startled her, I think. Then several of the dancers crowded around her and some of the girls had tears in their eyes.

"Annie," I heard one of them say, "I never heard you sing like that."

"Gee," one of the boys said, "we didn't know you could sing that way."

I smiled a smug little smile because I thought, "I can't believe how this happened." I was sure I had won the tug-of-war between Miller and Martin.

I arrived at the theater early that evening, all primed to enjoy my new victory. Ann came on stage looking like a Ziegfeld showgirl and started to sing. I couldn't believe my ears. She had gone right back to calling trains.

Chapter 47

Winding Down

*I*THOUGHT I WOULD MISS THE EXCITEMENT OF BROADWAY and Hollywood: the deadlines, the glorious sound of the orchestra at its first reading, seeing the costumes for the first time, and all that jazz. But I'm learning there are other things to love besides theater. I love an exquisite botanical garden[1] a couple of miles from where I live. I love my two cats, Maggie and Harlequin. I love the modest Hispanic church where I played for fourteen years, and walks on Neptune Avenue, and moments at Moonlight Beach. I love the marvelous California fruits and vegetables, and I love eating them in our large kitchen, facing a huge expanse of what appears to be the entire Pacific Ocean, complete with dolphins, little white sailboats, hang gliders, surfers, pelicans, and an occasional whale.

At night, I am often sung to sleep by a mockingbird just outside my bedroom window. Its music is sweet, melodic, and soothing and if I can't have pleasant dreams with a soundtrack like that, I would say I have a problem. I lived in the heart of Manhattan for 35 years, and the "Lullaby of Broadway" assaulting my eardrums at bedtime was a far cry from my mockingbird. For most of those 35 years in New York, I had no air

---

1 San Diego Botanical Gardens, Encinitas, California.

conditioning and in summer I had to sleep with my windows open. That, may I say, was quite a different sound track. My street, 55th, was a conduit to a popular freeway running parallel to the Hudson River. So the mixture of noises that sometimes put me to sleep consisted of grinding brakes, honking horns, toots, whistles, clangs, and curses. It seemed to go on all night, but since I adored New York and still do, it was a peculiar music that hypnotized and thrilled me and stimulated my soul.

On the whole, though, if I had to choose between the two background scores, I'd choose the mockingbird. In fact, I did.

I love living in Encinitas; it's a small beach town in southern California, and it boasts the friendliest residents I've ever encountered. I try to ignore my birthdays, but Agnes and John and Jane and Paddy never let me get away with it.

On one of my afternoon walks, a sheriff's patrol car suddenly pulled up beside me. Being human, my heart beat a little faster as I tried to recall what malfeasance I might have committed. I relaxed when the sheriff spoke to me. He asked, "Have you finished your book yet?"

I love the redwood house Elaine and Fred designed and built in 1968, and I love living in it. I love *them*, and I shudder when I reflect on where I'd be without their hospitality—in a nursing home, or a veteran's hospital, or a "hospital for the mentally disturbed," as my home away from home was called when I cracked up in England. Or more likely, dead. There's an option to consider. It probably sounds corny to say so, but I love life.

I'm on fairly good terms with being an old man. I love to play, I love my work more than the play, and I like walking best of all. I walk rather strangely, but I walk. A friend told me that my walk reminded him of the Titanic after it hit the iceberg.

We are blest here in our house on the ocean by visits from three topnotch interpreters of Gershwin. They have long since branched out to performing many other composers, but they all began as Gershwin specialists.

When Michael Feinstein sits at our piano, we feel we are in the third row center at one of George and Ira's opening nights. Everything that Michael sings and plays seems touched with the excitement of a Broadway premiere.

When Kevin Cole drops by, he takes us to a concert hall, where we can watch a magician with flying fingers set off musical fireworks or feed our romantic souls like a Rachmaninoff concerto.

When Richard Glazier is at our keyboard, we feel we are eavesdropping on George as he improvises poetic and lyrical phrases and cadences totally unlike the Gershwin stereotype. Three different and fascinating facets of George Gershwin, and we wonder how we ever got so lucky.

Just as Elaine and Fred have kept me alive for a few extra decades, there have been a handful of patron saints who have done the same for my songs. I would like to thank some of the craftsmen who have gone above and beyond are these.

Hugh Fordin, of DRG Records, has beautifully reissued *Martin & Blane Sing Martin & Blane, The Grandma Moses Suite,* and *The Girl Most Likely.*

George Feltenstein, has been a loyal supporter. He has been senior vice president of The Classic Catalogue of Warner Home Video. He gave the public a retrospective CD of *Best Foot Forward*; also a lovingly produced CD of *Athena.*

All of the above are audio, but there is one video so outstanding I feel it should be mentioned. George Feltenstein produced a DVD (also from Warner) of *Meet Me in St. Louis* that is exemplary in every respect. I have never seen such breathtaking color reproduction, and the sound is equally faithful. Thank you, George! You have blest me mightily.

Richard Tay, of Sepia Records in London, has brought out CDs of *Make a Wish* and *Love from Judy.*

And God bless Paul Christman and Judy Bell and Howie Richmond! When they found every songwriter from Tin Pan Alley had a sheet music folio except Hugh Martin, they drafted Dr. Terry O'Donnell and me, and it is in the music stores now.[2]

---

2 *The Songs of Hugh Martin.* Milwaukee, WI: Cromwell Music, Inc.: 2008.

Bruce Pomahac, The Rodgers & Hammerstein Organization Director of Music, conducting a rehearsal for Wedding Day.

Every songwriter dreams of finding the perfect music director. I didn't find mine until 1985 when Josh Logan introduced me to Bruce Pomahac.

I was collaborating with Josh at that time on *The Member of the Wedding* and I assumed two things: one, that Josh would probably want Bruce to conduct the orchestra, and two, that Bruce would be excellent because it seemed to me that everyone in the World of Joshua Logan was excellent: Rodgers and Hammerstein, Mary Martin, Henry Fonda, Jimmy Stewart, Helen Hayes, et al. Excellence seemed to be in the very air he breathed.

But I was to discover that Bruce was not only excellent and pro-ficient, he was as sweet as Josh and Josh's wife, Nedda, the ultimate compliment I can pay him. He is no longer available to me as musical

Backstage at the St. Louis Muny with Artistic Director Paul Blake, 1994.

director because he accepted an important position with the Rodgers and Hammerstein Organization as Director of Music. But he is still available as my friend and adviser. I run to him for guidance times without number.

Paul Blake's Company Store is the St. Louis Muny. (He threatens to retire in 2010.) I did two shows with Paul, and I admire him on four fronts—direction, production, script writing, and lyrics. Paul touched the hearts of theater-loving college students in 1997 when he was one of the speakers at a Hugh Martin Symposium at San Diego State University. He told of going with his aunt to see *Meet Me in St. Louis* again and again when he was a small child. He wished his family was like the one in the movie. Then he broke up the audience by adding in his impish way, "We didn't have people named Hugh in the Bronx."

With one of my favorite pianists, Richard Glazier, 2002.

The same year, Peter Jones asked me to participate in the filming of a two-hour biography of Judy Garland for the Arts & Entertainment Channel. The script was written by John Fricke, and our mutual love of Judy led to an exchange of letters. He wrote me one day that he had gone home to visit his mother for Christmas. She had asked him to sing a solo at their church. Rather than choose a hymn or a carol, he wrote some appropriate new lyrics for my Christmas song from *Meet Me in St. Louis.*

"I'm sending you what I wrote because it may give you a good laugh," he wrote to me. I read it, and it didn't give me a laugh. It gave me an idea.

I wrote to John, telling him what a great job he had done, and suggesting we collaborate on a version others might like to sing in church. When Dave Olsen of Warner Bros. Publishing read it, he said, "Why don't we publish the alternate lyrics directly under the traditional lyrics when we re-publish the song?" It is slowly finding

At home in Encinitas, California, age 88.

its way into a few churches, thanks largely to exquisite renditions by Sylvia Lange, Kevin Cole, and the Carolyn Mawby Chorale.

Another person who is invaluable to me is the previously mentioned Dr. Terry O'Donnell, Professor of Theater and Music at San Diego State University, a most skillful, computer-literate, and gifted musician, as pleasant and genial an Irishman as ever wore the green. I used to do all those little dots and flags and clefs and tails myself, but now that I'm older and lazier, I usually turn to Terry and retreat into a Turner Classic Movie. Terry and I speak a language that sounds like Sanskrit to those around us, but is perfectly clear to us.

"Do you want railroad tracks in that bar or an extra rest? What about the final chord? Aunt Harriet or just a plain tonic? Shall I put a bird's-eye over the quarter note? What about the accompaniment—just plain boom chick?"

Hugh and Michael Feinstein at a recording session for
Michael Feinstein Sings the Hugh Martin Songbook, *1994.*
(taken by Greg Henry)

Chapter 48

Michael Feinstein

W̲HEN MICHAEL PHONED ME IN 1986, I didn't know who he was. That seems almost incredible today when Michael Feinstein is a household name, but he wasn't quite so famous then. Besides which I was so out of it in 1986 that if President Reagan had phoned me, I might well have said, "Ronald who?"

A few years later, I realized that Michael had become not only one of our best-loved singers and pianists, but a tremendous force for good in the world of classic popular music. His reverence for what is truly excellent, plus his vast knowledge of the subject, have increased the love of the Golden Age repertoire of great songs in the hearts of millions of us.

It was an important day for me in 1988, when he invited me to become the fourth in a series of albums featuring songwriters from the Golden Age. He felt it important to capture the actual sounds, both pianistically and vocally, of the last few living composers of that fabulous era. He had done albums with Burton Lane, Jule Styne, and Jerry Herman.

He asked me to go through my archives and send him some of my songs that I particularly liked. He went through them during the next few weeks, then we made a date for him to drive down from

The cover of The Hugh Martin Songbook
(photo of Hugh on a Manhattan rooftop by Jerome Hill, sometime in the 1940s).

Hollywood to have our first rehearsal. Elaine and I found him irresistible from the first moment.

We transferred at that point to Hollywood, and started rehearsing with Michael at his home. Rehearsing with Michael is a joy. Our styles seemed to blend from the start, and we enjoyed ourselves so much that it was hard to cut down the list of songs to the twenty required for the CD *Michael Feinstein Sings the Hugh Martin Songbook.*[1] One thing that facilitated matters tremendously was his voice range; in almost every instance, it corresponded with my sheet music, so I had very little transposing to

---

1 *Michael Feinstein Sings the Songs of Hugh Martin,* TRO—Cromwell Music, Inc.: 2008.

With Michael Feinstein and Elaine Harrison, 1995.

do. This was a break for me because I had been sidelined for years and my pianistics were rusty.

I can't even begin to describe what this musician has done for America. Until "along came Michael" we were the beneficiaries of a matchless heritage of theater and film music and we didn't even realize it!

Before Michael, Leonard Bernstein had scratched the surface with some television programs, mainly for children. But they were elementary compared to the lovely, witty specials that Michael began to bless us with. His taste is impeccable, his memory, phenomenal. He has mined veins of gold and spread them at our feet like a beautiful carpet.

Josh and Nedda Logan.

(Photographed by Roddy McDowall)

Chapter 49

The Member of the Wedding

I REALIZE THAT MY FIFTEEN MINUTES OF FAME was the result of *Meet Me in St. Louis*. I will always be identified with that beautiful movie, and I'm eternally grateful to God and Arthur Freed and Judy Garland and Vincente Minnelli and Sally Benson. Call me irresponsible, call me unreliable, call me paranoid, too; but I sincerely believe I was treated shabbily on that production. Dick Rodgers and George Abbott had shown me respect and allowed me to be a partner, not a flunkey, on *Best Foot Forward*—an important Broadway musical—when I was a total neophyte, someone who had never written a show in his life. Ralph and I had the approval of all nine of those hard-boiled critics on the New York newspapers, and the show had been a hit. In my Hollywood ignorance, I thought I had earned the right to a chair at the conference table—a vote, no matter how humble, in choices about script and staff. Ignore my vote if you want to, but at least give me the fulfillment of being asked. I responded very childishly, sulking and bitching, all of which was a complete waste of breath and emotion because everyone was so wrapped up in himself that no one heard a word I said. So the only person I was hurting was myself; regretfully, I hurt myself rather deeply.

But *The Member of the Wedding* was a different story. No fame, no fuss, but it was my baby—mine and Josh Logan's—and Josh and I loved it with a very real love.

I brought Ralph Blane in on the project; don't ask me why—probably force of habit; he demonstrated the songs so superbly (I'd become accustomed to his voice), but his contribution was zero.

I got off to a bad start. Carson McCullers was the author of this masterpiece that had so hypnotized me as I gazed at Julie Harris and Ethel Waters and Brandon de Wilde from the balcony of the gorgeous old Empire Theater.

Carson had given me the rights to "have at" her marvelous play and had done so without any reservations. But after I'd been writing for a couple of months, her curiosity got the best of her and she wrote to me: "Would you be willing to let me in on where you're going? I don't insist on it but I'd love to get a glimpse of what you're doing."

I thought that what I was doing was just fine, so I sent my outline to Carson. She *hated* it; not just disliked it, she loathed it. I came across it months later and read it with unbelieving eyes. It was *awful*—the worst thing I'd ever written. Of course, she hastily withdrew the rights. I don't blame her; I would have done the same thing.

But by now I had fallen in love with the darn thing. I continued to struggle to repair the damage I had done. I sent it to my old friend, Joshua Logan, who wrote: "Come to New York immediately if you can. I want to talk about this with you."

I was, of course, thrilled out of my mind, and trusty Elaine volunteered to make the trip with me. When we turned up at River House, where he and his enchanting wife, Nedda, resided, we found that he had been hit with a debilitating nervous disorder called degenerative nuclear palsy. It was frustrating but not incapacitating; Elaine and I perceived immediately that his gifts for being theatrically powerful were all in place.

Josh: I like what you've done so far, Hugh; I like it even better than Carson's play. But it's very flawed; it's obvious that you've never written a play before and your lapses are showing. Would you be interested in collaborating on the script with me? I'm an old hand at pulling shows out of the fire.

I would have been an idiot to say "no," so I said "yes"—so quickly that it made him blink.

The next few weeks were as close to show-biz heaven as this old songwriter and would-be playwright will ever get. Josh was a joy to partner with: encouraging but firm with the convictions of a man who knows what he knows, and knows that he knows it.

Now a word about the songs: I ask you for the kind of indulgence you would give to a father with a wallet full of snapshots of his offspring; because they *are* my offspring and no proud papa could be any more pleased with his prowess than I. In my humble opinion, they are as good as I can do. I'm well aware that I'm not in the league with George or Ira, or Jerry, or Oscar, or Dick, or Larry, or Cole. But God in His wisdom gave me something that is all my own, and every now and then I am able to get it on paper. "When I Join the Circus" is so exciting I can hardly play it. "I Hate this Ol' Town" and "I Love this Ol' Town" tell me just a little bit more about Frankie than Carson did, and "Ludie and Me" tells me a lot more about Berenice. In truth, I believe this collection is character-revealing in a way that my other songs are not. "Night Music" makes us feel Honey's passion for jazz better than any dialogue could no matter how fine. I have to confess that I did lift it from "Here Come the Dreamers," so the rhythms, the syntax, the "flow" of the lyric belong to Marshall Barer and not to me. But the lyrics I wrote are entirely my own; I totally replaced Marshall's original.

The one I like best is "I Have Something to Say to You." I consider it the best song I've ever written—not as good as "The Folks Who Live on the Hill" or "Summertime" or "Wait Till You See Her," but it can hold its head up even in fast company. It was a huge problem. Frankie was twelve in Carson's version. Josh and I made her a tiny bit older, but the lyrics, although not overtly sexual, have an urgency that made some people nervous. I tried to rationalize the discrepancy by arguing that Southern gals mature earlier than their Northern counterparts, but I don't think I ever persuaded anybody that audiences would accept it.

A man convinced against his will
Is of the same opinion still.

Even in the light of the frustrating failure of our hopes, it was still a time to remember. The actual look of the Logan living room was part of the fun. It was a spacious room with a baby grand piano and nineteenth century French furniture. Every table top and mantle was covered with memorabilia from famous friends, plus the Logans' own collection of antique toys and dolls. There was one large window with a wide view of the East River. The draperies were designed to make the windows look like a proscenium.

The most unusual feature of the Logan living room was the color of the walls. They were dark red with a damask texture, and the effect was just the opposite of what one would expect. A dark red room sounds oppressive, even threatening. But such was not the case. It was warm, welcoming, wonderful. In that room I always felt like I was visiting royalty.

I can think of no more felicitous "freeze-frame" of my life than a typical scene during our work together in the Logan living room: Josh seated on the sofa, carefully propped up because of his disability; Elaine, sitting on a chair placed at a left angle to him, always the happy medium between Josh and me in case we had communication problems; and Nedda, darting in and out of the room, making sure her husband was comfortable and that all his needs were met. Sometimes immediately after we wrote a new scene, Nedda and Elaine would read it aloud, Nedda reading in an old-fashioned, almost Victorian, voice that thoroughly endeared her to us. I would sit at Josh's feet—physically and symbolically—as close to him as possible so as not to miss an elusive word or thought.

Looking back on my long and golden life, this little scene seems to me about as blissful a one as I could choose among all the others, and I wish I could freeze-frame it forever.

With Kevin Cole, four hands, one piano, and a single-minded devotion to
The Great American Songbook, 2005. Kevin calls me his mentor,
and I've never had a greater compliment!

(Photographed by Barbara Brill)

ACT THREE

*Afterthoughts:
Mostly about
Theater and
Music*

Entr'acte

My Music

(With apologies to Edna St. Vincent Millay)

My music often brought me tears,
At times I nearly drowned.
But oh, my pals, and ah, my peers,
It made a lovely sound.

My Favorite Prayer

I thank Thee, God, for the gentle ministry of
music and for all the wandering melodies
Thou hast loosed in the world.
I thank Thee for the people who have heard them
in the silences and caught them up and sung them back to me.

—Dr. Henry Edmonds

Pastor of the Independent Presbyterian Church
Birmingham, Alabama
(My minister during my teenage years)

Chapter 50

Beethoven & Bach, Picasso & Braque, Harnick & Bock

THE JOHN FRANKENHEIMER FILM, *THE TRAIN*, begins with a scene in the Musée du Jeu de Paume. The time is a few days before the liberation of Paris, August, 1944. The curator of the museum watches a band of German soldiers stripping the walls of the paintings she has lived with and loved for so many years.

"You have taken our food, our land, you have lived in our houses," she cries. "Don't take our art! It is our beauty, our heritage, our special vision, born out of France!"

She weeps as boxes upon boxes are crated up and ticketed for Berlin. They are labeled Renoir, Cézanne, Matisse, Monet, Manet, Braque, Degas, Picasso.

It started me thinking what is the special vision of America? Many thoughtful people feel it is our classic American popular songs evolving from minstrel shows, ragtime, spirituals, flowering into the rich lodes of jazz, Harlem night clubs, Broadway musicals, revues, singing and dancing movies.

This music is something Americans have done infinitely better than anyone else. Many of them have been my colleagues and friends. I had the enormous good fortune to know many of these songwriters and poets of the first half of the 20th century. Some I actually worked for, and some were acquaintances; some I merely admired from afar. Here are a few with whom I was lucky enough to share the work place:

Harold Arlen

An anomaly...his gregariousness...coupled with a seeming block about praising his songwriting colleagues . . . excepting the Chosen Ones: Harburg, Capote, Mercer, and of course above all, George Gershwin...his total devotion to his beautiful and beloved show girl wife, Anya... her mental illness, which never compromised his adoration of her . . . Ralph Blane's description of Anya chasing Ralph through the Arlen residence with a carving knife!...Harold's extraordinary singing: the voice, small but supercharged with emotion...Was the beauty he generated a fusion of genius and suffering? His score for *House of Flowers*, in my opinion, is the most beautiful ever written for a musical comedy.

Hoagy Carmichael

Finding him a country boy through and through, comfortable as an old shoe...his clothes, almost sloppy but wonderfully right for his angular Hoosier face and body...his acting and singing: no one played himself better than Hoagy...his heartwarming sweetness and generosity: Ralph and I ran into him one day on the streets of MGM. He was strolling with Johnny Mercer, and he said to Johnny, "Hey, these two boys sure made monkeys out of us!" (Ralph and I had just scored a hit with *Best Foot Forward* on the heels of Hoagy and Johnny's less than successful *Walk with Music* (title changed from *Three After Three*).

Noël Coward

His wit, the sharpest of any person I've ever known . . . his generosity, as infinite as his capacity to create laughter . . . the unexpected tenderness, the need to be loved, never (I'm only guessing) really requited . . . his feeling for the theater, genuine and intense—he felt it was a place for magic, not for grinding axes or mounting soapboxes . . . .his weakness in the area of casting, surprising in someone so intrigued by personality . . . his enormous versatility—was there anything he couldn't do? . . . his greatness, more valid, I believe, than any of us realize . . . posterity will have the last word.

Vernon Duke

The antithesis of Hoagy . . . his air of Russian aristocracy, intimidating but falsely so; underneath he was encouragement personified . . . his sartorial elegance and polished manners . . . his critical standards: fastidious yet open to new, unexplored musical ideas . . . his lyrics, so superior to what one would expect from an esteemed composer, "Autumn In New York" being Exhibit A . . . above all, his gorgeous music, rich and sophisticated yet as emotional as a child.

Yip Harburg

An imp, a sprite, a leprechaun right out of his own *Finian's Rainbow* . . . his lyrics, overpoweringly ingenious, fresh, and enchanting . . . his parties, small, intimate, noisy, full of friendly argument . . . his wife, Eddie (Edeline), so much a part of him that they seemed one person . . . his eagerness to help young people . . . his compulsion to make the world a little better.

Cole Porter

Until the devastating accident that crippled him for life, the complete hedonist . . . his courage in dealing with pain that was considerable and constant . . . his unfailing good manners even under duress . . . his (I hate to say it) superficiality, yet considering the pleasure he gave us all, it seems niggling to notice it.

Richard Rodgers

First, last, and in the middle, Richard Rodgers . . . mentor de luxe . . . wisdom unlimited . . . pearls without price . . . all suddenly available to a Johnny-come-lately who had never written a single song . . . his patience . . . his risqué but tasteful jokes . . . his respect for me . . . my astonishment at his respect for me, who, until I met Mr. Rodgers, had encountered mostly rejection, indifference, and even derision . . .his conservative clothes . . . his beautiful and charming wife, Dorothy . . . his vulnerability, surprising considering his stature in the field of music.

Arthur Schwartz

His persona more that of a successful businessman than the skillful composer that he was . . . everything about him—clothes, speech, deliberateness of manner, table manners—seemed more IBM than ASCAP . . . steady, conventional, ordinary, yet the possessor of exquisite taste in music.

Stephen Sondheim

I didn't actually have the honor of working with Steve, but he has played an important role in my life. Every once in a while (usually when I'm seeing the world through disaster-colored glasses), I'll get a tiny card from Steve, telling me how much he likes my work, then balancing the compliment by laughing at me. I tried to tell him once on the phone how in awe of him I feel, and he shut me up with, "Don't pull that Southern coquette stuff on me."

But how is it possible not to be in awe of a man who has single-handedly changed the world of theater music? Both his lyrics and his music are so fresh, so intricate, that my mind boggles when I attend a Sondheim musical. Yet he never becomes pretentious. The songs are always integrated perfectly into the story. This could cause his shows to be impressive rather than entertaining, but Sondheim never forgets to entertain, thanks to his uncanny theater instincts and his hilarious sense of humor.

And there are a few others I longed to work with but never got the chance:

Burton Lane

We were both at MGM at the same time but never had the opportunity to work together. *Finian's Rainbow* is one of the most fascinating scores ever written and he definitely belongs in the top echelon of songwriters.

Richard Whiting

This composer is one of the great unsung heroes of American popular song. He was at his best in the twenties and thirties, having written songs for a number of musicals at Paramount Studios. His lyricists included Johnny Mercer and George Marion, Jr. Some of his best songs include "Sleepy Time Gal," "Ain't We Got Fun?," "My Ideal," and "Hooray for Hollywood!" He was the father of the popular vocalist, Margaret Whiting.

In 1928, he surprised his peers by writing one of the greatest *lyrics* of all time. It is called "She's Funny That Way," and it's a killer!

In addition to Mr. Whiting, I yearned to work with George Gershwin and Vincent Youmans, naturally, but I was born a bit too late for those illustrious gentlemen.

We've only scratched the surface. Dig deeper and you will find many others of great stature:

Dorothy Fields
Ira Gershwin
Oscar Hammerstein
W.C. Handy
Ralph Rainger
Leo Robin
Willard Robison
Jule Styne
Harry Warren
Alec Wilder

The Genorisity of Musicians

I never cease to be amazed at how generous musicians are. Actors eye each other with suspicion; producers tend to be competitive; directors, less so; authors seem to enjoy being snide about each other's work.

Oh, but songwriters! A happy lot, I have found. There are exceptions: crusty old Irving Berlin, pinching pennies and sniping at his peers; Harold Arlen, so extravagantly talented that he could well afford to praise those less favored, but he didn't. Even George Gershwin; I didn't know him, but from all accounts he lived blissfully in a little world of George Gershwin.

They are in the minority. Look at Stephen Sondheim—he spends a good segment of his life advising, encouraging, and praising. This is the sign of a really great man.

Since inconsistency is a way of life for me, it's not surprising that, although my true love is theater music, two of my favorite songs are popular songs.

The music of the first one, "That's All," is by Bob Haymes, brother of the well-known singer, Dick Haymes, and the touching lyric is by Alan Brandt. The lyric of the final eight bars absolutely shatters me with its simple beauty. Here it is:

If you're wond'ring what I'm asking in return, dear,
You'll be glad to know that my demands are small:
Say it's me that you adore, for now and evermore,
That's all,
That's all.

The second song that I must confess I like, perhaps even more, is "Smile," music by Charles Chaplin (yes, *the* Charles Chaplin) and words by John Turner and Geoffrey Parsons. The music is part of the score for Chaplin's film, *Modern Times*. It is a hauntingly beautiful melody, and the Messrs. Turner and Parsons found inspired lyrics to match it. This song helps to banish my occasional blues better than anything else ever written.

A Decade of Great Singers

It wouldn't be fittin' to write a chapter on the 1940s without mentioning the quality, not only of its songs (which is generally acknowledged), but also of its troubadours. Good singers have a way of coming along in every decade, but the fabulous forties surely had more than its share. Space prevents an analysis in depth; I can only raise my glass to a handful who have given me special pleasure. In order not to play favorites, I list them in alphabetical order.

On Broadway

Pearl Bailey
Kaye Ballard
Alfred Drake
Dolores Gray
Ella Logan
Mary Martin
Ethel Merman
Ezio Pinza
John Raitt
Ethel Waters

In Hollywood

June Allyson
Fred Astaire
Rosemary Clooney
Bing Crosby
Doris Day
Alice Faye
Judy Garland
Lena Horne
Betty Hutton
Mario Lanza
Jeanette MacDonald
Gordon MacRae
Tony Martin
Ann Miller
Carmen Miranda
Dennis Morgan
Harold Nicholas

Virginia O'Brien
Jane Powell
Martha Raye
Shirley Ross
Dinah Shore
Ginny Simms
Frank Sinatra
Dooley Wilson
Jane Wyman

In the Ballrooms, Night Clubs, Recording Studios, and on the Airwaves

Harold Arlen
Mildred Bailey
Tony Bennett
Connee Boswell
Cab Calloway
Nat "King" Cole
Matt Dennis
Bob and Ray Eberle
Anita Ellis
Ruth Etting
Ella Fitzgerald
Helen Forrest
Dick Haymes
Louis Jordan
Peggy King
Frances Langford
Peggy Lee
Julie London
Ella Mae Morse

Loulie Jean Norman
Anita O'Day
Kate Smith
Keely Smith
Georgia Southern
Jo Stafford
Kay Starr
Maxine Sullivan
Kay Thompson
Martha Tilton
Mel Tormé
Sarah Vaughan
Bea Wain
"Fats" Waller
Clara Ward
Fran Warren
Dinah Washington
Margaret Whiting
Lee Wiley

All of the above seem to me to possess certain virtues that flourished in that swingy, zingy decade: beautiful sonorities, excellent intonation, superior rhythm, great sense of humor, and intelligent phrasing. They seem unusually gifted when it comes to understanding and communicating the marvelous lyrics of the period.

There was also in the forties, a group of people who were noteworthy less because of the beauty of their voices than for other reasons. Some of these reasons might include humor (Johnny Mercer, Hoagy Carmichael, Louis Armstrong), dramatic talents (Édith Piaf, Mabel Mercer), and blend and ingenuity of arrangements (The Andrews Sisters, The Hi-Lo's, The Martins, The Mel-Tones, The Modernaires, The Pied Pipers, The Williams Brothers).

What a perverse creature I am, at least when dealing with singing. It seems to me God's greatest gift, yet I am wildly inconsistent on the subject. When I'm casting a musical, or buying a recording, or selecting singers for an ensemble group, I'm tough about intonation—I do like my vocalists to sing on pitch. When someone like Ella Fitzgerald comes along who is infallible in that area, I cheer.

On the other hand, quite a few singers with a pitch problem have a secure place in my heart. I don't go so far as to condone people who sing sharp. Singing sharp affects me like squeaking chalk on a blackboard.

But there are a few performers who have such charisma that they can get away with murder. Édith Piaf, for instance, sang flat frequently, but she riveted me just the same. Dinah Shore's sweet tones sometimes slipped a little, but never lost the tenderness of her expression. Maurice Chevalier played fast and loose with pitch, but did anybody care? I didn't. Ella Logan often fell short of the on-the-nose intonation we all desired, but when she sang "How Are Things in Gloccamora?," our tears were the credentials of her greatness. When Gertrude Lawrence died, I happened to be in London and heard Noël Coward give, on the BBC, the first tribute to his most famous leading lady. "It must be admitted," Noël said, "that Gertie sang flat. But that did nothing to detract from the fact that she was always a star of the first magnitude."

Fortunately, my two favorite singers had no problems with good intonation. They are the wives of David Rose, the conductor-composer who wrote and conducted "Holiday for Strings." Mrs. Dave Rose Number One was Martha Raye, an unsurpassable singer, and Mrs. Dave Rose Number Two was Judy Garland, who surpassed the unsurpassable! You can pick 'em, Dave, old boy!

Funny Folks

There has been a long roster of truly funny folk with whom I've had the great privilege of working. Ed Wynn was the first; Nancy Walker was the second. Following them have been Lucille Ball, Mickey Rooney, Judy Garland, Robert Morse, Nanette Fabray, Jimmy Durante, Ethel Merman, Phil Silvers, Beatrice Lillie, and Noël Coward. How lucky can a songwriter get?!

Not only has my theatrical life been blest with gifted purveyors of laughter, on-stage, so to speak, but also I've had more than my share of that wonderful commodity off-stage. All three of my writing partners, for instance, have tickled my funny-bone. Ralph Blane was funny without trying to be. He had a way of expressing himself that doubled me up—me and everyone around me. Conversations with Ralph were often unhampered by logic. It was a little like talking to Gracie Allen.

Here is an example (I memorized this exchange because it is so quintessentially R.B.):

Ralph: I forgot my comb, Hugh. May I borrow yours?

Hugh: No, Ralph, I don't lend my comb, because of scalp diseases and things.

Ralph: Oh, do you have a scalp disease?

Hugh: No!

Ralph: Then why should I give you mine?

Marshall Barer was a truly witty man, and wrote marvelous comedy songs. Timothy Gray made me laugh more than anyone else in my life, even Noël Coward. His humor was unique, bizarre, and hilarious, and not even hurricanes in Florida and cancer could quench it.

Memories of Richard Rodgers

A mixed bag of memories concerning Richard Rodgers: He was about 39 years old when we started working together on *Best Foot Forward*—still quite good looking with a razor-sharp brain, especially when anything musical was concerned. He was of medium height, but, of course, he looked like a midget standing next to Mr. Abbott as did we all.

He surprised me one day by asking me whom I'd like to orchestrate our songs.

Hugh: Dick, I never thought anyone would ask me such a question—least of all you. You're the master.

Rodgers: When I write, I have a pretty good idea what the sound in the pit should be. You probably do, too.

Hugh: Yes, I do. Do you think I could have Don Walker?

Rodgers: Who is Don Walker?

(Aficionados of Richard Rodgers will smile at this because only four years later, Dick chose Don Walker to orchestrate *Carousel*, possibly Rodgers' finest musical.)

I told him that I had worked with Don on a show by Johnny Green, *Hiya Gentlemen!* It had closed after a brief road tour and never reached Broadway, but I had been impressed with the Don Walker orchestrations and had hoped that some day we might work together again.

Hugh: Johnny's a great pal of yours. Why don't you ask him what he thinks of Don?

Rodgers: I don't need to do that. I trust you. But are you sure you don't want Russell? Or Hans?

(Robert Russell Bennett and Hans Spialek were tops at that time in the hierarchy of orchestrators.)

I said I was sure. I reminded him that he had told Ralph and me that the reason he and Larry had not written the songs for *Best Foot Forward* (Mr. Abbott had asked them to) was that he felt fresh blood was needed for this very youthful show. Don Walker was engaged to orchestrate *Best Foot Forward*—his first Broadway musical—the first of a long series of memorable assignments.

One of the songs I submitted was "I Know You by Heart," a simple, sweet ballad for Bud Hooper, our principal male character. Dick was somewhat taken by it, but after I sang it, he was silent and frowning.

Hugh: You don't like it.

Rodgers: I like it.

Hugh: What then?

Rodgers: Are you familiar with a song called "I See Your Face Before Me?"

Hugh: Lovely song. Dietz and Schwartz.

Rodgers: Does your song sound a bit like it?

I said I didn't really think so, but that if he was worried about it, I'd write another song.

Rodgers: No, hold on.

He thought a minute. I learned to revere the expression on Dick's face when the muse was hovering over him. "Excuse me," he said, replacing me on the piano bench. "Do you like this?"

He played my melody with a new twist. "I do," I said. Into the score it went, a Martin tune with a Dick Rodgers patina.

Ralph Blane

When I came to the end of writing this memoir, I had mixed emotions; it had been great fun recalling "my life and good times," but there had been a certain amount of stress, also. So when I was finally able to write "THE END," I felt a great sense of relief.

Unfortunately, it was short-lived. Something happened that might qualify as being what the news channels like to call "Breaking News." It is definitely not world-shaking; I would call it a "tempest in a teapot;" but in my psyche it's a full-blown hurricane.

I learned that an Oklahoma lady named Phyllis Braunlich had published a biography of Ralph Blane that we refer to as "the Ralph Blane novel." It is a small paperback book that doesn't attempt to be an in-depth bio— more of a local-boy-makes-good story. She reports that Ralph had claimed (in taped interviews) to have written many of the lyrics of my songs, including my special "baby," "Have Yourself A Merry Little Christmas" and its various versions. I, of course, went through the ceiling. I have spent a lifetime trying (and occasionally succeeding) to write songs of quality—songs that would give the world some pleasure and perhaps even be remembered after I pass on. Now it comes out, in print, that my partner and (I thought) friend had betrayed me big-time!

When MGM offered me a contract in 1942, I firmly rejected it, explaining that I would only sign their seven-year contract if they would offer one to Ralph as well.

I wouldn't be troubling the waters now if Ralph's greed had not grown to such outlandish proportions. I was reasonably content to let him receive equal screen credit, sheet music credit, ASCAP royalties, etc., mainly because this bizarre situation was caused by my naïve and atrocious lack of business acumen. But when I learned that Ralph had told fantastic lies about the songs I had written after Best Foot Forward, I finally lost my cool!

As I delved deeper into the extent of Ralph's lies, I discovered that he had built his whole career on claiming to have written the lyrics to many of my songs. This was ridiculous right at the start because after Best Foot Forward (except for some of the shows I wrote with Timothy Gray and the one show with Marshall Barer), I always wrote my own lyrics. When Ralph came to MGM, the songs he submitted for Meet Me in St. Louis were rejected and Ralph stopped writing. He was suddenly very much the "party boy"—all play and no work. So all three of the St. Louis songs were written entirely by me, words and music, and indeed all of the so-called Martin and Blane songs (except for Best Foot Forward) were written by me, solo, without help from Ralph or anybody else.

Another thing that was ridiculous was Ralph's claim to be a Vocal Arranger. Ralph couldn't have made a vocal arrangement if his life depended on it. He didn't know one chord from another, but I shared the credit with him because his beautiful voice was useful to me in teaching the harmonies to the various singers.

Never in a million years would it have occurred to me that anyone in his right mind would try to steal the whole career of an honest, hard-working little citizen of Tin Pan Alley like me. I sweated blood over many of those songs and I'm not about to give up without a struggle to a compulsive liar who claims that he wrote them.

I feel a deep sense of relief. Elaine has been absolutely irreplaceable in all this. For one thing she was on board when some of the songs I wrote turned out to be songs that Ralph claimed he had written. He once remarked in front of both of us, "Elaine knows our secret." To paraphrase a famous remark by Ethel Waters, "God don't sponsor no liars."

Timothy Gray

It was with Timothy Gray that I probably found my greatest fulfillment. When I was writing with Ralph and Marshall, we worked separately. But with Timothy, the collaboration was urgent, excitable, sometimes angry, sometimes ecstatic, and always very vital. And no else's wit has so convulsed me.

His suggestion, for instance, for an inscription for the urn in which my ashes will eventually be contained. I had mentioned to him casually that I had decided cremation nowadays seemed to make more sense than burial since the earth is so over-populated and land is at such a premium.

"I have a suggestion for the inscription on your urn, Hugh," he volunteered. I waited.

"Here lies Hugh Martin; he finally got warm enough."

"How about *your* urn, Tim?" I asked.

"Oh yes," he said cheerfully. *"Here lies Timothy Gray; he finally got enough sleep."*

Timothy Gray died March 17, 2007. We all had known it was coming; cancer had long since broken his health but not his spirit. It was a beautiful spirit, one that lit up my sky for 59 years.

Like many friends with close bonds, we clashed a lot, but seemed to be fed creatively by the pressure, and we wrote well together. I enjoyed the work—it was more fun than play, emotional and visceral and synergistic, and I shall always be grateful for it and for his friendship.

Postlude

I'M VERY BIG IN THE WISHFUL THINKING DEPARTMENT. The rose-colored glasses are never very far away, and very often I see things as I'd like them instead of seeing them as they are.

Broadway today is not the Broadway I grew up with and loved. It is like a different planet, and I sometimes feel like an alien from outer space. Gone are the backers' auditions that went on sometimes for months. That, I suppose, is an improvement, though I sometimes think anything is better than dealing with large, faceless corporations like Disney and CBS.

Gone are the nice Wall Street types, some of whom really loved the theater, others who just had a weakness for chorus girls.

Gone is the freedom to try something new. "Don't you know we've got twelve million tied up in this show? Can't take a chance!"

Gone are the standard out-of-town tryouts—three days in New Haven, two weeks in Boston, and two weeks in Philly. It was a sensible way to get the kinks out of the show, so much better than those hateful previews attended by high-society types who paid too much and ate too much. I heard of one such where the curtain went up on a set, no actors, just a living-room. Before the play even began, a dowager in the third row said "Deadly!" in a voice that reached to the second balcony.

Gone is wonderful Gray's Drug Store, right on Times Square. When I went to New York the first time, I could go to Gray's basement and get a cheap ticket for a play by Eugene O'Neill or Maxwell Anderson or Noël Coward, or a musical by the Gershwins or Porter or Rodgers and Hart for fifty cents if it was nearing the end of its run.

I hope there are kindred souls who remember delights such as these. I assure you that a night at a Broadway show was more exciting – and a darn sight cheaper – than some of the shenanigans that are going on in New York's theater district these days.

Will the pendulum swing? I have to say I don't think it will. I'm an optimist about almost everything, but I fear Broadway has slowly metamorphosed into something that doesn't turn me on.

Good luck, everybody. I hope you enjoy your falling chandeliers and your rock music and your on-stage helicopters. As for me, I'll settle for an evening at the Princess Theater with some really funny dialogue by Guy Bolton, captivating lyrics by P.G. Wodehouse, and a sheaf of gorgeous Jerome Kern melodies.

I had intended to end my book here with a whimper instead of a bang, but I suddenly remembered an email I received from a colleague named Josh Ellis, a publicist of note on the theater scene in New York. He was relaying to a few of his buddies a letter he had received from a friend. It was headed:

What a Difference Half a Century Doth Make

And it called to our attention the contrast between the winners in the Best Song category in the Academy Awards of 1936 and 2006.

He printed out verbatim the lyrics of the two songs. First, the elegant and lovely one Dorothy Fields created to match one of Jerome

Kern's most richly melodic inventions, a song called "The Way You Look Tonight" from *Swing Time.* Right under it he put the lyric for the song that won in 2006, called "It's Hard Out Here for a Pimp" from a movie called *Hustle and Flow.*

I wonder what song will win the Oscar in 2011.

Draw the veil!

—— *Hugh Martin*
June, 2010

Index

K

L

O

P

Q

R